ADOPTION-SPECIFIC THERAPY

ADOPTION-SPECIFIC THERAPY

A Guide to Helping Adopted Children and Their Families Thrive

JILL WATERMAN
AUDRA K. LANGLEY
JEANNE MIRANDA
DEBBIE B. RILEY

AMERICAN PSYCHOLOGICAL ASSOCIATION
Washington, DC

Published by
American Psychological Association
750 First Street, NE
Washington, DC 20002
www.apa.org

APA Order Department
P.O. Box 92984
Washington, DC 20090-2984
Phone: (800) 374-2721; Direct: (202) 336-5510
Fax: (202) 336-5502; TDD/TTY: (202) 336-6123
Online: http://www.apa.org/pubs/books
E-mail: order@apa.org

In the U.K., Europe, Africa, and the Middle East, copies may be ordered from
Eurospan Group
c/o Turpin Distribution
Pegasus Drive
Stratton Business Park
Biggleswade Bedfordshire
SG18 8TQ United Kingdom
Phone: +44 (0) 1767 604972
Fax: +44 (0) 1767 601640
Online: https://www.eurospanbookstore.com/apa
E-mail: eurospan@turpin-distribution.com

Typeset in Meridien by Circle Graphics, Inc., Columbia, MD

Printer: Sheridan Books, Chelsea, MI
Cover Designer: Beth Schlenoff, Bethesda, MD

Library of Congress Cataloging-in-Publication Data

Names: Waterman, Jill, 1945- author. | Langley, Audra K., author. | Miranda, Jeanne, 1950- author. | Riley, Debbie B., author.
Title: Adoption-specific therapy : a guide to helping adopted children and their families thrive / Jill Waterman, Audra K. Langley, Jeanne Miranda, and Debbie B. Riley.
Description: Washington, DC : American Psychological Association, [2018] | Includes bibliographical references and index.
Identifiers: LCCN 2017061356| ISBN 9781433829246 | ISBN 143382924X
Subjects: LCSH: Adopted children—Counseling of. | Family counseling. | Adoption—Psychological aspects.
Classification: LCC HV875 .W38 2018 | DDC 362.734—dc23 LC record available at https://lccn.loc.gov/2017061356

British Library Cataloguing-in-Publication Data
A CIP record is available from the British Library.

Printed in the United States of America
First Edition

http://dx.doi.org/10.1037/0000096-000

10 9 8 7 6 5 4 3 2 1

To adoptive parents, who are willing to open up their homes and their hearts to provide permanency, stability, security, and love to often traumatized and hurt children, and to the foster and adopted children who blossom and develop in families sensitive to their history and adoption-specific needs.

To my children and grandchildren, present and future, who bring me much joy and whom I love so dearly; to the hundreds of children and families I've seen in psychotherapy at UCLA TIES for Families and elsewhere who have taught me about the resilience and capacity for growth and connection of vulnerable children; and to the memory of my beloved father, who aged out of an orphanage after eighth grade without having known the love and security of a family.
—Jill Waterman

To my children, adopted and otherwise—Ansel, Teagan, and Neve Garcia-Langley—the best part of my day, every single day. May you always be there for each other through triumphs, big and small, and to put one another back together if the world tries to tear you down. And to the dedicated, multidisciplinary staff at UCLA TIES for Families, whose unwavering belief that every child deserves a stable, nurturing family changes and heals lives.
—Audra K. Langley

To my roots (Naomi and Norman Miranda) and my shoots (Diego and Xiomara [daughter-in-law], Juan Camilo and Angie Klein). My amazing adopted children have taught me the strength of the human spirit given rough beginnings, as well the capacity to form loving adoptive family bonds that nourish me daily and bring amazing joy to my life.
—Jeanne Miranda

To all of the clinical staff at the Center for Adoption Support and Education who have deeply influenced the C.A.S.E. therapeutic model and value of adoption-specific therapy and the impact it has had on the children and families we serve.
—Debbie B. Riley

Contents

List of Online Handouts

The treatment protocol presented in this book uses many handouts with both parents and children. The handouts are listed below and referred to in the text by their name and number. All handouts can be found online (http://pubs.apa.org/books/supp/waterman) to allow for easy reproduction and use with families.

Preface

This book developed gradually over a period of almost 10 years as a collaboration between University of California Los Angeles Training, Intervention, Education, and Services (UCLA TIES) for Families in Los Angeles, California, and the Center for Adoption Support and Education (C.A.S.E.) in Maryland. We'd like to share a bit about how each center was formed and how the synergy in our approaches led to this book. Interestingly, all the authors' lives have been touched by adoption. Three of the authors are adoptive mothers, one through adoption from foster care, one through infant domestic adoption, and the third through international adoption from Peru and Colombia. The other author's father grew up in an orphanage in St. Louis, Missouri, and never had the opportunity to be adopted into a family.

TIES for Adoption (now called UCLA TIES for Families) was founded in 1995 as a collaboration between UCLA and the Los Angeles County Department of Children and Family Services through an Adoption Opportunities grant from the federal government. It originated in the middle of the crack cocaine epidemic when Susan Edelstein—TIES' founder and a social worker with the UCLA SCAN (Suspected Child Abuse and Neglect) team and the Neonatal Intensive Care Nursery—noticed that babies and children who had experienced prenatal substance exposure were not being adopted. Prospective adoptive parents were afraid to risk providing permanency for these very vulnerable children because of unsubstantiated reports in prominent newspapers and other publications that these children would never be normal, could not attend regular schools, and were doomed for life (Besharov, 1989; Brody, 1988; Chasnoff, Burns, Schnoll, & Burns, 1985). Prospective parents reported that the risks were just too large, and they worried about potential serious consequences of these terrifying claims. Moreover, parents who overcame their fears and fostered or adopted these vulnerable children were often unprepared to meet the unique challenges of parenting these children, and sometimes their lack of knowledge and support led to unintentional negative outcomes. For example, one foster parent complained about an 18-month-old who was throwing feces. When TIES' clinicians made a home visit, they found that the foster mother had isolated the child in a crib in a dark room because she had heard that children prenatally exposed to substances did better with a minimum of stimulation. It was not surprising that the child was throwing feces because there was nothing else for him to play with or focus on.

In response to this widespread lack of accurate information regarding the needs of prenatally exposed children, Ms. Edelstein started PREP, three 3-hour preplacement education sessions for prospective foster and adoptive parents considering adoption from foster care through the Los Angeles Department of Children and Family Services (DCFS). Later research showed PREP helped prospective parents gain knowledge about prenatal substance exposure and substance-using birth parents and that it significantly increased their willingness to adopt children with prenatal substance exposure as well as other high-risk conditions such as parental mental illness and attention-deficit/hyperactivity disorder (Edelstein et al., 2017). Also in 1995, Dr. Jill Waterman and Ms. Edelstein developed the TIES interdisciplinary treatment model, which has expanded greatly over the years and formed part of the basis of adoption-specific therapy. TIES is supported primarily through public funding from DCFS and the Los Angeles Department of Mental Health.

UCLA TIES for Families' mission is to optimize the growth and development of children from birth to age 21 with special needs who are, or have been, in foster care and are in some stage of adoptive or other permanency planning option. The program supports the children and their foster and/or adoptive families with an array of high-quality, interdisciplinary, accessible, and free comprehensive services, including comprehensive mental health, pediatric, educational, and speech and language consultation; occupational therapy; youth and parent mentorship; and therapeutic behavioral services to address the wide range of psychological, psychiatric, social, and educational needs presented by children and families. TIES has provided training to social workers, attorneys, and judges locally and to mental health professionals and students locally, nationally, and internationally. Dr. Audra Langley, a clinical child psychologist and adoptive parent, is the director of UCLA TIES for Families and has been an integral part of developing adoption-specific therapy.

C.A.S.E. was cofounded in 1998 by Kathleen Dugan, an extraordinary woman and mother of 12, and Debbie Riley, LCMFT, an adoptive parent, mental health provider, and administrator. Always knowing she would adopt one day after giving birth to four daughters, Kathleen and her husband Mike adopted eight older children placed through the public child welfare system. They knew how difficult it was for older children to find permanent homes. Many had histories of traumatic beginnings and years of deprivation. As they matured, the children's troubled emotions often resulted in challenging and, at times, dangerous behaviors. Kathleen's search for the support and help their children and family needed too often ended with a recommendation to return their children to foster care.

Frustrated by the lack of support available, Kathleen invested her own financial resources and engaged the passion and expertise of Debbie Riley to establish and become the chief executive officer of C.A.S.E. Debbie had worked in a variety of mental health settings—from community-based mental health to inpatient and residential treatment center settings—so she was acutely aware of the overrepresentation of adopted youth in higher levels of mental health care and the lack of treatment programs available to address the inherent issues in adoption.

Together, Kathleen and Debbie established C.A.S.E. to provide pre- and post-adoption counseling and education services to families in Maryland, Northern Virginia, and Washington, DC. They wanted a free-standing organization not connected with a placement agency to enhance the accessibility of adoption-competent mental health services to families of all foster care and adoptive backgrounds. C.A.S.E.'s mission is to improve the lives of adopted and foster children through counseling, lifelong education, and a growing national network of trained professionals.

Since its inception, C.A.S.E. has served over 6,000 foster and adoptive families ensuring improved child well-being and adoption permanency. C.A.S.E. staff is a multidisciplinary team bringing together expertise in the field of social work, family therapy, expressive therapy, and education to address the unique needs of this population through a trauma-informed, adoption competent framework. C.A.S.E.'s expert clinical team has received training in the growing field of adoption using the C.A.S.E. national model, Training for Adoption Competency (TAC), which is being replicated in 17 states nationally.

In 2007, Dr. Jeanne Miranda approached the TIES staff about developing a manualized version of their adoption treatment so that it could eventually be studied and disseminated to others. She was an established researcher in the area of depression treatment and mental health care disparities who had developed an interest in furthering the field of adoption psychotherapy after seeking services for her adopted children. She was surprised to find that many therapists knew little about adopted children. Because she was a psychotherapist herself, was well-connected in the therapy community, and had insurance, she felt it would be easy to get appropriate care for her children. Given that it was so difficult to find adoption-competent care, she contacted TIES about beginning to manualize the therapy.

As a preliminary step to develop and manualize an adoption-specific therapy, Dr. Miranda organized a conference, funded by the Annie E. Casey Foundation, with a stellar list of psychotherapy developers from areas close to adoption, including representatives from both TIES and C.A.S.E. As TIES and C.A.S.E. staff attended each other's trainings, it became clear that they shared some basic principles for helping children and families in the process of adoption. For example, both agencies believe that children deserve all information about their background at developmentally appropriate times, that it is helpful for families to talk openly from the beginning about adoption, that children who have had traumatic histories and multiple placements may not respond to standard mental health treatment that does not take into account how their dysfunctional behavioral responses may have been adaptive in a previous traumatic context, that there is no "quick fix" for longstanding developmental trauma, that activity-based curriculum is most helpful for these vulnerable children, that a family-based approach where parents receive as much treatment as the children is helpful, and that children are exceptionally resilient and we can build on their strengths.

Given the similarity in these underlying theoretical and philosophical views, the four authors of this volume worked together to develop this manualized version of our shared mental health treatment approach. With additional funding from the Annie E. Casey Foundation, the authors developed the intervention, pilot-tested it in several agencies, developed training workshops for therapists, and endlessly revised the treatment and associated activities as more experience and data accumulated. The adoption-specific therapy presented here—which we call ADAPT—was the result. All the authors care passionately about adopted children and their parents, both for personal reasons and as the focus of our professional lives. We hope this book will help adoptive and foster families thrive.

Acknowledgments

In the development and writing of this book, we received assistance from many people, whom we would like to acknowledge. Most important, we thank the families who participated in our adoption-specific therapy (ADAPT) curriculum over its long period of development and helped us refine and improve our intervention. These families, adopting older children from foster care, received adoption-specific therapy in Los Angeles through University of California Los Angeles Training, Intervention, Education, and Services (UCLA TIES) for Families, TIES for Families South Bay, and Children's Bureau; in the Washington, DC, area through Center for Adoption Support and Education (C.A.S.E.); and in North Carolina through Children's Home Society of North Carolina. Additionally, we thank the therapists who learned and administered the intervention for their faithful adherence and enthusiastic support.

In translating and refining our intervention for presentation in this book, we would like to give special thanks and acknowledgment to Ellen Singer, LCSW-C, senior adoption competent therapist and training coordinator at C.A.S.E. for her incredible hard work in helping to write and edit this manual, as well as to her colleague at C.A.S.E., Penny Zimmerman, LCSW-C, who helped develop case examples for the child sessions. Ellen's expertise has been impactful throughout our work on this book. We are also very grateful to Erum Nadeem, PhD, for a previous review of the literature on adoption that we drew from liberally. In addition, Austin Blake at UCLA TIES for Families provided invaluable help in many ways, including preparing references, formatting handouts, proofreading, and being available to do anything asked, always in her efficient and pleasant manner. Finally, we want to acknowledge Susan Edelstein, LCSW, founder of TIES for Adoption, for her vision and dedication to bringing interdisciplinary adoption-specific services to children transitioning from foster care and their families.

ADOPTION-SPECIFIC THERAPY

Introduction

Adoption-specific therapy was developed from our experience treating children who had been adopted past infancy, either through foster care or internationally. We noticed that often these children had very specific kinds of symptoms and that they frequently did not respond to standard evidence-based mental health interventions in the same way as children who did not have disrupted attachments and trauma histories. Most adopted children and families are resilient and successful, and children who are adopted do much better than children who have never had a permanent family, instead aging out of foster care (Triseliotis, 2002; Vinnerljung & Hjern, 2011) or remaining in institutions (van IJzendoorn, Juffer, & Poelhuis, 2005). However, overall, children who have been adopted have more mental health issues than do children raised in their biological families (Miller, Fan, Christensen, Grotevant, & van Dulmen, 2000). Although families usually came to treatment for help with particular behavioral concerns and problems and not to deal with issues related to adoption, we began recognizing that these serious behavioral and emotional symptoms such as stealing, lying, aggression, running away, hoarding food, depression, and so forth that some children present with, particularly those adopted at older ages, were connected to what had happened to them prior to joining their adoptive families.

http://dx.doi.org/10.1037/0000096-001
Adoption-Specific Therapy: A Guide to Helping Adopted Children and Their Families Thrive, by J. Waterman, A. K. Langley, J. Miranda, and D. B. Riley

We realized that there were strategies and interventions that seemed to be quite effective when used to enhance standard psychotherapy techniques with adopted children; the common element had to do with redesigning interventions to take into account the child's past history of abuse, neglect, and/or trauma and their developmental understanding of adoption.

For example, Josie, 7 years old, was brought to treatment by her adoptive parents because they were concerned that she was very friendly to everyone, and they worried that she was an easy target for kidnapping or a sexual predator. She had come to the family from foster care 2 years prior, having already lived with eight different caregivers, including several previous foster placements and various maternal relatives. Although she generally obeyed her parents' rules and tried to please, the parents didn't feel like they really knew her at a deeper level despite her living with them for several years. The other problem they presented was that Josie lied whenever she might be in trouble and was unable to back down even after it was clearly evident that what she said was untrue. When about to be interviewed, Josie eagerly held the therapist's hand and did not look back at her parents as she left the waiting room. She was friendly and outgoing, and said she wanted to stop lying but she just didn't know how. In treatment, her parents worked diligently to set appropriate limits and develop a reward system for being truthful, and Josie seemed to be on board with joint plans, but whenever she thought she had done something wrong, she felt she could not stop herself from lying about it, and this behavior remained unchanged.

In another case, Willie, 10 years old, and his two dads came in because of his aggressive behaviors at home and in school. He also was stealing from his parents and brother as well as occasionally stealing from peers at school. Willie had been with the family for 14 months and although they had become very attached to him, they were hesitant about finalizing the adoption because of his behavior problems. The parents were concerned that the closer it came to finalizing the adoption, the worse Willie's behaviors were becoming. Once again, standard evidence-based behavioral strategies were not effective in decreasing Willie's aggression and stealing. Although Willie felt he benefitted from learning relaxation and calming strategies such as deep breathing and muscle relaxation in sessions with the therapist, his aggression had not diminished significantly. He had been rejected by several previous potential adoptive placements because of fighting and was able to say that he was sure these parents would reject him too. He also felt that his prospective adoptive parents did not understand the importance of his African American culture, and he was concerned about how others would judge him for having two dads. Finally, he hated the organic food served in the house.

Mai Lei, age 9, had been adopted from China when she was 5 years old and had lived with her Caucasian American single mother for 4 years when they came in for therapy. Mai Lei had a great deal of difficulty speaking English correctly even after 4 years, though she understood everything that was said to her, and she was failing in school. Despite a great deal of tutoring and educational therapy, she had improved very little. Additionally, Mai Lei was quite withdrawn and wanted to be alone in her room. There was another Chinese girl in her condominium complex, and whenever possible, Mai Lei spent time with that family, leaving her adopted mother feeling left out and rejected. Despite the best intentions of both her mother and her therapist, attempts to encourage more family interaction and closeness were not successful. For example, setting up rewards for spending time with her mom and not in her room did not help.

Through seeing cases such as those described here, clinicians at both University of California Los Angeles Training, Intervention, Education, and Services (UCLA TIES) for Families on the West Coast and Center for Adoption Support and Education (C.A.S.E.) on the East Coast recognized that such families needed a different approach to standard interventions. We noticed common patterns in these children who had known other caregiving situations than their adoptive families, many of which involved situations traumatic for the children. Believing that children are naturally resilient, we began to recognize that the behaviors that were so problematic in their current homes had almost always been adaptive in a previous traumatic or dysfunctional setting. So in looking at the examples described previously, review of records and interviews with parents almost always gave us a clue about the meaning of the children's difficult behaviors and how they may have helped the child cope and even survive in a previous abusive or neglectful situation. This provided the spark for our development of new interventions that took the child's traumatic history into account, both in tweaking evidence-based behavioral interventions and in introducing some attachment-based interventions consistent with the rich clinical literature on adoption dynamics.

For Josie, we realized that having been in at least seven different homes in 5 years, superficial friendliness to everyone was very adaptive. Such behaviors elicited positive reactions from constantly changing caregivers, and it would be dangerous to become too attached to any one person because her experience had been that the caregiver was likely to soon disappear. We also recognized that in her original home, her birth mother had been addicted to methamphetamines, and when high, she often became abusive to Josie when she sought attention or disturbed her, screaming and hitting her. One instance in the records described a situation (which led to her removal from the home the first time) in which her birth mother asked Josie whether she had taken a box that held some drugs. When Josie said she did, she was beaten severely. As a result, it became highly adaptive for Josie to deny any wrongdoing because admitting it led to traumatic consequences. Although lying also led to punishment at times, she sometimes did not get caught. The intensity of her anxiety would lead her to lie whenever confronted with possible undesired behavior.

Understanding these dynamics was necessary for the family and the therapist to be able to intervene in ways that took Josie's previous traumatic context into account in developing a therapeutic behavior plan, recognizing that her problematic behaviors had been adaptive and protective in a previous abusive caregiving environment. The adoptive parents learned not to confront Josie and ask if she had done something she was not supposed to, but instead to deal with it matter-of-factly so she did not have to lie. When the adoptive parents responded calmly and rationally to Josie's behavior and gave reassurances that she is loved and wanted no matter what her behavior, along with appropriate consequences, Josie gradually learned that this family environment is safe and loving. Over time and with consistent safety and security in the adoptive family, her need to lie diminished greatly, and her sense of safety and security increased. Similarly, her need to be superficially friendly to people diminished as she developed a deeper attachment to her parents. For example, she began to have trepidation around certain strangers and would want to hold the hand of a parent in those situations.

In Willie's case, his behavior problems of aggression and stealing needed to be seen through the lens of his past history. His birth family had been gang involved, and he had witnessed a great deal of violence both at home and in his community by the time he entered foster care at age 5. At one point, his birth mother had taken Willie and gone to live on the streets to escape ongoing domestic violence from his birth father. After that, they were homeless for about 18 months before she returned to the birth father. During that time, she and Willie survived by stealing food from stores, combing through dumpsters, and begging on the street.

When considering his past history, it was clear that responding to strong feelings with aggression was normative in Willie's previous living situation and was modeled by his caregivers. Additionally, his stealing behavior (often stealing food or money to buy food) can be understood as an adaptive response to being homeless and hungry that helped Willie survive on the streets. Assisting the prospective adoptive parents to understand that these behaviors were helpful to Willie in his previous caregiving environment and to look at them from Willie's point of view allowed the dads to experience increased empathy for him. They were then more open to learning new strategies to manage his difficult behaviors. For example, Willie's parents acknowledged to him that they understood he sometimes had not had enough to eat or even warm clothes at times in the past. Noting that he must be afraid of being hungry and not having enough food, they provided a large bowl of acceptable snacks that he liked and made it available 24/7 and also brought some to the school that he could get from his teacher if he felt the need to steal food. They also decided to learn to make some of the foods that he had loved from his original family, such as shrimp and grits, and this turned out to be an important way in which the family incorporated Willie's birth culture into their lifestyle, helping him feel more connected to the adopting family. They also attended a support group made up of other same-sex couples and their children so that Willie could gain support from other children about issues that come up around being in a nontraditional family. Additionally, Willie's parents told him that they would always take care of him and make sure his needs were met. Although there were a couple of hiccups along with way, Willie's stealing decreased dramatically.

With regard to his aggressive behaviors, his parents came to understand both that aggression had been a problem-solving strategy in Willie's birth family and that his aggression had seemed to increase in his previous prospective homes as the adoption had begun to approach finalization, probably as a way of helping him feel he was rejecting the family before they could reject him. Armed with this new understanding, they were able to talk with him about the pattern and assure him that they wanted him as part of their family regardless of how he might try to push them away. They noted how scary it must be to think that this might be his forever family.

With Mai Lei, it appeared that she and her mother had not really developed an emotional connection, which left Mai Lei unmotivated and depressed and her mother alienated and frustrated. It seemed as if Mai Lei still did not feel comfortable in the United States and held onto her language by avoiding learning English partly as a way of continuing to feel Chinese. After some initial defensiveness, her mother was able to look at their lifestyle and see that no aspect of Mai Lei's heritage was honored in their home. After brainstorming with the therapist, the mother decided that if Mai Lei was having trouble learning English, maybe she should learn Mandarin. After talking it over with Mai Lei, she enrolled in a conversational Chinese class. Mai Lei made fun of her efforts to speak Chinese at home but enjoyed giving her mom pointers on both vocabulary and pronunciation. The more her mother worked on her Chinese, the warmer and more animated Mai Lei became. Mai Lei's mother decided to subscribe to a Chinese language cable station and they were able to watch simple shows together with pleasure. Interestingly, as her mother's Chinese became better, Mai Lei's English proficiency improved as well. This intervention, although certainly not standard, addressed both the lack of attachment in the family and the child's mourning for her original culture.

As these examples show, we believe that to best serve adopted children, especially those most at risk for serious behavioral and emotional distress, the most useful treatment protocol is one that uses an adoption lens that takes into account the child's past history and addresses behavioral, developmental, and attachment-related concerns while building on the child's natural resilience, coping, and competence. We have developed an adoption-specific therapy protocol and named it adoption-specific therapy (ADAPT). This book presents clear, step-by-step instructions for delivering ADAPT, as well as an ongoing case example to illustrate activities and concepts. The book is intended for therapists who treat adopted children and their families.

ADAPT, developed over many iterations, combines what we know about evidence-based behavioral treatments for children and parents (e.g., Chorpita, Daleiden, & Collins, 2014; Eyberg, 1988; Webster-Stratton, 2011) with consideration of the child's past trauma history and adoption dynamics culled from best practices and the adoption literature. Although not yet subjected to rigorous research, the rich past literature on adoption dynamics (e.g., Barth & Miller, 2000; Brodzinsky, 1993; Fahlberg, 1991, 2012; Kerman, Freundlich, & Maluccio, 2009), widely accepted by practitioners specializing in this work, allows us to bring this piece of the puzzle into child behavior treatments. ADAPT was developed to standardize and to test this integration of adoption-specific therapeutic practices with evidence-based behavioral treatments. Interestingly, the large literature on adoption dynamics is targeted almost exclusively to parents (e.g., Berry & Berry, 2016; Caughman & Motley, 2009; Eldridge, 1999; Gray, 2002), and there are few studies to our knowledge that seek to systematically evaluate adoption-focused treatment programs, especially for older children adopted from foster care or orphanages.

Three Kinds of Adoption in the United States

There are three routes to adoption used by American families: domestic infant adoption, international adoption, and foster care adoption. In domestic infant adoption, a birth mother is matched with a family interested in adoption, usually through lawyers or adoption agencies specializing in this field, and they receive the child immediately after release from the hospital. Often the adopters pay the medical bills and living expenses of the birth mother and may be present at the birth. In 2014, approximately 16,312 infants were adopted through private agencies and 5,944 through private individual adoptions (Jones & Placek, 2017).

In international adoption, prospective parents usually work through an international adoption agency in, or with ties to, a particular country. Once a child is identified for them, they travel to the country and after a few days to weeks take the child home with the adoption complete from the providing country's viewpoint. Children are often infants but can be much older. Over the years, fewer countries have participated in international adoption; for example, China, which once was a prolific source, now prefers to keep the children in China, and Russia has also stopped adoptions to the United States. Statistics show that 5,370 children were adopted from other countries in 2016 (U.S. Department of State, 2017); international adoptions have declined steadily from a high of 22,989 children in 2004 (Leinaweaver, 2017). Of those adopted in 2016, the largest group were 5- to 12-year-olds, followed by 3- and 4-year-olds. Despite great decreases in the number of children available for international adoption, China sent the most children: 2,231.

In foster care adoption, children are removed from the birth parents because of abuse or neglect, and if there is not an appropriate birth family member to care for the children, they are placed with a foster family who may or may not wish to adopt. The birth family then receives reunification services, including possible drug treatment, psychotherapy, parenting assistance, and so forth, and is granted progressive visitation with the children. If this is successful, the child returns to the birth family. If the birth parents are not able to provide a safe home, other relatives may step up and provide permanency for the child, either through kinship adoption or legal guardianship. If reunification with a family member is unfortunately not possible, family reunification services are terminated and a permanency plan such as adoption is made. Birth families may still have visitation while the decision about whether to terminate the birth parents' rights is being made. Furthermore, even if the birth parents' parental rights are terminated and the child joins an adoptive family, the birth parents sometimes remain connected to the child by some means, whether sharing photos or special events or having ongoing visitation if that is safe for the child. More and more, this arrangement, called "open adoption," is advocated. In 2015, almost 270,000 children entered foster care, with neglect (61%) and parental drug abuse (32%) accounting for the lion's share of new cases. Of the 427,000 children in foster care in 2015, 111,820 were waiting for adoptive families, and 53,549 children were adopted from public foster care during 2015. The number of adoptions from foster care has been quite stable over the last decade, with about 21% of children who exit foster care being adopted. According to The Adoption and Foster Care Analysis and Reporting System, in 2015 the mean age of adoption from foster care was 6.2 years (Child Welfare Information Gateway, 2017; U.S. Department of Health and Human Services, 2016).

This book focuses mostly on children adopted past infancy through foster care or internationally because they are among our most vulnerable children. Not only have they lost their birth family and often a cultural heritage, but many have also suffered multiple placements or orphanage care that may lead to repeated loss of caregivers, abuse and neglect, and trauma in their homes and their communities. As discussed further in Chapter 1, children adopted at older ages experience significantly more behavioral and educational problems (e.g., Gleitman & Savaya, 2011; Nadeem et al., 2017; Sharma et al., 1996b; Waterman et al., 2013).

However, although ADAPT's focus on loss, grief, and trauma will be most relevant to families adopting from foster care or internationally, many of the exercises are useful for any adoptive child or parent, regardless of how old the child was at the time of adoption or how much trauma they have experienced. These exercises will help families understand adoption, form close bonds, and deal with others' attitudes about adoption.

Adoption-Specific Therapy: The ADAPT Curriculum

As illustrated by the case examples presented here, we have come to realize that it is necessary to process certain common aspects of these children's experiences as well as those of the adoptive parents who care for them to optimize successful family formation and to heal past deeply felt wounds. For example, we support open discussion about all aspects of adoption and believe that all information about the child's past, no matter how heinous or painful, should be shared with the child as developmentally appropriate. We also believe that the grief and loss about previous caregivers must be honored and facilitated. Often parents want to reassure children that now that they are in their adoptive home, everything will be fine. We want to help adoptive parents accept and understand the sadness and yearning that most adoptees feel for their birth families even if the birth parents were highly abusive to the child. Although these feelings are most pronounced for older children who have memories of living in and leaving their previous caregiving situation (birth family, foster family, or orphanage), children adopted at birth also feel similar feelings and wonder what was it about them that led their parent to give them up or be unable to care for them. There are also significant identity issues that arise for adopted children as they get older, particularly in transracial adoptions, and these must be addressed as well. If there is significant trauma in their backgrounds, children need to be able to process these with the therapist and view their parents as a supportive resource when they are experiencing posttraumatic stress.

Dealing with such adoption- and trauma-related issues is necessary to successfully treat the significant behavioral and emotional symptoms that bring adoptive families to seek treatment. ADAPT combines evidence-based child coping strategies and positive parenting approaches—largely from cognitive behavioral therapy and modified to take into account the child's past history—with resiliency-focused, trauma-competent, attachment-based treatment that addresses adoption-related issues of parent–child bonding, loss and grief, developmental understanding of adoption dynamics, identity development, and birth family connections. In each of the seven modules of adoption-specific therapy (20–24 sessions total), parents and children meet separately for several sessions and then come together for a family session. Although the focus of the ADAPT intervention is on children adopted past infancy, we have found that children adopted at birth and their parents can also benefit significantly from adoption-specific therapy.

In Chapter 1, we discuss the theoretical and empirical underpinnings of our approach. Chapter 2 presents an overview of ADAPT, including our basic beliefs about adoption, a summary of module content, and who should use this approach and how. In Chapters 3 through 9, we present the modules with detailed instructions for therapists on how to use the approach with families, along with the ongoing case example of the Springfield family, which illustrates how each session may unfold. In Chapter 10, we discuss the termination session.

Many of the treatment activities described in this book involve handouts. There are 60 handouts in total, all of which can be downloaded for free from the book's companion website (http://pubs.apa.org/books/supp/waterman). Interested readers may also purchase a supplemental ADAPT toolkit from C.A.S.E. for $95.99 (see http://www.adoptionsupport.org).

We are passionate about supporting the resilience of adopted children and their families and hope that you will find adoption-specific therapy very helpful in your own work.

FOUNDATIONS

I

1 Theoretical and Empirical Underpinnings of Adoption-Specific Therapy

In this chapter, we provide information that forms the basis from which adoption-specific therapy developed. First we present basic data about adoption. Then we discuss the mental health needs of adopted children, reviewing the literature on psychological and psychiatric issues of both domestic and international adoptees, as well as preplacement predictors of mental health concerns, documenting the need for mental health services for adopted children and families. We note that children adopted at an older age are particularly vulnerable. Next, school and cognitive challenges are reviewed, along with protective factors. After a discussion of data on identity issues for adopted children and adoption dynamics, we look at studies of postadoption services. There is a paucity of interventions designed for families after adoption, which adoption-specific therapy seeks to change by our intervention to help families build positivity, develop coping skills, discuss adoption parameters sensitively and openly, cope with loss and grief, and increase attachment. We then discuss our approach to treatment, with an emphasis on supporting adopted children's resiliency while helping families understand children through the lens of their past often-traumatic history.

http://dx.doi.org/10.1037/0000096-002
Adoption-Specific Therapy: A Guide to Helping Adopted Children and Their Families Thrive, by J. Waterman, A. K. Langley, J. Miranda, and D. B. Riley

Adoption Basics

The 2000 census was the first census in which adoption statistics were collected. The estimated number of children adopted in the year 2000 was slightly over 128,000, bringing the total U.S. population of adopted children to 2,058,915. The number of children adopted in the year 2008 increased to nearly 136,000 (Children's Bureau, 2011). As a result of the rising rates of adoption, Americans have reported an increase in their experience with adoption in recent years. In fact, 65% of families in a national survey reported that they had experienced adoption either through their own families or their friends (Dave Thomas Foundation for Adoption & Evan B. Donaldson Adoption Institute, 2002). The majority of Americans feel favorable toward and supportive of adoptive families (Dave Thomas Foundation for Adoption & Evan B. Donaldson Adoption Institute, 2002).

In the past 15 years, adoptions from foster care have increased. The Adoption and Safe Families Act of 1997 (ASFA), along with subsequent Congressional initiatives, has provided incentives to states to increase adoptions from foster care and subsidies for parents adopting older children from foster care. This resulted in increased rates of adoption of children in foster care from 26,000 in 1995 to 50,000 beginning in 2002 (U.S. Department of Health and Human Services, 2010), with increased rates continuing to date. The mean age at adoption from foster care is now 6 years (U.S. Department of Health and Human Services, 2010). Seventeen percent of international adoptees are over the age of 5 at adoption. These older children can have histories of physical and sexual abuse, neglect, multiple placements, and prenatal substance exposure, all factors that if left untreated, can contribute to subsequent risk for mental health issues and substance abuse (Pilowsky & Wu, 2006).

Mental Health Challenges of Adopted Youth

Although children who are adopted fare better than those who age out of foster care, consistent evidence from both international and domestic studies indicate that adoptees remain at higher risk for both psychiatric and behavioral problems than children raised in their biological families. Given their risk for early adversity, older adopted children's difficult histories could easily result in increased risk for mental health and behavioral challenges. The most comprehensive study of this issue to date is a meta-analysis in which data from all available studies of this issue were combined to form a sample of 25,000 adoptees from across different countries. This study concluded that adoptees have more behavioral problems compared with nonadoptees (Juffer & van IJzendoorn, 2005). Furthermore, domestic adoptees have more behavioral problems than international adoptees (Juffer & van IJzendoorn, 2005). International adoptees are often in need of families because of poverty within their countries, whereas domestic adoptees who have experienced foster care are often removed from their families because of problems related to substance abuse and mental health that may lead to higher rates of child exposure to trauma, abuse, and neglect. Those involved in private domestic adoption are usually voluntarily relinquished by their birth parents.

Overall, in both international and domestic studies, adoptees are more likely to differ from their nonadopted peers in externalizing problems compared with internalizing problems (Juffer & van IJzendoorn, 2005). On the basis of their review of the literature, taking into account study selection criteria and sample characteristics, Bimmel and colleagues (Bimmel, van IJzendoorn, Bakermans-Kranenburg, Juffer, & De Geus, 2008) concluded that it is not adoption per se that puts children at risk for psychiatric and behavioral problems, but rather the adversity, trauma, disrupted attachments, and maltreatment that many adopted children face prior to adoption. Given this, it makes sense that age at adoption is consistently found to be a risk factor for mental health problems, with higher age related to increased risk (Bimmel et al., 2008; Hjern, Lindblad, & Vinnerljung, 2002; Verhulst, Althaus, & Versluis-den Bieman, 1990b).

INTERNATIONAL STUDIES OF PSYCHIATRIC DISORDERS

Studies carried out in Scandinavian countries have been able to provide very strong evidence about mental health diagnoses of adoptees because they have national registries of adopted children and are able to link this registry with public health registries. Verhulst and colleagues (Verhulst, Althaus, & Versluis-den Bieman, 1992) in the Netherlands found that adoptees from other countries are twice as likely to be in the clinical range for externalizing disorders—such as attention-deficit/hyperactivity disorder (ADHD) and oppositional defiant disorder (ODD)—than are nonadoptees (Verhulst, Althaus, & Versluis-den Bieman, 1990a). A Swedish cohort study examining over 11,000 intercountry adoptees found that adoptees were three to four times more likely than the Swedish-born children to commit suicide or attempt suicide and five times more likely to be hospitalized for a psychiatric or substance abuse problem (Hjern et al., 2002). Similarly, another Swedish study reported that adoptees were up to three times as likely to have psychiatric and substance abuse problems, were more likely to receive social welfare, and were less educated (given the socioeconomic status [SES] of their adoptive families) than were their nonadoptive peers from similarly high SES families. Nonetheless, those who were adopted were average on each measure, such as education level, for their country (Lindblad et al., 2003).

U.S. STUDIES OF PSYCHIATRIC DISORDERS

Studies in the United States have shown the same general pattern of higher rates of psychiatric diagnoses among adopted compared with nonadopted youth. For example, Keyes and colleagues (Keyes, Sharma, Elkins, Iacono, & McGue, 2008) compared domestic and internationally adopted adolescents (adopted before age 2 years) to nonadopted adolescents in the United States and found that adopted adolescents had more symptoms of externalizing disorders (ODD, ADHD, conduct disorder). Adoptees were also rated as being more anxious by teachers. Domestic adoptees and children who were older at the time of placement were at higher risk for psychiatric and school problems (Keyes et al., 2008). An examination of 292 adopted children in Illinois whose families were taking part in a state adoption preservation program revealed that over half of the children had externalizing problems (Smith et al., 2006). With regard to psychiatric problems, a statewide study of adopted youth 8 years after placement showed that 30% of the sample exhibited symptoms consistent with ODD, ADHD, or both according to parental report (21% had ADHD symptoms and 20% had ODD symptoms; Simmel, Brooks, Barth, & Hinshaw, 2001). It is important to note that having externalizing symptoms was associated with other biological and environmental risk factors that are common for children in foster care such as prenatal substance exposure, traumatic experiences, abuse and neglect, older age at adoption, and having endured multiple placements and separations from attachment figures (Simmel et al., 2001). Brodzinsky and colleagues (1984) found in a study of 260 adopted children that they were rated higher in externalizing psychological problems and school-related behavior problems (parent and teacher reports) than were nonadopted children. Berry and Barth (1989) studied 85 children adopted at age 3 or older and found that the average externalizing score on a common child behavioral problem measure (Child Behavior Checklist; Achenbach & Edelbrock, 1983) was near the clinical range, higher than found in nonadoptive samples. It is important to note that adopted children had more problems than nonadopted children but still fared better than youth who remain in foster care (Brand & Brinich, 1999).

DIFFERENCES IN RATES OF PSYCHIATRIC DISORDERS

Differences in rates of psychiatric disorders between adoptees and nonadoptees appear to be relatively stable over time, with evidence continuing into adulthood for those who are adopted as children. A study in the Netherlands found that adult adoptees were more likely to meet criteria for an anxiety disorder or substance abuse disorder than nonadoptees and that adopted men were more likely to have a mood disorder than nonadopted men (Tieman, van der Ende, & Verhulst, 2005). There is also evidence that behavior problems and mental health difficulties among adoptees persist over time. In interpreting these findings, it is important to note that rates of disorders among those adopted were 29.6% compared with 21.6% of nonadopted individuals. Clearly, the vast majority of adopted individuals do not suffer from mental disorders. Although the rates of psychiatric disorders are higher among those who are adopted compared with those not adopted, the percentage difference is quite small.

Several international studies (Netherlands, New Zealand, Norway) reported that adoptees' externalizing problems persist into adulthood. Versluis-den Bieman and Verhulst (1995) found increased problem behaviors through later adolescence and early adulthood in a Dutch longitudinal study. Similarly, a longitudinal study in New Zealand found that adoptees' higher externalizing behaviors were present even 16 years later (Fergusson et al., 1995). Verhulst and colleagues (1992) reported that international adult adoptees in Norway had higher scores on hyperactivity than did their nonadopted peers. In the United States, Simmel (2007) conducted a study of almost 300 youth adopted from foster care (at 2, 4, and 8 years postadoption). Behavior problems tended to be stable over time (Rosenthal & Groze, 1994).

SUBSTANCE ABUSE AND ANTISOCIAL BEHAVIOR

Substance use and antisocial behavior also appear to be higher in adopted youth than their nonadopted peers. In a matched control study of U.S. adoptees (predominantly Caucasian), Sharma, McGue, and Benson (1996a) found that adoptees demonstrated significantly higher rates of drug use, antisocial behavior, and lower levels of optimism/self-confidence and school adjustment. On the other hand, those who were adopted reported higher rates of some prosocial behaviors (e.g., church or synagogue attendance, giving money or time to a charity, spending time helping people who are poor, hungry, or sick) than nonadoptees.

PREDICTORS OF PSYCHIATRIC PROBLEMS AMONG ADOPTEES

National surveys have indicated that approximately 11% of pregnant women used alcohol or drugs while pregnant (Vega, Kolody, Hwang, & Noble, 1993; Young et al., 2009), and 50%–79% of children in foster care have been prenatally exposed to substances (Testa & Smith, 2009). Because of the parental difficulties of overcoming substance abuse, a disproportionate percentage of foster children with prenatal substance exposure do not return to birth families and become available for adoption. Prenatally substance-exposed infants have increased biological risk factors (higher prematurity rates, smaller head circumference, and lower birth weight) than nonexposed infants (Fanaroff et al., 2007; Irner, Teasdale, Nielsen, Vedal, & Olofsson, 2012). Substance use during pregnancy is also associated with environmental risk factors. Compared with nonexposed children, those exposed to substances were placed in adoptive homes at an older age, had multiple foster placements, experienced abuse or neglect, and had birth families with lower SES (Barth & Brooks, 2001). Although prenatal substance exposure is sometimes associated with physical, developmental, learning, and behavioral issues (e.g., Bada et al., 2007; Simmel, Barth, & Brooks, 2007), these issues occur in the context of the risk factors. Because of variation in these risk factors, children with prenatal substance exposure are not a homogenous group; outcomes can range from no apparent effects to considerable short- and long-term harm (Marcellus, 2010). Helping families understand these multiple interacting risk factors and how to build in protective factors is important.

Given their risk for early adversity, it is not surprising that children's difficult histories seem to predict high rates of psychiatric problems and use of mental health services. For example, many youth in foster care have multiple placements, with one study reporting that 41% had more than three foster placements. Children with multiple placements and older children have higher use of mental health services than younger children with fewer placements (Rubin et al., 2004). One of the strongest predictors of psychiatric disorder was the rate of maltreatment (McMillen et al., 2005). High rates of trauma in foster youth are also related to increased mental health problems. A recent study examined complex trauma exposure, including physical abuse, sexual abuse, emotional abuse, neglect, and domestic violence, in foster youth ages 0–21. Extremely high rates of trauma exposure were noted, with 70.4% of the sample reporting at least two of these traumas and 11.7% reporting all five types (Greeson et al., 2011). Data from the Patterns of Care study (Hazen, Hough, Landsverk, & Wood, 2004) showed that children in the child welfare system had higher rates of use of residential treatment centers, group homes, emergency shelters, and specialty mental health outpatient services compared with children not involved in the child welfare system (controlling for age, gender, and diagnosis). Interestingly, they had lower odds of using school-based and juvenile justice services.

MENTAL HEALTH SERVICE USE BY CHILDREN WHO ARE ADOPTED

Large meta-analytic studies that put together many individual studies have documented that children who are adopted use more mental health and substance abuse services than those who are not adopted. There is also evidence that adoptive parents refer their children for services more than nonadoptive parents and that adopted children are overrepresented in clinical settings (Juffer & van IJzendoorn, 2005; Miller, Fan, Christensen, Grotevant, & van Dulmen, 2000; Wierzbicki, 1993). Many adoptive families and children could benefit from additional support because of the often difficult backgrounds of older children and children adopted from foster care. The National Survey of Adoptive Parents (www.cdc.gov/nchs/slaits/nsap.htm) inquired about rates of seeking counseling for 2,089 adoptive parents (923 with children under age 10 and 1,161 with children aged 10 and older). Of children adopted from foster care, 44.7% of those adopted at ages 0–2, 60.4% of those adopted at ages 3–5, and 69.8% of those adopted at ages 6+ had sought counseling. Among children adopted internationally, 40.3% of those adopted at ages 0–2, 48.5% of those adopted at ages 3–5, and 40.6% of those adopted ages 6+ had sought counseling.

A U.S. study of international and domestic adolescent adoptees who were adopted in infancy reported that adoptees had two times higher odds of having seen a mental health professional than nonadoptees (Keyes et al., 2008). Similarly, adoptees use more special education services and counseling than nonadoptees (Miller et al., 2000). Adoptees were also overrepresented in a study of psychiatric inpatient admissions; adopted and foster youth had the longest inpatient stays (Dickson, Heffron, & Parker, 1990). Children in foster care and those adopted are more likely to have used mental health services in the past 12 months than children residing with their birth parents (Brand & Brinich, 1999). However, the differences between adopted children and birth children lost significance when outliers were removed (Brand & Brinich, 1999), suggesting that a small number of children are high-service users and account for these differences. A Swedish study reported that children adopted under 7 years old and currently over age 10 were five times more likely to be placed in residential treatment and three times more likely to be placed in foster care than their comparison peers (Elmund, Lindblad, Vinnerljung, & Hjern, 2007). Older age at adoption and single parent adoption were associated with increased service use.

CONCLUSIONS REGARDING NEED FOR MENTAL HEALTH CARE

The research on children who are adopted would suggest that there is significant need for mental health care for these children, given the generally higher rates of mental disorders among this population and the high rates of service use by these children and their parents. Because some of these behavioral problems continue and standard mental health treatments may not address the trauma-related and adoption-specific experiences, especially for children adopted at older ages, new approaches that view the children's behaviors through the lens of their past history and trauma are necessary. These approaches consider the children's problematic behaviors in the context of their previous dysfunctional and often abusive caregiving experiences where these very behaviors may have been adaptive coping strategies that enabled the child to survive. In addition to helping children develop coping skills and helping parents with behavioral plans, treatment must look at issues of attachment, grief and loss, child identity, and adoption dynamics to be optimally successful.

School Challenges of Adopted Youth

Research has examined the extent to which adopted children have problems with cognitive development and school outcomes. Adopted adolescents are at higher risk for poor school achievement, skipping school, more negative feelings about school (Miller et al., 2000), and having lower grades (Sharma et al., 1996a) than are their nonadopted peers. These effects are larger for those with later age at adoption than for those adopted at younger ages (Sharma, McGue, & Benson, 1996b). Adopted youth with ADHD and/or ODD (29% of the sample) had more frequent complaints from teachers; more special education services; and more learning disabilities, suspensions, and impaired peer relations compared with the rest of the sample (Simmel et al., 2001). Again, those with difficult preadoption histories, such as abuse or neglect, later age of adoption, prenatal drug exposure, or multiple placement, were at greatest risk for poor outcomes (Simmel et al., 2001).

With regard to cognitive functioning, a meta-analysis of 62 studies that compared adoptees with children who remained in institutions or grew up with birth families showed that adoptees had higher scores on IQ tests and had better school performance than those who remained in institutions or with birth families. Their IQ was similar to their nonadopted siblings in their adopted homes and current environmental peers, but their school performance was poorer. These children needed special education services at twice the rate of their nonadopted peers. Not surprisingly, older age at adoption predicted poorer school achievement (van IJzendoorn & Juffer, 2005).

Children who are adopted, particularly those children who were adopted at an older age, are at higher risk for negative school outcomes than their nonadopted peers. This disadvantage is often due to older children having experienced multiple placements and therefore a disrupted school history. This would suggest that it is important for interventions to help families adopting children, particularly those adopting older children, to be aware of the potential extra services and supports that their child may need to succeed in school. For example, research by current authors (Waterman et al., 2013) examined the trajectory of cognitive development over the first 5 years of adoptive placement among children adopted from foster care. Overall, children's cognitive scores increased significantly over the 5-year period, with the most rapid improvement occurring in the first year after adoptive placement. By 5 years post-placement, children's mean cognitive and achievement scores were in the average range. Similar to van IJzendoorn and colleagues' findings (van IJzendoorn, Juffer, & Poelhuis, 2005), adopted children were referred for special education more often than their nonadopted peers, despite comparable cognitive scores.

Encouraging parents to support their child's individual strengths, even if they are not in the area of academics, is critical to building self-esteem and mastery for each child. Even if school is challenging for an adopted child, parents can focus on the positive things about the child such as characteristics of working hard, social skills, or having a good sense of humor, and they can support their other talents, strengths, and passions such as athletics, music, martial arts, theatre, dance, art, science, and building things. This is essential to helping adopted children feel loved and valued even if they struggle with school.

Adoptive Parent SES and Adoption Outcomes

High parental SES, in general, leads to better health, mental health, and functional outcomes for children. Maternal education predicts child health and achievement, with higher maternal education related positively to child health and overall achievement. These almost universal good outcomes are not true for all adoptees. For example, Tieman and colleagues (2005) found that for all psychiatric diagnoses together, adoptees with low and middle parental SES in childhood did not differ from the comparison subjects, whereas adoptees with high parental SES were twice as likely to meet the criteria for a disorder as nonadoptees with high parental SES. Similarly, among adoptees, living in a "white collar household" was associated with greater risk for social maladjustment, including alcohol abuse, drug abuse, criminal offense, or imprisonment (Hjern et al., 2002).

Review of the literature on child outcomes and parental SES suggests that children in adoptive families respond differently to family status than do nonadoptive children. Because adoptive children appear to fair better in less-affluent settings, it is important to help families know each child's unique strengths and develop appropriate expectations of their adopted children. Children need to feel that they are valued and respected, and positivity on the parents' part can help mitigate any concerns children may have that they are not "good enough" for their adopted family.

Identity and Adoption Dynamics

In addition to issues such as mental health, behavior problems, and school performance, issues directly related to adoption are important to consider in developing interventions for adoptive families. Children who have information about their birth parents also report knowing more about why they were placed for adoption and are more likely than children with less information to have both positive and negative feelings about their adoption (Wrobel, Grotevant, & McRoy, 2004). Adoptive parents who provide their children with information about their birth parents have children who demonstrate more curiosity about their adoptions and ask more questions of their parents about their birth families and adoption. A study of the adolescents' desire to search for birth parents (which ranged from having no information about their birth parents to those who had information but no direct contact) found that those with more open adoptions were more likely to search or be interested in searching for birth parents. Desire to search for birth parents was unrelated to behavior problems of family functioning (Wrobel et al., 2004). Over time, families report more satisfaction when the adoption is open than when there is no contact with birth parents (Grotevant, McRoy, Elde, & Fravel, 1994).

Many adopted children spend time thinking about their birth parents, even when they do not share these thoughts with their adoptive parents. Adolescents with very high levels of preoccupation with their adoption tend to feel alienated from both parents (Kohler, Grotevant, & McRoy, 2002). Interestingly, adolescents in confidential adoptions were not found to have more preoccupation than those in open adoptions. Girls tend to be more preoccupied with their adoptions than boys. Overall, over half of adolescents think about their adoptions once a month or more, and almost 30% think about them once a week or more (Kohler et al., 2002).

Many adopted children have intense feelings about their birth families at all levels of contact. These issues may be different for children who have lived with their birth families and been removed because of abuse or neglect versus those who know very little about their background but yearn for more information and connection. There is a trend now toward open adoption in child welfare, with an increased emphasis on the importance of birth family connections. With the advent of social media, it has become much easier for adoptees to connect with their birth family, with or without knowledge or consent of adoptive parents.

Transracial adoptive families experience unique challenges, including feeling "different" and experiencing discrimination and microaggressions. For example, in a U.S. study of perceived discrimination, in a sample of 1,579 internationally adopted children ages 5 to 18 years, adoptive parents with Asian and Latin American children reported more discrimination than parents with Eastern European children (Lee, 2003). Internationally adopted children may have particular issues associated with being from a different country and culture. Intercountry adoptees in Sweden reported feeling conscious of being "foreign," being teased about their backgrounds, had lower self-esteem, and had higher rates of behavioral problems than those born in Sweden (Cederblad, Höök, Irhammar, & Mercke, 1999). The majority of parents of internationally adopted children hold beliefs consistent with enculturation and racialization (vs. being "colorblind"), and parents with these attitudes engaged in more culture socialization parenting behaviors (Lee, Grotevant, Hellerstedt, Gunnar, & the Minnesota International Adaption Project Team, 2006). Lee's (2003) review of the literature on racial/ethnic identity development and cultural socialization of cross-racially/culturally adopted children concluded that most children are well-adjusted and, along with their parents, engage in a variety of cultural socialization strategies to help them feel comfortable with their birth and adoptive identities. Clearly, helping parents recognize these issues and talk openly with their children around them is important. Adoption-specific therapy for transracial families should include helping parents to understand and support their child's racial identity, develop a transracial family identity, and prepare children to deal with potential discrimination and microaggressions.

Parent Characteristics as Protective Factors

Although later adopted children often have traumatic backgrounds and many risk factors, the adoptive family's nurturance, compassion, and security can be healing. In the Netherlands, both current and past maternal sensitivity were found to predict social development in adolescence (Jaffari-Bimmel, Juffer, van IJzendoorn, Bakermans-Kranenburg, & Mooijaart, 2006). Specifically, early sensitive parenting influenced adolescent social adjustment mediated through middle childhood adjustment. In addition, adoptive maternal sensitivity mediated the impact of early difficult temperament on later adjustment (Jaffari-Bimmel et al., 2006). The role of parents is also evident in U.S. studies, with self-rated parental readiness for adoption as an important mediating variable for outcomes over time (Simmel, 2007). Families who provide unconditional acceptance and love, provide safety and security, and take into account the child's past history can help ameliorate children's emotional pain and behavioral difficulties. A therapeutic treatment that involves adoptive parents as healing agents along with providing support and skills to children could be very useful in assisting families in this regard.

Postadoption Services

Very minimal work has been done on adoption-related psychotherapy. Welsh and colleagues (Welsh, Viana, Petrill, & Mathias, 2007) reviewed the literature on various interventions currently used with internationally adopted populations and concluded,

"Surprisingly, very little systematic information exists regarding the effectiveness of interventions designed to prevent and remediate these difficulties (including behavioral, attachment, medical, etc. issues) in internationally adopted children" (p. 285). A UK study surveying parents about postadoptive care reported that although over half of the families who adopted children from public care used mental health, educational, and health care supports, they often were dissatisfied, feeling that services were not offered in a timely fashion and that they wanted more education and parenting support (Sturgess & Selwyn, 2007).

Many more treatment programs with clearly defined goals, treatment descriptions, and evaluation methods have focused on foster care than adoption, perhaps assuming that once children get adopted, they will do well. Some foster care interventions have focused on attachment and parental responsiveness (e.g., Dozier, Lindhiem, & Ackerman, 2005). Other interventions have focused on teaching foster parents behavior management skills and the importance of maintaining a consistent, positive environment, working from a cognitive–behavioral perspective (e.g., Fisher & Kim, 2007).

For example, Fisher and Kim (2007) conducted a randomized trial focused on improving attachment-related behaviors among foster preschool children with the Multidimensional Treatment of Foster Care for Preschoolers (MTFC-P) program. The intervention uses a team approach and provides parents with 12 hours of intensive preplacement training. After placement, parents receive phone consults, support groups, and on-call staff support. The basic model focuses on helping parents to maintain a positive, consistent home environment with reinforcement of positive behavior and limit setting for problem behaviors. Children also received playgroups and behavior specialists. The study found that intervention cases showed more secure attachment behavior over time and less avoidant behavior over time. Age at first placement was also a significant predictor of change, with children placed younger having greater increases in secure behavior. In the intervention condition, those who were older experienced greater increases, and the opposite pattern was true in regular foster care. In an evaluation of EIFC (Early Intervention Foster Care, which is the same as MTFC-P), Fisher, Gunnar, Chamberlain, and Reid (2000) found that EIFC parents showed rates of monitoring, consistent discipline, and positive reinforcement similar to a community control group and that regular foster care parents were less likely to show these behaviors. Additionally, the children showed improvements in behavior over time, as well as decreases in salivary cortisol over time, suggestive of lower physiological arousal. In another study, Fisher, Burraston, and Pears (2005) found that children in EIFC had more permanent placements (birth parent, adoption, etc.), and it did not matter how many prior placements children in the treatment condition had.

In a study of MTFC in regular foster care in San Diego, Chamberlain and colleagues (2008) found that MTFC reduced child behavior problems and improved parental use of positive reinforcement. They also found that improvements in child behavior were mediated through parental behavior. In an application of MTFC for adolescent girls in juvenile justice, Chamberlain and colleagues (2007) found that the intervention group had less delinquency. The intervention was modified from one that has been implemented with boys and addresses coping skills, emotion regulation, limit setting, and anxiety related to trauma. The prior studies with delinquent boys showed similar findings (Chamberlain & Reid, 1998; Eddy et al., 2004).

Price and colleagues (2008) evaluated the KEEP intervention with children between ages 8 and 12, which is related to MTFC, to look at changes to placement status on children already in foster care. It was a support-group type of intervention with a focus on understanding risk and protective factors, positive reinforcement, monitoring, and so forth. Number of prior placements was related to a greater number of negative exits from the foster placement (e.g., disruptions). The intervention group was more likely to make positive exits from placement (e.g., reunification or adoption). Finally, there was an interaction such that the intervention group was less likely to be impacted by a history of multiple placements compared with the regular foster care group.

Dozier's (2003) work is more attachment focused. The Attachment and Biobehavioral Catch-Up (ABC) intervention is designed to "help caregivers provide an environment that helps children develop regulatory capabilities, re-interpret children's alienating behaviors, and over-ride their own issues that interfere with providing nurturing care" (Dozier, Peloso, Lewis, Laurenceau, & Levine, 2008, p. 851). The intervention has the goal of enhancing parental nurturance and following the child's lead, with the expectation that these parental behaviors would lead children to develop more secure and organized attachments, more normative regulation of cortisol production, and better regulation of emotions than the behaviors of parents not using this intervention. All were found. This intervention is designed for very young children in foster care. Some of the same principles seem very important in working with older adopted children as well and have been incorporated into our adoption-specific therapy.

Our literature review only came across a couple of adoption-specific studies that evaluated the outcome of the interventions. Juffer, Hoksbergen, Riksen-Walraven, and Kohnstamm (1997) conducted a study of a maternal sensitivity training program that involved videotaped feedback sessions and found that the intervention group had greater maternal sensitivity, infant competence, and secure attachment; this study looked at important variables in connection between parent and child but was focused on infants and was not appropriate for older children. Rushton, Monck, Upright, and Davidson (2006) described an effectiveness study of two parent-focused adoption interventions in the United Kingdom; the first is a cognitive behavioral therapy (CBT)-type parent training (enforcing positive behavior, ignoring negative), and the second is focused on understanding the meaning of children's behavior. They did not report results in this manuscript. One program in England, AdOpt, is a 16-week group prevention program for adoptive parents of 3- to 8-year-old children (Harold, Hampden-Thompson, Rodic, & Sellers, 2017) that has had success in increasing perceived parental competence and adoption satisfaction; behavioral outcomes are mixed with decreases in conduct but not emotional problems, impulsivity, or peer problems. The program stresses relevant concepts to our intervention but is not tailored for older children and provides no child or family treatment.

As noted previously, very few evidence-based studies of older adopted children are available to date. In this book, we present a comprehensive therapy, drawing on evidence-based effective child therapeutic techniques combined with an adoption-specific, attachment-based, trauma- and resiliency-informed lens.

Our Approach in Adoption-Specific Therapy

Our intervention draws on effective prevention intervention principles (Griffin, Botvin, Nichols, & Doyle, 2003), as follows: We provide a comprehensive intervention, focusing on an array of precursors and mediators of mental health and substance abuse issues, intervening in both direct and indirect pathways. We provide an array of methods, including active, skills-based components, with hands-on experience for both parents and children. Our approach is theory driven, with social learning theory (Bandura, 1977) and social control theory components (Hirschi, 2002), and builds on positive relationships enhancing family attachment and bonding (Fahlberg, 2012). Our program is socioculturally relevant, with a focus on helping families understand their child's behavior through his or her past experiences prior to entering the family while helping the family deal with adoption relevant social issues such as transracial adoption.

Our intervention includes indirect interventions for increasing child resiliency. Masten's (2001) review of converging findings on resiliency highlighted a critical phenomenon: that resilience occurs through ordinary processes, even in the face of severe adversity. Family characteristics (e.g., close relationships with caring adults, authoritative parenting) enhance child resilience. Our intervention focuses on improving family interactions and attachment to improve resilience of youngsters, as well as developing parental skills at behavioral management and monitoring. We draw from the existent evidence-based interventions that have been found effective for treating specific mental health issues in children, such as trauma, externalizing behaviors, internalizing behaviors, and anxiety (Cohen, Mannarino, Berliner, & Deblinger, 2000; Sanders et al., 2000). We also draw on preventive interventions for children in foster care and bereaved children (Chamberlain, 2003; Cohen et al., 2000; Sandler et al., 2003; Scott, Spender, Doolan, Jacobs, & Aspland, 2001; Webster-Stratton, 1984). We use three broad strategies derived from this literature. First, a positive approach to parenting is important to child outcomes in general and is particularly so for foster families (Kaminski, Valle, Filene, & Boyle, 2008; Sanders et al., 2000). We help parents to increase praise, rewards, encouragement, positive events, child-led play, and family rituals. Second, the strong cognitive behavioral literature in adoption-specific therapy (ADAPT), our adoption-specific therapy protocol, includes teaching children coping strategies to manage negative affective states (Cohen et al., 2000) and increase their awareness and identification of emotions in self and others (Cohen et al., 2000), as well as to open lines of communication between children and parents (effective listening and expression skills training with role play). We draw on the strong behavioral literature (Chamberlain, 2003) to help families manage difficult child behaviors, but we modify these interventions to take into account the child's past traumatic history. Third, we focus on open communication about all aspects of adoption and help parents and children increase their connection and attachment.

Adoption is conceptualized as a significant emotional event in the lives of children. Children understand and deal with their adoption differently depending on their age and developmental stage, and often struggle with issues related to loss, abandonment, and rejection. Although we do not believe that adoption is traumatic for children, we model our approach in a manner similar to the exposure elements of trauma-focused cognitive behavioral therapy (TF-CBT; Cohen, Mannarino, & Deblinger, 2006). Similar to their approach, we help children develop coping strategies and work with parents on increasing positivity in their relationship with their children prior to addressing the more emotionally laden material. Then, in parallel fashion to TF-CBT, the child gains an understanding of the adoption, creates a narrative of their adoption story, and can discuss it comfortably with adoptive parents and the broader community. These strategies are used to normalize concerns about adoption (psychoeducation); increase child and parents' knowledge of and comfort with the child's adoption history (exposure); create a narrative (adoption story) parents and children can share with each other (including difficult topics such as birth parent histories of abuse/neglect, mental illness, incarceration, substance abuse, etc.); help parents view children's behavior problems from the perspective of their history; and increase awareness of the effects of adoption history on the child's sense of self, identity development, emotion regulation patterns, and family interactions. The importance of this approach was exemplified by the words of a child participant who said in the first session, "Adoption is the nightmare of my life. How can I listen in school when I'm wondering who is my real mom?" Our exposure approach was very helpful for him.

Adoptive children experience divided loyalties to birth and adoptive families and experience unique identity formation issues relative to integrating their biological background, the influence of their adoptive families, and their own unique qualities. Children adopted transracially have particularly unique experiences in integrating their cultural background with their adoptive background, as well as developing skills to manage societal responses to their appearance that is different from their adoptive family. ADAPT includes opportunities for adoptive families to discuss these issues and help build resilience in youth through strengthening family relations and child identity formation.

Overview of Adoption-Specific Therapy

2

In this chapter, we first present some of the basic beliefs that guide adoption-specific therapy (ADAPT) and the ADAPT curriculum. Next, we present an overview of ADAPT, including its structure and important features. Finally, we discuss the details of implementing ADAPT.

Basic Beliefs in ADAPT

Following are some basic principles that underlie our approach to working with adopted children and their families (adapted from Riley, 2005, and expanded).[1]

ADOPTIVE FAMILIES FACE UNIQUE CHALLENGES INHERENT IN ADOPTION AND DIFFERENT FROM THOSE IN BIRTH FAMILIES

Although many of the issues and concerns experienced in the course of growing up are similar for birth and adopted families, there are extra challenges

[1]From *Beneath the Mask: Understanding Adopted Teens* (pp. 35–36), by D. Riley with J. Meeks, 2005, Silver Spring, MD: C.A.S.E. Publications. Copyright 2005 by Debbie Riley and John Meeks. Adapted with permission.

http://dx.doi.org/10.1037/0000096-003
Adoption-Specific Therapy: A Guide to Helping Adopted Children and Their Families Thrive, by J. Waterman, A. K. Langley, J. Miranda, and D. B. Riley

for adopted children with regard to identity, loss, and self-esteem. These issues are especially salient for children adopted after infancy who have known a birth family whose members were unable to care for them and for children who have spent significant time in environments such as orphanages that may not have been able to provide stable, nurturing caregivers. Longitudinal studies such as those conducted with children from Romanian orphanages have shown that remaining in group care rather than living with a family after about the age of 2 years often causes long-lasting deficits in many areas of development, including cognitive, physical, and psychological areas (Gunnar, Bruce, & Grotevant, 2000).

ADOPTION AND REACTIONS TO IT ARE NOT PATHOLOGICAL

In most instances, adoption is a positive and sometimes life-saving intervention for children. It is not a diagnosable condition, a weird family format, something that needs to be secret, nor is it a category of trauma (though the transition from birth family, long-term foster family, or other caregiving situation may be difficult). In a large-scale study comparing 900 adopted children with 3,100 children who aged out of foster care, both adopted and foster care children had weaker outcomes than the general population of 900,000 peers in Sweden to whom they were compared. However, adoptees had significantly better outcomes on cognitive competence, educational attainment, and self-support capacity than those who had remained in foster care (Vinnerljung & Hjern, 2011).

LOSS IS UNIQUE AND PERVASIVE IN ALL ADOPTION ADJUSTMENT

In adoption, gaining a family always means losing a family. Children inevitably wonder, "Why didn't she/they want me?" "Why couldn't they take care of me?" "Do I have brothers and sisters, and will I ever get to know them?" By the time children have been adopted, they may have lost several families (birth and foster). Additionally, children may have experienced other losses as a result of various moves—loss of extended family members, teachers, friends, religious leaders, coaches, pets, culture, neighborhood, or country. For many parents who are adopting as a result of infertility, loss of their potential birth child may also lead to unique and significant emotional pain. Many birth parents also experience an intense and overwhelming sense of loss when their child is adopted.

CHILDREN MUST GRIEVE THEIR LOSSES TO FORM HEALTHY NEW ATTACHMENTS

Adoptive parents often want to believe that now that they are parenting the child, providing love, nurturance, and stability (and possibly greatly enhanced resources), the child should be happy and grateful. However, it is natural for children to be sad at losing their previous caregivers, regardless of possible past deprivation, abuse, or neglect. New attachments build when caregivers sensitively respond to the emotional and physical distress of the children. So although it may be painful for parents to see their child distressed, and especially painful if it seems that the child prefers the previous caregiver, allowing the child to express grief and sadness while providing nurturance and understanding is the basis of developing an ever closer relationship. Children's feelings of loss and grief about their birth family are likely to reemerge at different developmental stages, particularly in adolescence, and sometimes also around later major transitions such as marriage and birth of a child. The therapist's task is to help parents understand the depth of the child's loss and grief; see it as normal and not a threat to their relationship with the child; and help them emotionally tolerate the child's divided loyalties, as well as validating, processing, and normalizing these feelings for the child.

ADOPTIVE PARENTS NEED TO RESPECT AND HONOR THE CHILD'S PREVIOUS ATTACHMENTS; CHILDREN SHOULD NOT BE ASKED TO FORGET

Regardless of adoptive parents' feelings about the birth parents, it is important to recognize their importance to the child. Especially if there has been a contentious relationship between birth and adoptive parents (most likely in foster care situations), adoptive parents need to respect the children's feelings toward their previous caregivers and facilitate the children feeling comfortable about discussing their feelings toward these previous attachment figures. Some ways in which this can happen involve keeping and safeguarding any toys or clothes or pictures that the child may have from previous important caregivers; bringing up birth parents in a positive manner ("You are such a good runner; I bet your dad was really athletic," "You clearly got your artistic talent from your birth mother because you certainly didn't get it from me," "I remember how beautiful your birth mother was, and you have the same beautiful eyes and hair"). If no information is known about the birth family, empathizing with this loss can be very helpful, as well as acknowledging what the child might have in common with the birth family members, as noted previously.

PARENTS NEED TO UNDERSTAND THEIR CHILD AND THE CHILD'S BEHAVIOR IN LIGHT OF THEIR PREVIOUS HISTORY

This is one of the major goals of adoption-specific therapy, and it was discussed in detail in the Introduction. Children's backgrounds of trauma, loss, abuse, and neglect lead to increased needs for stability, predictability, consistency, nurturance, and security. Using the lens of the child's past history can help adoptive parents understand that many problem behaviors were adaptive in the child's previous dysfunctional caregiving environment. Taking this knowledge into account can then assist them in developing sensitive and effective parenting strategies.

TALKING ABOUT ADOPTION IS POSITIVE AND CREATES A HEALTHY ADJUSTMENT

We believe that children do best when they grow up knowing they were adopted. The *fact* of adoption is not usually an issue for children adopted after about age 4 or 5 because the children are aware of and often involved in the process. Even with older children, we find that many have misunderstandings around their adoption story. However, for those adopted as infants and toddlers, an active effort should be made early to assure that adoption is a fact of the child's life of which they were always aware. Particularly for children who are not adopted transracially and look as if they might have been born to their adoptive parent(s), it is sometimes tempting to hide the adoption and lead the child and others to believe the child was born into their family. We have worked with many parents who come to us when the child is 7 or 9 or 11 or 13 years old saying, "I always meant to tell him he was adopted, but there never seemed to be the right time to do it. And the longer I waited, the harder it became." Adoption is not a secret, it is nothing to be ashamed about. However, when it is not discussed and is hidden, it may feel like a shameful secret to the parents and/or the child. We advise parents to mention adoption in casual conversation at least once a month to let the child know it is OK to talk about any aspect of adoption. Parents might say, "When we adopted you, we lived in Fresno," "I can't wait until the judge says our adoption is final and you will be with us forever," "When we met you for the first time in the orphanage, we gave you a pink bunny that you took everywhere." Many families celebrate the child's adoption day much the way they celebrate the child's birthday as a special and meaningful occasion, and some have pictures of the child's adoption day prominently displayed in their home. Talking about the child's birth family in a positive manner is also helpful, and some families have ongoing contact with birth parents or with other family members, such as grandparents or siblings, even if there is no contact with their birth mother or father. In this intervention, we prepare and help families to tell their child's adoption story in a positive and healing manner.

ADOPTION IS PROCESSED WITHIN A DEVELOPMENTAL FRAMEWORK

The fact and meaning of adoption are understood and processed differently at various developmental stages. As noted previously, early on, children know they were adopted but may not understand what that means. As children mature, their understanding of adoption increases, and they ask more sophisticated questions, with the most basic one being "Why couldn't I stay with my birth parents?" Although the standard answer, "Because she/they couldn't take care of you," satisfies young children, older school age and adolescent children want to know why and at increasing levels of complexity. Parents are encouraged to answer the questions asked at the time and to give developmentally appropriate responses, knowing that at an older age, there will be more sophisticated and difficult questions.

ADOPTED CHILDREN NEED TO FEEL ACCEPTED FOR WHO THEY ARE, WITH HELP IN FINDING THEIR OWN UNIQUE STRENGTHS

All parents have hopes and dreams for their children. Because of genetics and inborn temperament, children in birth families are more likely to share talents and characteristics with their parents than they are in adoptive families. In addition, adoptive parents are often from more economically privileged and/or outwardly accomplished backgrounds than the birth parents. Although parents may have graduated from Harvard and wish their adopted child would follow in their footsteps, setting rigidly high expectations that the adopted child may not wish to or be capable of living up to can lead to significant disappointment on the parents' part and in turn to low self-esteem and feelings of failure in the child. Parents are strongly encouraged to look at what the child's interests and talents are, even if very different from their own, and to support the child's unique skills and interests. For example, one mother reported that she was extremely liberal politically and had gone with her own mother to several civil rights marches on Washington. When her teenage son developed a strong interest in policing and chose to join the Police Cadets as his main extracurricular activity in high school, she really had to reflect on her own feelings to provide her full support for what her son wanted to do. He is now in college and very involved in The Reserve Officers' Training Corps, and his mother could not be prouder of him.

ADOPTIVE FAMILIES NEED ALL AVAILABLE INFORMATION ON THE CHILD

The better prepared parents are for caring for a child, the better the outcome of the adoption. Parents should be given all information about the child's background, strengths, and needs so that they can make an informed decision about whether they are able to successfully care for and meet the needs of this particular child. This includes information about difficult parental background such as mental illness, parental substance abuse, criminal history, sexual abuse, neglect, domestic or community violence, etc., as well as full disclosure about what is known about the child's development and behavior in all aspects, including juvenile justice issues, medical problems, educational needs, etc. It is much better for parents to have all the information about the child and to feel able to make a decision that is right for their family based on that without coercion or judgment from the placing agency. It is much better for the family to decide they cannot meet the child's needs for whatever reason *before* they have met the child, avoiding a potential rejection that could feel devastating for the child.

CHILDREN HAVE THE RIGHT TO ALL INFORMATION ABOUT THEMSELVES AND THEIR PAST, INCLUDING DIFFICULT INFORMATION, AS IS DEVELOPMENTALLY APPROPRIATE

We believe that children's stories belong to them. They deserve to know all the information we know about them, at developmentally appropriate times. Details about really difficult information, such as maternal prostitution, child sexual abuse, paternal schizophrenia, father murdered mother, etc., require the emotion regulation and abstract reasoning skills that only develop in mid- to late adolescence or early adulthood. It is very important not to lie to children about their background. If they find out (and they often do because relatives or friends may tell them), they will feel deceived, and the trust between child and parent will be seriously impacted. If they are not old enough or mature enough to handle the difficult aspects of their story, it is fine to say something less detailed but still true, such as "She had mental health problems," "Your birth father made a poor choice and got in trouble with the law." It is also fine to say, "That's something we can discuss when you are older." Additionally, as children "own" more of their stories, they will need to make choices about what to tell to whom, to feel entitled to share nothing if they choose, and to learn skills to manage at times very intrusive questions.

Overview of ADAPT

The modules of ADAPT are as follows:

1. Trust, Positive Coping Strategies, and Behavior Management
2. Developmental Understanding of Adoption Experience
3. Loss and Grief Issues in Adoption
4. Attachment and Joining With the Adoptive Family
5. Search for Identity and Transracial Adoption (extra sessions for families adopting transracially and nontraditional families)
6. Adoption and the Outside World

An additional seventh module on Trauma Treatment is given as needed. The modules and the sessions within the modules are listed in Exhibit 2.1.

A version of this outline for parents, including goals and number of sessions in each module, is given in Handout 1 (Modules of ADAPT) in the first parent session of Module 1. As noted previously, almost all modules consist of an equal number of individual child and parent sessions, followed by a joint family session. Module 1 is always presented first, as it involves foundational material and positive parenting and child coping strategies from which the rest of the intervention flows. After the first module, the modules can be switched around to best meet the needs of the children and families. The most common reasons that modules are given out of order are the following:

1. If there is a risk of adoption disruption, Module 2 (Developmental Understanding of Adoption Experience) is delayed, and either Module 3 or 4 is given first, depending on the family's situation. Module 2 is then implemented if and when it becomes clear that the adoption case plan will proceed.
2. If it is clear that there are major trauma issues that need to be addressed before the adoption issues, Module 7 on Trauma Treatment can be inserted any time after Module 1 is completed.

EXHIBIT 2.1

Modules and Sessions of ADAPT, Adoption-Specific Therapy

Module 1. Trust, Positive Coping Strategies, and Behavior Management

Purpose of parent sessions: To form a therapeutic, supportive relationship and working alliance; to discuss basic premises of adoption; to help focus on children's strengths and engender positive interactions; to assist parents in developing appropriate behavior management plans.

Purpose of child sessions: To form a therapeutic, supportive relationship and working alliance; to assist child with feelings identification; to aid child in strengthening current and developing new adaptive coping strategies.

Purpose of joint session: To lead families in an activity to increase positivity among family members; to develop a shared set of coping strategies that are appropriate for children and parents alike that will be helpful in dealing with emotionally powerful content in the following modules.

Sessions:
Parent Session 1: Program overview, positive coping strategies, and behavior management
Child Session 1: Overview and rapport building
Parent Session 2: Child-led play and reflective listening
Child Session 2: Feelings identification
Parent Session 3: Focusing on the positive
Child Session 3: Coping strategies of deep breathing and muscle relaxation
Parent Session 4: Developing adoption-specific discipline strategies
Child Session 4: Problem-solving strategies
Joint Session: Sharing positives and coping strategies

Module 2. Developmental Understanding of Adoption Experience

Purpose of parent sessions: To assess parents' comfort with, awareness of, and understanding of the adoption experience for them and their child; to help parents tell or cocreate the child's adoption story; to help parents develop comfort with and skill in talking with their child about difficult information in their past at a developmentally appropriate level.

Purpose of child sessions: To assess children's understanding, comfort, and awareness of why they are or were being adopted and to clarify information about their adoption story; to facilitate children's ability to tell their story within an appropriate developmental level; to understand the meaning of adoption and to validate adoption as a valued family form.

Purpose of joint session: To enable the joint sharing and processing of the parents' story of the child's adoption as well as the child's Lifebook; to discuss child's unanswered questions.

Sessions:
Parent Session 1: Parental path to adoption
Child Session 1: Normalizing and understanding adoption
Parent Session 2: Understanding the child's path to adoption
Child Session 2: Child's adoption story and unanswered questions
Parent Session 3: Parental fears about birth parent contact
Child Session 3: Child's adoption story and unanswered questions (continued)
Joint Session: Sharing adoption story and unanswered questions

(*continues*)

EXHIBIT 2.1 ***(Continued)***

Modules and Sessions of ADAPT, Adoption-Specific Therapy

Module 3. Loss and Grief Issues in Adoption

Purpose of parent sessions: To facilitate parents' understanding of their child's losses; to help parents learn to assist children in the grieving process; to help parents deal with their own adoption-related losses; to assist parents in dealing with feelings of rejection.

Purpose of child sessions: To help children identify and acknowledge their previous losses; to assist children in understanding the circumstances surrounding their losses and support exploration of feelings; to assist in the grieving process.

Purpose of joint session: To assist children in sharing with their parents their losses; to honor children's past losses through making a Tree of Remembrance.

Sessions:
Parent Session 1: Understanding the child's losses and grief reactions
Child Session 1: My losses and Loss Box activity
Parent Session 2: Dealing with rejection by child
Child Session 2: The task of grieving (continuation of loss box activity)
Joint Session: The Tree of Remembrance

Module 4. Attachment and Joining With the Adoptive Family

Purpose of parent sessions: To assist parents in understanding the attachment process; to discuss mechanisms to facilitate attachment; to help parents "claim" the child and feel entitled to parent their child; to facilitate positive family interactions.

Purpose of child sessions: To help children talk about their feelings about safety, trust, and security (or lack thereof) in their adoptive family; to facilitate a strong sense of identification with their adoptive family.

Purpose of joint session: To help the family focus on what they like and would want to change about their family; to firm up new family ritual; to help family members talk about what they would like to change in their family in a positive and constructive manner.

Sessions:
Parent Session 1: Understanding attachment styles
Child Session 1: *The Invisible String* and child's web of connections
Parent Session 2: Ways to encourage attachment
Child Session 2: Family activities cards and matching game
Joint Session: Family rituals/what I like about our family/what I would like to change about our family

Module 5. Search for Identity and Transracial Adoption

Purpose of parent sessions: To help parents understand the complexities of identity development for adopted children in integrating a sense of self that involves birth family, foster family, adoptive family, and the child, particularly as they approach adolescence; to explore special issues of identity for children adopted transracially; to help transracial and same-sex families develop strategies to deal with discrimination and microaggressions.

Purpose of child sessions: To assist children in developing an integrated identity that includes birth family, adopted family, and children's own uniqueness; to help children adopted transracially or in same-sex families develop strategies to deal with discrimination and microaggressions.

Purpose of joint session: (for transracial and nontraditional families) To develop an integrated family identity; to role play handling discrimination.

EXHIBIT 2.1 *(Continued)*

Modules and Sessions of ADAPT, Adoption-Specific Therapy

Sessions:
Parent Session 1: Understanding adopted children's search for identity
Child Session 1: Identity exploration through Game of Discovery
Parent Session 2: Game of Discovery/positive similarities with birth family
Child Session 2: My Self chart
Parent Session 3: Racial/ethnic identity, supporting child's cultural heritage (given if adoption is transracial)
Child Session 3: Racial/ethnic identity (given if adoption is transracial)
Parent Session 4: Preparing for and dealing with discrimination and microaggressions (given for transracial families and other diverse families, e.g., LGBT)
Child Session 4: Handling discrimination and microaggressions (given for transracial families and other diverse families, e.g., LGBT)
Joint Session: Developing an integrated family identity, dealing with discrimination

Module 6. Adoption and the Outside World

Purpose of parent sessions: To help parents and children deal with questions about the child's background and adoption that come from other children, other parents, and strangers; to help parents in deciding whom they tell (e.g., extended family members, pediatricians, teachers) about difficult past history of the child.

Purpose of child sessions: To empower children to handle the intrusive and sometimes aversive questions others ask about adoption, using the *W.I.S.E UP! Powerbook*.

Purpose of joint session: To help parents and children practice W.I.S.E. UP! program together.

Sessions:
Parent Session 1: Dealing with difficult adoption-related questions, deciding what information to share and with whom
Child Session 1: W.I.S.E. UP! program for responding to difficult questions
Parent Session 2: Helping child use the W.I.S.E. UP! program
Child Session 2: Practicing with W.I.S.E. UP!
Joint Session: Practicing W.I.S.E. UP!

Module 7. Trauma Treatment

(Optional—May Be Inserted as Needed Any Time After Module 1)

Purpose of parent sessions: To help parents understand that children being adopted past infancy are likely to have experienced traumatic events that will take time, love, and probably therapy to heal; to assist parents in coping with and accepting children's disclosures of trauma, providing a safe and trusting environment for them to talk about (or draw or play out for younger children) what happened to them.

Purpose of child sessions: To help children who have experienced physical and/or sexual abuse, neglect, deprivation, domestic violence, and other violent events process and cope with the trauma. If a child is experiencing posttraumatic stress symptoms that are upsetting and interfering in any way, to help the child engage in the trauma narrative process with the therapist in combination with other coping and adoption-specific skills from previous modules.

Purpose of joint session: To facilitate children sharing their trauma story with their parents.

(continues)

EXHIBIT 2.1 ***(Continued)***

Modules and Sessions of ADAPT, Adoption-Specific Therapy

Sessions:
Parent Session 1: Trauma education, child's trauma history
Child Session 1: Trauma education, trauma history, reactions, and coping strategies
Parent Session 2: Processing child's trauma history
Child Session 2: Trauma narrative
Child Session 3 (and as many extra sessions as needed): Continue completion of child's trauma story book (note session sequence exception)
Parent Session 3: Sharing child's trauma story with parents and processing reactions
Joint Session: Child shares trauma story with parents

Termination Session

Purpose of parent session: To help parents focus on gains they and the child have made during ADAPT, discuss what they have learned, and share their feelings about ADAPT.

Purpose of child session: To help children process not only this goodbye, but also past goodbyes, which often have been abrupt and traumatic for children; to review ADAPT activities, what they have learned, and make goodbye cards.

Purpose of joint session: Eat, celebrate termination, and have fun.

Note. LGBT = lesbian, gay, bisexual, and transgender.

Generally, the overall ADAPT intervention is about 20–24 sessions (about 6 months of weekly parent and child sessions and family meetings), depending on the age of the child and the particular issues involved. Following are a few important features of ADAPT.

THERE ARE AN EQUAL NUMBER OF CHILD AND PARENT SESSIONS

Unlike many treatments that mainly target the child, we see the issues at both the time of transition to adoption and postadoption as family concerns, and we feel that work with the parents is as important or sometimes even more important than work with the child. We also feel that both parents and children need separate time (and sometimes separate therapists) to address their unique concerns. Parents need space to vent about their doubts about the adoption and whether they can manage (very frequently expressed in the first year after placement of older children), and children need space to talk freely about missing birth or foster families or other caregivers (e.g., orphanage workers, friends) without worry of hurting the feelings of their adoptive parents. In this model, we often find it helpful to use separate parent and child therapists who consult regularly and jointly lead the family sessions that conclude most modules.

ALL CHILD SESSIONS AND MANY PARENT AND FAMILY SESSIONS ARE ACTIVITY BASED

To be engaging for children, each child session and most family sessions involve specific activities—these may include art, role play, games, etc. All the necessary materials for these activities are listed in an online handout (Handout A: Materials

Needed for ADAPT Toolkit) and can also be purchased from the Center for Adoption Support and Education (C.A.S.E.; http://www.adoptionsupport.org) in a toolkit that makes administration of the intervention very easy.

FOUR PARENTING STRATEGIES AND FOUR CHILD COPING STRATEGIES ARE INTRODUCED IN MODULE 1 AND REINFORCED REGULARLY THROUGHOUT THE REST OF THE CURRICULUM

At the end of each succeeding session for parents and for children, one of the four core strategies is discussed again in rotation, and participants are asked to practice it during the following week. We have found that recurrent discussion of and practice with these core strategies greatly improves their implementation and therefore leads to better outcomes.

The recurring parenting strategies to increase positivity in parent–child relationships are

1. child-led play and reflective listening,
2. praise and encouragement,
3. preteaching, and
4. de-escalation.

The recurring child coping strategies to increase emotion regulation are

1. deep breathing,
2. muscle relaxation,
3. guided imagery/mindfulness, and
4. problem solving.

PARENTS CHOOSE MEASURABLE GOALS AND REVIEW THEM REGULARLY

Parents are encouraged to identify three problematic child behaviors at the start of treatment and review progress at the beginning of each new module.

Parents select three problematic child behaviors to work on, and the therapist helps the parents address these behaviors using an adoption lens. Parents and therapists review progress on these behaviors at the beginning of each parent session, which helps to maintain focus throughout the treatment. If any of the behaviors are fully eliminated, new goals are set at the beginning of each new module. We have included a brief measure in the online resources—Handout 4: Parent Progress Report (PPR)—that we encourage therapists to have parents fill out weekly to help measure progress.

Implementing ADAPT

In the following sections, we give information about the nuts and bolts of implementing ADAPT. This includes which clients the intervention is intended for, what the necessary therapist characteristics are, and details about things like location of services and how to treat sibling sets.

FOR WHICH CLIENTS IS ADAPT APPROPRIATE?

ADAPT was originally developed for children adopted from foster care past infancy and their families, as these are the children for whom standard interventions are least likely to work and who are highly overrepresented in outpatient, inpatient, and residential treatment settings. However, almost all of the content is equally appropriate for families who have adopted internationally or through private domestic adoption. We have also used ADAPT very successfully with families who have adopted very young children, including infants, omitting or making changes to those parts of the curriculum that involve losses of previous caregivers, multiple placements, etc. (most notably in Module 2, Developmental Understanding of Adoption Experience; Module 3, Loss and Grief Issues in Adoption; and Module 7, Trauma Treatment).

Additionally, there are developmental considerations in using ADAPT. The usual age range for children participating in ADAPT is from 5 to 14 years of age. However, the majority of the parent sessions are appropriate for families with children of all ages. Children under 5 years of age generally do not have the cognitive capacity to effectively use most of the curriculum and, in general, cannot participate appropriately in many of the activities. In addition, certain issues are less salient for younger children, and we advise that a few child sessions be omitted for younger children; these suggestions are noted in the module content. Some of the sessions also have different activities that are developmentally appropriate for younger and older children. We have several children's books in the curriculum that are meant for younger children (e.g., *Murphy's Three Homes: A Story for Children in Foster Care* by Jan Levinson Gilman, 2009), but our experience has been that even the young teens enjoy these books.

We have used ADAPT with a few youth older than 14 years of age, and it has required some adaptations to the child sessions, whereas most of the parent sessions could be used with minor changes (e.g., for child-led play, brainstorming about possible activities with the child would look very different for a 6-year-old and a 15-year-old). For children 7 or 8 years old or younger, we have often found it helpful to leave a few minutes at the end of each session for a reward of free play if therapist and child work through the agenda items for that session. For extremely active or inattentive younger children, we have also used stickers as rewards for staying on task, talking about difficult feelings, etc.

For children with significant developmental problems (e.g., mild intellectual disability, autism), we have found that ADAPT can be successful. Minor modifications are needed for the parent sessions, and we have found that often extra sessions are required in the child component to accomplish the goals.

WHICH THERAPISTS SHOULD USE ADAPT?

ADAPT is meant to be used by licensed mental health professionals (e.g., social workers, psychologists, marriage and family therapists) and by students in these areas under clinical supervision of licensed professionals. Good counseling skills such as rapport building, empathy, reflection, warmth, and acceptance are necessary, as well as cultural competency, case conceptualization and problem-solving skills, and knowledge of child/family psychotherapy. It is extremely useful to have awareness of adoption dynamics and experience with child trauma, although the ADAPT protocol guides the therapist through the actual interventions. Especially because working with this population can be very emotional as a result of painful loss and trauma histories, it is helpful if several colleagues in an agency or practice are all using this approach and can provide support for one another.

SHOULD THERE BE ONE THERAPIST OR TWO?

ADAPT can involve either one or two therapists (one for child or children, one for parents). The advantages of two therapists are that all parties can be seen at once, there is no need for arranging child care, parents and children each feel like they have a safe and trusted advocate who is there just for them, and the therapist only needs to learn half of the curriculum. On the basis of our experience, the two-therapist option is preferable for families who are able to come to our offices. However, ADAPT can be delivered by a single therapist and can be beneficial in private practice settings as well as public agencies.

SHOULD THERAPY TAKE PLACE AT HOME OR IN AN OFFICE?

In-home sessions with ADAPT have been carried out in several different ways, most often using one therapist. Sometimes, parent and child are seen back-to-back. This option is most feasible if there are not young children in the home, because older children are better able to occupy themselves while parents are being seen. A second strategy is to see parents at home when the children are at school or afterschool programs and then to see the child separately at an afterschool time. The advantages of home sessions are avoiding transportation and organization problems for families, usually better attendance, and a more naturalistic setting. Advantages of office sessions are a more economical use of therapist time, a more controllable and usually more private setting, and a greater likelihood of being able to use two therapists.

SHOULD SEPARATE THERAPISTS OR THE SAME THERAPIST TREAT SIBLINGS?

If there is more than one child in the family who needs individual treatment, several options are again possible. One is to appoint different therapists for the different target children; we recommend this option when the adoption is not finalized, when more than one child has very significant needs, or when significant sibling issues would prevent them from trusting each other and working cooperatively. If one therapist must see more than one child, he or she has the option to see both children at once or to split the time between them.

WHERE CAN I FIND THE MATERIALS NEEDED FOR ADAPT?

All materials, including books, handouts, and materials for games and activities, are contained in the ADAPT toolkit. It can be obtained from the C.A.S.E. online store (http://www.adoptionsupport.org; click on "Store"). In addition, copies of the handouts for therapist use with as many children and parents as needed can be found online (http://pubs.apa.org/books/supp/waterman). Therapists have found the toolkit to be invaluable, allowing them to easily administer the ADAPT intervention with fidelity to the model, and users of the manual are urged to either purchase the toolkit or make their own. If therapists prefer to make their own toolkit, a list of what is needed can be found in online resources for Chapter 2, Materials Needed for ADAPT Toolkit (Handout A). All handouts for the curriculum are sequentially numbered, with a list of handouts at the beginning of the book.

Conclusion

Developing ADAPT has been a long-term labor of love for its authors, culminating many years of work with adopted children, often with many risk factors, and the families who adopt them. Qualitative interviews with parents who have completed ADAPT indicate very high satisfaction with the program; parents feel they are less stressed, more understanding of their child, more positive, and closer as a family. In addition, all family members report being more comfortable discussing adoption. Therapists also have high regard for the ADAPT program. They note that it focuses on the most critical areas that need to be covered with adopted children and their parents and especially mention the importance of the sessions that work on building family positivity, understanding the developmental stages of adoption, communicating about the child's adoption story, processing grief and loss, and building family attachment. Therapists report that ADAPT is easy to use, is meaningful for themselves as well as the children and families, and helps them bring up and process difficult issues that often are avoided (either consciously or unconsciously).

THE ADAPT CURRICULUM

II

3 Module 1
Trust, Positive Coping Strategies, and Behavior Management

The goals of Module 1 parent sessions are to form a therapeutic, supportive relationship and working alliance; to discuss basic premises of adoption; to help parents focus on children's strengths and engender positive interactions; and to assist the parent in developing appropriate behavior management plans, taking into account the child's past history. The goals of Module 1 child sessions are to form a therapeutic, supportive relationship and working alliance; to help children develop skill in feeling identification; and to aid child in developing coping and problem-solving strategies. Module 1 consists of five sessions. Sessions 1 through 4 involve separate sessions for the child and the parent(s). Session 5 is a joint session for all family members.

Parent Session 1: Program Overview, Positive Coping Strategies, and Behavior Management

In the first parent session, there are four main goals. First, parents are asked to share information about the child's current problems and functioning, as well as a brief summary of the child's adoption history. Obtaining this

http://dx.doi.org/10.1037/0000096-004
Adoption-Specific Therapy: A Guide to Helping Adopted Children and Their Families Thrive, by J. Waterman, A. K. Langley, J. Miranda, and D. B. Riley

information allows the therapist to begin to think about the connections between the child's current issues and previous traumatic experiences. Second, an outline of adoption-specific therapy (ADAPT) and module content is introduced. Third, activities aimed at building positivity in the parent–child relationship are presented. In this first session and throughout Module 1, the focus is on developing a more positive atmosphere in the family because it helps the child and the parents feel good about themselves and builds a foundation for family closeness and cohesion. Additionally, these positive experiences and feelings build goodwill, which then can be drawn on later when dealing with limit setting and problem behaviors. Fourth, homework about supporting the child's strengths and looking at a behavioral problem through the lens of the child's past history is discussed.

Materials for this session include

- a notebook for parent handouts and homework,
- Handout 1: Modules of ADAPT (Adoption-Specific Therapy),
- Handout 2: Basic Beliefs of Adoption-Specific Therapy,
- Handout 3: What Parents Can Expect During the Transition (given to parents with pending or new placements),
- Handout 4: Parent Progress Report (PPR),
- Handout 5: My Child's Positives, and
- Handout 6: My Child's Strengths/Concerning Behaviors.

DISCUSSION OF CHILD'S CURRENT FUNCTIONING

Begin by warmly introducing yourself to the family, and try to connect with each family member. Tell parents that you will be gathering information about the child and family, discussing the ADAPT program, and looking at the child's strengths. If this is your first contact with the family, conduct a full intake interview with the parents. In this case, an extra session may be needed to discuss ADAPT and build parent–child positivity. If someone else has already conducted an intake, acknowledge your awareness of the information gathered.

Ask in an open-ended fashion, "What concerns are you having about (child's name) now?" Elicit details such as how long the problem has existed, what the parents think might be the cause, and how they have tried to deal with it. Make sure to ask for additional concerns or problems and gather details about them. Assess the child's functioning in the following areas, as well as others brought up by parents: school (academic and behavioral), peers, family relationships, outside activities, and hobbies. Elicit details about current and former psychological and pharmacological treatment. During the interview, reflect and validate feelings, summarize issues, and communicate your understanding of the problems.

STORY OF CHILD'S ADOPTION

Next, ask "How did (child) come to be part of your family?" Elicit details about type of adoption (foster care, domestic, international), how long ago child came to live with them and when the adoption was finalized (or when they expect it to be finalized), why the child was available for adoption, what other types of placements the child has had and for how long, and what traumas the child may have suffered. Although the adoption story will be discussed in much greater detail in Module 2, it is important to get the basic history in the first session. Also make sure to confirm that children know they are adopted. This must be established before proceeding with the ADAPT program. If the child does not know about his or her adoption, explore why, and ask what the parent's feelings are about keeping the adoption a secret. Work with the parent(s) to process these feelings and see if parents are willing to work toward the goal of sharing information about the adoption. You cannot proceed with the child's sessions until the child is aware of their adoption, and it may take several sessions of working with the parents and gently exploring their resistance to sharing the information.

Begin to wonder with the parents how this past history might help with understanding the child's symptoms. In many cases, the problematic behavior may have been adaptive in the context of the child's past experience. For example, if a child has had many placements or multiple caregivers, or was passed around from one relative to another, developing quick but superficial connections might have helped the child to get their needs met. Being willing to go off with anyone is maladaptive in the context of a safe and secure family, but it could have been very helpful in the earlier context of chaotic caregiving or multiple placements. In this first session, you are trying to plant the seed that examining what has happened to the child in their early years can help the adoptive parents make sense of troubling behaviors, build empathy for the child, and develop parenting strategies tailored for this particular child. Make sure to be accepting, reflective, and nonjudgmental, with the aim of building the therapeutic alliance.

OUTLINE OF TREATMENT

Having set the stage for thinking about the child in the context of that child's specific adoption and trauma history, introduce the ADAPT treatment outline. Give parents a copy of Handout 1: Modules of ADAPT (Adoption-Specific Therapy). Go through the outline with parents, noting that most modules involve individual parent and child sessions along with a joint family session. At the end of the presentation of Modules 1, 4, and 7, ask the parents about what questions and reactions they have if these have not already arisen spontaneously.

After reviewing and discussing the ADAPT module outline, give Handout 2: Basic Beliefs of Adoption-Specific Therapy. Read each belief aloud and ask for feedback. Answer parents' questions briefly and, if appropriate, reflect the feelings expressed. Let parents know that the various activities in ADAPT further explore these beliefs. If a parent has major objections to these beliefs, you will need to discuss them in detail, as it may be difficult to go through ADAPT if parents are strongly opposed, for example, to sharing the child's information with them or talking openly about adoption. In these cases, try to obtain the parent's buy-in to be open to thinking about these concepts as they go through the program. In many instances, parents came in opposed to sharing any information with the children about their past but as they became more comfortable with the therapist and began exploring these issues, significant change occurred.

For example, one adoptive mother was adamantly opposed to sharing any information about the birth family with her 9-year-old daughter, whom she had adopted at age 18 months, and in fact the girl did not know she was adopted when they entered treatment. Her mother knew that she should have told the girl earlier, but "there never seemed like the right moment." As we went through the curriculum, the mother decided to contact the birth aunt with whom she had talked once or twice and who was raising the girl's half-sister and half-brother. She was gradually able to tell the girl about her adoption, and when her daughter asked what her birth mother looked like and whether she had any siblings, the adoptive mother was able to answer these questions and asked the aunt to send pictures.

Module 1 does not address adoption issues in depth, instead focusing on increasing positivity in the parent–child relationship and helping the child develop or expand coping strategies. This allows reluctant parents to become comfortable with the treatment and the therapist before processing the many issues and beliefs about the child's adoption in Module 2.

If the child has entered the home in the last 9 months, give parents Handout 3: What Parents Can Expect During the Transition. Discuss the points, with particular focus on the helpful hints for the transition, and ask the parents about what transition behaviors or feelings of the child have arisen.

Introduce the Parent Progress Report (PPR) measure (Handout 4), give parents a copy, and let parents know they will fill this out at the beginning of every session. Help the parents to identify the three main concerning child behaviors, and let them know that you will be going over these again at the beginning of each module to track progress. Tell parents that research has shown that regular monitoring of symptoms and concerns leads to more positive outcomes.

MY CHILD'S POSITIVES ACTIVITY

Discuss the need to focus on and support things the child does well, both to build the child's self-confidence and to increase family closeness. Ask: "What do you see as (child's name) areas of strength? What does (child's name) do particularly well?" Sometimes the child's strengths may not match the parent's own goals and dreams. For example, the child's strengths may lie in ability on the soccer field, whereas parents' goals for the child may be highly academic ("I want her to go to an Ivy league school like I did," "I think computers will be the wave of the future and I hope she'll be an engineer").

Ask parents: "How do these strengths match your goals and dreams for your child?" Bring up that often the child may have very different, but meaningful and important, strengths and interests from theirs. Discuss and validate their feelings about the child having different strengths than they had hoped, being accepting of all the feelings expressed. Note that biological parents may be more likely to have similar strengths and talents with the child than adoptive parents do. Wishing that this child would be more like their fantasized birth child (and therefore more like themselves) is often an underlying adoption-related loss for adoptive parents.

If appropriate, note that issues may arise for the child when the adoptive parents are obviously doing better emotionally and materially than their birth families. This is most likely if the child has spent considerable time with their birth families prior to foster care/adoption or the child's story involves impoverishment as a reason for relinquishment as is often the case in international adoption. For example, one teenager noted that he often felt lost and out of place when his parents, who both had doctoral degrees, began discussing political or scientific issues. The parents saw his silence and boredom during these dinnertime talks as a sign of sullenness and disdain, but these behaviors actually reflected the son's feelings of inadequacy.

After eliciting the child's strengths, ask each parent to use Handout 5: My Child's Positives, to list the child's positive personal attributes, areas in which the child does well, and activities that the child enjoys. Go over the lists with the parents, reflecting and emphasizing the strengths of the child. If the parents cannot come up with positives, brainstorm with them to think about and notice the child's personal attributes, areas in which the child does very well, and activities that the child enjoys. If there are two parents, talk about similarities and differences in their lists.

HOMEWORK: MY CHILD'S STRENGTHS AND CONCERNING BEHAVIOR

Give parents a folder in which to keep handouts and homework. Ask each parent to do the following:

1. Take one step this week to support a strength or interest of the child.
2. Look at and reflect on one child behavior of concern through the lens of the child's past history to develop an adoption-specific strategy to address the concerning behavior in the next session.
3. Fill out Handout 6: My Child Strengths/Concerning Behaviors, and bring it to the next session.

Ask for parental feedback about the homework. Make sure they understand what you mean by looking at the child's behavior through the lens of the child's past history. If needed, refer back to the example given in the section, Story of Child's Adoption, or use the case example that follows to help parents look for ways in which the child's current maladaptive behavior may have been adaptive in the context of the child's previous life experience.

CASE EXAMPLE: THE SPRINGFIELD FAMILY

Throughout the modules of ADAPT, we will illustrate the activities with the clinical example of the Springfield family, a composite of many families with whom we have used ADAPT. At the end of each session, some aspect of the Springfield family's experience with the session will be discussed to illustrate how ADAPT activities are used.

Rachel Springfield, a 42-year-old Caucasian woman, and her husband Lewis Springfield, a 44-year-old African American man, have been married for 12 years. Rachel works as a preschool teacher, and Lewis is a sales representative for a large roofing company in the Los Angeles area. For the last 6 years, they have tried unsuccessfully to conceive a baby. The process of trying to have a child without success has been very upsetting for both of them, and Rachel often experiences anger at herself for not starting to try when she was younger and theoretically more fertile. They tried reproductive assistance up to IVF, for which they did not have the funds. International adoption was also out of their price range, so they decided to explore adoption from foster care. They were open to any age and gender, with a slight preference for a child past infancy. After their preadoption classes, they had hoped to be matched immediately and were offered a 16-year-old who was living in a group home. After much soul-searching and discussion, they both decided that they really wanted younger children; the behavioral problems and difficult history of the teen were frightening to them. So they waited, and waited, and waited. About 13 months later, they were matched with Carlos, 6 years old, and his half-sister Maria, 11 years old, who are Hispanic. Although Rachel and Lewis had assumed they would adopt one child, they decided that a sibling set might be the right option for them because they had already waited over a year and eventually wanted two children. Lewis especially wanted more than one child because he had three brothers and a sister, whereas Rachel was more hesitant because her relationship with her only sibling, an older sister, was quite rocky.

Maria and Carlos had entered foster care 3 years previously when at age 3, Carlos was found wandering in the street, hungry and filthy. A stranger who noticed him tried to comfort him, bought him a hamburger, and called 911. In canvassing the neighborhood, police found Maria frantically looking to find her half-brother. She had been left in charge of him by their birth mother while she attempted to buy methamphetamine. Maria was watching TV and didn't notice that her brother had walked out the door. They lived in a motel room that was dirty, with feces in the corner and roaches everywhere. The children were taken to an emergency shelter for 2 days, then placed with an aunt, their mother's sister. However, after a domestic violence report at her home 4 months later, the children were placed in a foster home, where they remained for 1 year. However, because of concerns about Maria's aggressive behavior, the single foster mother asked that the children be moved. They then resided in another foster home for about 15 months until they were placed with prospective adoptive parents Rachel and Lewis. The children had only sporadic contact with their birth mother and with Carlos's birth father during placement with the aunt and during their first foster placement, but there had been no contact with the birth mother and only one visit with Carlos's birth father during their last foster placement. Maria's birth father has never had contact with her and is in fact unknown.

In the last foster home, both children gradually grew attached to the foster parents and their 14-year-old biological son. Maria has had academic problems in school, possibly because of her multiple moves and is thought to have attention-deficit/hyperactivity disorder. She is always moving and shows inattention and impulsivity at times. She used to get in many fights with other children on the playground, but since she became a star on a soccer team through the park in her last foster home, her aggressive behaviors have diminished. Maria expresses a great deal of longing for her birth mother and experiences periods of sadness. Carlos, on the other hand, says he barely remembers his birth mother and was extremely clingy to his last foster mother, having difficulty with separation at the beginning of kindergarten. He exhibits symptoms of anxiety in new situations and is reluctant to attend birthday parties or other events outside the home. In school, Carlos often asks for help from the teacher and appears to be functioning at grade level.

The children had been with Rachel and Lewis for 14 months when they began ADAPT. The adoption had been finalized 3 months prior; Rachel particularly feels that Maria's behavioral issues have escalated since the finalization, and she is seeking help to contain her increasingly aggressive behavior at school and with Carlos. In addition, Maria had recently been caught stealing food from the middle school where she had entered sixth grade the previous September. The parents want help with managing Maria's behaviors, and they also feel that she might be regretting the adoption and missing her birth mother, although she denies it and shuts down if they try to talk about it. Rachel is very sad that she is less close to Maria than before, and she and Lewis do not always agree on how to handle issues that arise with the children; sometimes she wonders if the adoption was a mistake and will end up hurting her marriage.

In the Module 1 Parent Session 1, the mother Rachel took the lead in talking mostly about her concerns with Maria's increasing aggression at school and with her brother Carlos. The previous night, when Carlos came into Maria's room, she screamed at him and physically threw him out of her room, which terrified Carlos who began sobbing hysterically. Rachel reported being both angry and scared by this incident. The father Lewis was mostly concerned about Maria's stealing behavior at her new middle school; she recently stole food from the cafeteria, and the parents were called into the vice principal's office. Lewis was worried that Maria might get a bad reputation at school.

The parents generally seemed comfortable with participating in ADAPT, although Rachel had some concerns about discussing issues of loss of the birth parents with Carlos. Because he didn't remember being with his birth parents, Rachel felt that he might be upset by talk of them. She noted that when Maria brought up her feelings of sadness about missing her birth mom, she always drew her into a room separate from Carlos so he wouldn't hear. The therapist empathized with her concern for Carlos and noted that they would be talking more about these issues over the weeks of ADAPT.

In the My Child's Positives activity, both parents found it very easy to list Carlos's strengths. Rachel said that he was warm, affectionate, and sensitive to other's feelings. Lewis added that he had a great sense of humor. Both felt he excelled in block building, learning his ABCs, and kicking a soccer ball. They took longer to answer about Maria's strengths, giving strengths that could also be a weakness; for example, they noted that she was strong-willed and determined, and she never gave up in getting what she wants. The therapist emphasized the determined, persevering portion. It was also difficult for them to come up with things she did very well, especially because she was having academic problems in school. The therapist was encouraging, and finally Lewis noted that she was a good artist and Rachel commented on her ability to come up with unusual but cool and hip outfits. In discussing the homework about supporting a strength, the parents said they would look into possibilities for an after-school art class for Maria.

Because one of the goals of ADAPT is to help parents view and react to children's problematic history through the lens of their past history, the therapist asked Rachel and Lewis if they could see one of the children's behaviors through the lens of their past history. Rachel quickly noted that she thought Carlos's anxiety and clinginess in new situations must be related to having moved homes so many times in his young life. The therapist praised her perceptiveness. They saw less clear connections between Maria's aggressiveness, impulsivity, and stealing behavior but agreed to think about it over the week and write down their ideas on the homework sheet given.

Child Session 1: Overview and Rapport Building

The first session with the child has four main goals. First, the focus is on building rapport and beginning to develop a positive relationship. Next, the therapist discusses with the child a basic outline of what ADAPT treatment will be like. It is important to explain right from the start that this program is especially for children who have been adopted or are in the adoption process. Third, the Clay Animal activity is presented as a fun way to learn more about the child and build rapport. The animal they choose, the reasons they chose this animal, and what they say about where the animal lives and with whom (or with no one) can help the therapist begin to understand the child's world view and feelings about themselves. Finally, the child is given a homework folder and encouraged to decorate it.

Materials for this session include

- a folder for homework and handouts,
- art material (e.g., blank paper, markers, glitter glue, feathers),
- modeling clay (Model Magic recommended or Play-Doh), and
- feeling cards/feeling faces.

BUILDING RAPPORT

The first task is to develop a positive relationship with the child and build rapport. Beginning in the waiting room, work on building rapport by trying to connect immediately with the child. For example, if they are wearing a basketball jersey, you might ask what their favorite team is, or if they play on a team. You can also ask about family, school, pets, favorite activities, etc., as you get to know the child.

OUTLINE OF TREATMENT

Prior to the session, make sure that children know they are adopted; this should have come up in the first session with the parents. Present the basic outline of ADAPT. Points to mention include (a) ADAPT is especially for children who have been adopted or are in the process of being adopted; (b) there are six or seven modules on different topics, each with several sessions; (c) the child will be seen separately and do activities, and the parents will have their own sessions as well; and (d) every three or four sessions, there will be a family session where child and parent(s) will meet together with you. Explain that you and the child will be working together to deal with feelings about the child's family, adoption, worries and concerns, behaviors, and self. Be sure to ask if the child has any questions about what you'll be doing together over the next few months.

If the child seems to be warming up, ask: "What did your parents tell you about why you are coming to see me?" Reflect the child's feelings and be welcoming. You might say something like, "I'm glad you're here and we can work together on that problem." If it feels like the child is not ready to discuss any possible areas of concern, omit this section and come back to it later, possibly at the end of this session when the child is decorating the homework folder.

CLAY ANIMAL ACTIVITY

Introduce the Clay Animal activity by asking: "If you could be any animal in the world, what animal would you be?" Give the child a package of Model Magic clay (or Play-Doh if Model Magic clay is not available) and encourage the child to create that animal out of clay. We suggest Model Magic because it is easier to handle and less messy, but Play-Doh can also be used. If the child asks for assistance, give help with the animal, but do not do it all for them. Have markers available to decorate the animal. Praise the child's efforts and/or creation. If the child refuses to make an animal because it seems too hard, ask if the child would prefer to draw the animal instead. If they child refuses to make any representation of the animal, then explore their animal choice verbally.

Once the animal is developed, ask the child the following questions: (a) "Why did you choose this animal?" (b) "What is it about this animal (e.g., dog, bear) that you like? What other traits of this animal did you like?" Possible answers include: can fly, is strong, can camouflage themselves, is pretty.

Next, give the child a piece of paper and markers and ask them to draw the place where the animal lives. Allow them a few minutes to draw the animal's habitat. Then ask the child to tell you about the animal's home and how the animal feels about living where it does. Inquire about whether the animal lives with anyone else, if it is not obvious from the drawing. If the child says the animal lives alone, ask how the animal feels about that and wonder if the animal ever gets lonely. If the child says the animal lives with others, explore what the relationships are like between the animal and the other creatures. Reflect the child's feelings and provide validation through this process.

DECORATE HOMEWORK FOLDER

Give the child a folder to hold handouts and homework. Say the following:

> Some weeks I will be giving you handouts, and sometimes I will give you an easy homework assignment to do before the next session. Here is a folder to keep those things in. You can decorate it however you want with these markers and art materials. Please make sure to put your name on it somewhere.

Allow the child time to decorate the folder, and if this isn't finished by the end of the session, let the child know they can continue to decorate it at home. Ask the child to bring the folder back each session along with completed homework. Collect homework each week and keep it until the end of treatment when the child can take it home if they wish. At the end of the session, mention the homework folder to the parent and ask the parent to help the child remember to bring it back each week.

CASE EXAMPLE: THE SPRINGFIELDS

In Maria's first session, she engaged fairly easily with the therapist, who had started a conversation about Maria's outfit—she was wearing a tie-dyed long tunic with striped leggings and a faux fur jacket that was very stylish and hip. The therapist complimented her for the cool outfit and asked about her interest in fashion. Maria told the therapist she hoped one day to try out for Project Runway or another fashion reality show and noted that she had made the tunic out of an old bedspread that her adoptive mother had.

When discussing the ADAPT program, Maria expressed ambivalence about talking about adoption. She mentioned that she thought she'd feel better once she was actually adopted, but instead it had caused her to think more about her birth mom and therefore miss her more. The idea of discussing it a lot in the therapy sessions did not seem like fun to Maria, who said it helped to avoid thinking about any of her past. The therapist normalized Maria's feelings, saying that many kids want to avoid the possible pain of talking about their past and upsetting events. The therapist reassured Maria that the next four sessions would focus on coping skills to help deal with uncomfortable feelings and that adoption would not be the focus until after those sessions.

Maria loved the Clay Animal activity, as she enjoys art. After thinking about it for a bit, Maria began to make what looked like a lion or tiger. After shaping it out of bright pink Model Magic, she took a black marker and made spots on it. Maria identified it as a cheetah named Emily and said she liked that animal because it was fast and could get away easily if in danger. She drew the cheetah's habitat to include a river and jungle-like trees, saying that Emily could hide among the trees if a lion was after her and was glad she had the river to drink from. When asked if Emily lived with anyone, Maria said that she lived alone and that Emily liked it that way because then no parents were around to nag her and no sisters or brothers could tease and annoy her. She reported that Emily thought the jungle was very peaceful.

Carlos was more reluctant to make a clay animal. He said clay made his fingers feel weird and that he did not want to do it. The therapist asked if he'd rather draw the animal instead, and he said he wasn't a good drawer. With empathy and encouragement from the therapist, he finally did draw a dog. He said that he chose a dog because he likes dogs and had one at his last foster home. When asked what he liked about dogs, he said they get petted a lot and taken for walks, and also they have a good sense of direction so they can find their way home. Carlos drew two houses for the dog. When the therapist asked him about the two houses, he said that the dog lived some of the time with one family and then, when he wanted to, he could walk over to the house of his other family. He said that one family was the dog's foster family and the other one was the dog's adoptive family, and that the dog liked to stay with them both. The therapist reflected that the dog loved both of the families and wondered if he ever missed one family when he was with the other one.

Parent Session 2: Child-Led Play and Reflective Listening

The overall goal of Parent Session 2 is to continue building a positive parent–child relationship to provide a foundation of affection and connection between the child and the adoptive parents from which to explore the myriad issues that are discussed in the following modules of ADAPT. There are three subgoals. The first goal is to review the homework about supporting the child's unique strengths to continue to encourage parents to enhance the child's self-esteem and emphasize to the child how much the parent appreciates and notices these strengths. The second goal is to help the parents develop skills for child-led play. This special type of play allows the child to be seen and heard as a unique and valued individual, in contrast to the much more frequent parent–child interaction that involves the child responding to the demands that parents constantly need to put on the child (e.g., do your homework, get dressed, go to bed now, pick up your toys). We aim for 10–15 minutes daily of child-led play and work in this session to help parents develop their abilities to listen reflectively, respond to the child's lead rather than directing the play, and make descriptive comments rather than asking questions. These skills are first discussed and then role played. The third goal of this session is to review the parents' homework about reflecting on one child behavior of concern through the lens of the child's history and to help parents develop adoption-specific strategies to address this concerning behavior.

Materials for this session include

- play materials for role playing (e.g., LEGO blocks, play food, puppets),
- Handout 7: Child-Led Play Skills,
- Handout 8: Adoption-Specific Behavior Record, and
- Handout 9: Child-Led Play Record Sheets (homework).

REVIEW SESSION 1 PARENT HOMEWORK: MY CHILD'S STRENGTHS AND CONCERNING BEHAVIORS

Review with the parents their homework of supporting an area of strength of the child. Go over the handout and see what concrete action the parent has taken to support the child's strength listed. Make sure to discuss how it went, how the child reacted, and how the parent felt about supporting that strength. Some concrete examples of supporting the child's strength may be enrolling the child in a class for pottery making or martial arts, spending an afternoon playing catch with the child in the park, or cooking a special dessert that the child has wanted to try to make. Process with the parent feelings that may have arisen during the activity, such as pride at how quickly the child's skill level developed in the class, guilt that they had not done anything to nurture this skill previously, and feelings of joy when they saw how much the child enjoyed the activity. Be sure to praise the parents for taking these new steps and encourage them to continue.

If the parents did not do the homework of encouraging a strength of the child, inquire what happened that prevented this by asking, "What got in the way of accomplishing this?" If it was a matter of not enough time, brainstorm with the parents how they can work the activity into their schedule or help them pick another way to support the strength. If they could not figure out how to support the child's strength, work with them to develop options for doing so. If they say they couldn't figure out what strength to support, go back to the My Child's Positives handout from Module 1 Session 1 of what the child does well and what activities the child enjoys to nail down the strength they will support and what concrete step they will take in the next week to support it. The second part of the homework about concerning behaviors will be reviewed later in the session.

CHILD-LED PLAY AND REFLECTIVE LISTENING SKILLS DEVELOPMENT

Begin by saying,

> Today we will be working on developing skills for what may feel like a different kind of play with your child. We will focus on following the child's lead doing an activity that the child chooses. As we continue to work on increasing the positive relationship between you and (child's name), child-led play may at first feel very different and kind of awkward. The good feelings that this kind of

play brings about help the child tolerate other times when parents have to set limits. In other words, when children know they can count on having regular special fun time playing with parents, it is easier for them to accept the times that parents do have to place demands on them (i.e., school work, bedtime) or say "no" to something.

Ask parents about their experiences doing child-led play (if any) and how they have felt about it. This often causes parents to talk about how their parents never played with them in this way and provides an opportunity for them to think how they might have felt if their parents had done this. Often parents who have busy schedules and many conflicting demands will say there is no time in their day for such activity that has no concrete goal. Note that this play does not have to take a long time and that it tends to be pleasurable for the parent as well as the child; work with the parents to find a time of day to do this play for 10 to 15 minutes. If parents absolutely feel they cannot commit to doing child-led play daily, try to elicit a commitment to do it a minimum of three times per week to start. Give parents Handout 7: Child-Led Play Skills, and go over the specific Dos and Don'ts with them. Make sure that parents have the idea that the play is to be directed by the child, not them, that it is not a teaching opportunity, and that they simply describe what they see and reflect the child's feeling with lots of praise and encouragement.

ROLE PLAY OF FOLLOWING CHILD'S LEAD IN PLAY

Say: "Let's try out these child-led play skills through doing a role play. First you can be the child and I'll be the parent, playing two different ways. Then you can take a turn being the parent doing child-led play." Give the toys you have brought for this activity to the parent and encourage the parent to play. As the parent, begin by being directive and teaching, and not following the child's lead. For example, if the parent is playing with dolls, say something like, "No, no, don't do it that way, do it this way" or "I think you should play with the LEGOs," pushing the LEGOs on the child, or "What color is that? What does it do?" Continue for 3–5 minutes, then ask the parent what it felt like to be the child. Reinforce how as the child, the parent may have felt angry and unheard, and might not have wanted to play. Next, as the parent as child continues to play, model following the child's lead, using descriptive comments and reflecting feelings, as noted on the handout. After 3–5 minutes, ask the parent how this play felt and process his or her reactions.

Next, ask the parent to take the parent role while you take the child role, with the parent attempting to follow the child's lead and reflect the feelings they see and hear. Continue for about 5 minutes, and then ask the parent what the experience was like for them. Also share honest feedback about what it felt like to be the child in that situation, such as "I felt you were really interested in what I was doing," "I was sorry the time was up." If there are two parents, make sure that each parent takes a turn in this second part, role playing appropriately following the child's lead.

DEVELOPMENT OF AN ADOPTION-SPECIFIC PLAN FOR CONCERNING BEHAVIOR

In the final activity, help parents examine a concerning child behavior in the context of the child's past history, using information from the homework for Session 1. If you think it would be helpful, also incorporate information from the PPR in picking a target behavior.

Discuss and brainstorm appropriate adoption-specific behavioral strategies that might be helpful given the context. For example, a parent would deal differently with the behavior of stealing food from school if the child has been homeless and living on the streets or deprived of sufficient food in an orphanage than if the child had lived in a safe and secure home. If the child had to forage for food, the parent might put out a bowl of healthy snacks that the child could have whenever desired to decrease stealing and hoarding of food (and even allow the child to have a supply of these snacks in the backpack). You might also encourage the parent to help the teacher at school understand the context under which the child might be stealing food (e.g., child was homeless and did not have enough to eat, child was not given much food in orphanage) so that the school might also handle the stealing food less punitively.

Similarly, time-out might not be a good strategy for a child who had previously been abandoned and left alone by a substance-abusing parent or orphanage caregivers, as time-out might also be viewed as abandonment and be triggering for the child. Another example would be if a child with a history of major deprivation steals from the parent or others, the parent might fill a box with the type of things the child steals (e.g., quarters, small toys, etc.), hide it in a closet, and let the child know that if they feel like stealing there are things in the box that are OK to take. Emphasize positive strategies including praise, encouragement, parental positive attention, and reward in planning the strategy. Begin the discussion of various types of incentives and when they would be useful (e.g., praise, encouragement, tangible rewards, points, stars, etc.), and let the parent know that these will be discussed in greater detail during the next session.

Collaboratively set up a simple plan for how the parent will handle the concerning behavior during the upcoming week that takes into account the child's past history, letting parents know that it is likely they will need to work on revising and refining the plan over the next few weeks. Go over Handout 8: Adoption-Specific Behavior Record, to make sure parents are clear about what behavior they are targeting, what the intervention plan is, and what information to write down on the Behavior Record.

HOMEWORK: SETTING ASIDE A TIME AND DOING CHILD-LED PLAY

Ask the parent to set aside a period of time each day of the following week to engage for at least 10 minutes in child-led play and to note what happens on Handout 9:

Child-Led Play Record Sheets. If in the earlier discussion parents felt they could only commit to doing child-led play three times a week, accept that as the goal for now.

Remind parents about the adoption-specific plan for the concerning behavior and ask them to make sure to fill out the Adoption-Specific Behavior Record (Handout 8).

CASE EXAMPLE: THE SPRINGFIELDS

The therapist asked Rachel and Lewis how it had gone last week with the homework of supporting a strength of the children. They both started laughing. Rachel explained that they had broached the idea of an after-school art class with Maria, as they had planned in the last session. She soundly rejected the idea, saying she didn't want to be in a class with little kids, didn't like painting, and yelled at them that they didn't understand her at all. "Not a good beginning," commented Lewis. However, a few days later, Maria told Rachel that she had a better idea than an art class. She had found an online fashion design class that she was interested in. Lewis checked out the school and discovered that it was legitimate, and so they enrolled Maria, who was very excited about it and had already done the first lesson.

In talking about child-led play, both parents felt it would be weird, as neither had experienced one-on-one time with their own parents. Lewis noted that his mother would tell all the kids to go out and play, but the parents never joined in. Rachel said that she had longed for special time with her mom, whom she felt liked her sister better than her, and felt rejected whenever she tried to get this. She mentioned that her mom told her that her grades were so bad that all her time with her had to be in doing homework; the therapist reflected Rachel's sadness about this.

Lewis played the child in the first part of the role play when the therapist as parent was being directive. At one point, he began bashing a toy truck onto the floor and later said how much he hated being told what to do. He reported feeling much calmer when the therapist followed his lead in the next role play. Both were reluctant to role play the parents, but finally Rachel started out. She chose LEGOs because Carlos really likes LEGOs. The therapist playing Carlos wanted mom to find different shapes and colors of LEGO blocks to help build his structure, and mom as parent several times gave him suggestions to make the structure better, which therapist as child vociferously rejected. In debriefing, Rachel stated how hard it was to simply find the LEGO pieces, make comments on what he was doing, and reflect his feelings of frustration; she so much wanted to give directions.

When Lewis was the parent, he did an excellent job of allowing the therapist as child to lead the play, commenting enthusiastically, and the therapist as Carlos responded very positively. Both parents expressed that it would be much harder to do child-led play with Maria, who didn't really "play" anymore. The therapist and parents brainstormed ways to creatively engage Maria in activities she might want to do if she herself did not come up with anything. Some ideas Rachel generated were reading fashion magazines and painting each other's nails. Lewis wondered if Maria and he might take an early evening walk to the convenience store, which Maria likes to do.

In working on a concerning behavior, Rachel wanted to start with Maria's aggression to Carlos, which has continued. She thought maybe Maria's anger at Carlos's wanting to be near her and cuddle was related to when she and Carlos lived with their birth mother and she always had to take care of him. The parents decided to note to Maria that it must be difficult to develop a new kind of relationship with Carlos when she used to have to almost be his mom. They decided to see if she would like to have a "Carlos-free hour" every evening when he was not allowed in her room and to institute a system where she could earn a point toward a clothing purchase for each day that she was not physically aggressive toward Carlos.

Child Session 2: Feelings Identification

The rest of the child sessions in Module 1 are meant to build skills and coping strategies that will help the child in dealing with more emotionally laden material in later modules such as feelings about birth parents and their family background, grief and loss, identity concerns, and divided loyalties. The goal of this session is to help children build a vocabulary of feeling words that they can use to describe their emotions. Children's level of awareness of their feelings and ability to express them vary greatly, both as a result of temperament and as a result of their past possibly traumatic history. Therefore, we provide several different activities to stimulate feeling identification. Although one activity may be enough to help some children identify and talk about feelings, other children may need to use several of the activities described next. In this session, children also learn to use the Feelings Thermometer to help them recognize when their "temperature" is rising, as well as what triggers such rise in intensity of feelings and where they experience this in their bodies.

Materials for this session include the following:

- feelings flashcards (cut out and laminated images of child and adult faces showing varied emotional expressions). These are available in the toolkit or can be made by the therapist.
- Handout 10: Feelings for Feelings Grab Bag
- construction paper and pencils, crayons, or markers for my feelings poster
- Handout 11: Feelings Thermometer
- feelings cards (therapists can use their own feelings cards, if available)
- Handout 12: Adoption Fill-in-the-Blank (for children 8 and older)

FEELINGS EXPLORATION

The activities listed next all involve the child (a) learning to identify various feelings presented in different ways and (b) talking about when they themselves have felt that feeling. Depending on time and developmental understanding of feelings, you may engage in one or all of the activities presented next. In general, focus on simpler feelings such as happiness, sadness, anger, fear, and worry for children under age 7 or 8.

For older children, add to these feelings more complex and subtle feelings such as embarrassment and pride. Use Handout 10: Feelings for Feelings Grab Bag, to help with which feelings to use with a particular child. As noted on the Grab Bag chart, use the feelings on the left side only for the younger children and include all the feelings listed for children ages 8 and above.

The Feelings Flashcards activity is a good place to start with young children or with children that you feel may be inhibited or delayed in their understanding of feelings identification. For older children or those who seem more aware of their feelings, you may want to start with the Feelings Grab Bag activity.

Feelings Flashcards

The goal of this activity is to begin a nonthreatening discussion about feelings by trying to identify feelings in others. For this activity, you can either use the Feelings Flashcards available in the optional toolkit, or you can make your own Feelings Flashcards by collecting pictures of faces of children and adults expressing different feelings from magazines or the Internet or other sources, and then either copying them onto cardstock or laminating them to make them sturdy enough for repeated use.

Put the stack of Feelings Flashcards on the table with the faces down, and say, "We're going to play a game about feelings." Ask the child if they would like to go first or prefer that you go first. Take turns choosing a card from the table, looking at the face pictured, and guessing what that person is feeling. Say, "What do you think this person is feeling?" With each card, talk about what clues the picture gave about the feeling generated. Was it the expression on the face? The person's body posture? Other hints from context in the picture? You will probably need to model this part of examining why the child thought of that feeling, and then guide the discussion. For example, if the child says the person is mad, you might ask, "What about her face made you think she was mad?" If the child cannot come up with anything, you might say, "I wonder if it's because her eyebrows come together here or maybe because her teeth are clenched?" Or if the child cannot come up with a reason a child is sad, you might wonder if it is because there are tears coming out from her eyes.

Feelings Grab Bag

The goal of Feelings Grab Bag (adapted from Pedro-Carroll, 2010)[1] is to increase awareness of one's own and others' emotions. It is similar to Charades. This activity requires the child to read feelings words, and while it can be done with you reading

---

[1]From *Putting Children First: Proven Parenting Strategies for Helping Children Thrive Through Divorce* (pp. 216–218), by J. Pedro-Carroll, 2010, New York, NY: Penguin/Avery. Copyright 2010 by Joanne Pedro-Carroll. Adapted with permission.

the words to the child, it is most effective if the child can read simple words and therefore is generally not appropriate for children under 7 unless you are sure they are reading. For younger children, use the simpler words in the left column of the Feelings for Feelings Grab Bag chart (Handout 10); include all words for older children.

Use a bag, hat, or envelope for the grab bag and place the papers with the appropriate feelings words in the receptacle, folded so that the word is not visible until you or the child unfolds the paper. Say the following:

> We're going to play a game called Feelings Grab Bag, and it is kind of like Charades. Have you ever played Charades? We will take turns pulling a card out of the bag, looking at it so the other person can't see, and then acting out the feeling written down on the paper. The other person will then guess the feeling. We can give hints to each other if we can't guess. After the other person guesses the feeling, then we will each say a time we had that feeling.

Ask the child if they would like to go first or prefer that you go first to pick a word to act out. You and the child take turns drawing a feeling out of the grab bag and acting it out. Tell the child that you won't be using any words, just actions to try to help the other person guess the feeling. If the child asks if it is OK to make noises like crying sounds or growling, say that those kinds of sounds are OK, but it's not OK to say something like "I'm really feeling brave right now."

The actor acts out the word, and the other person tries to guess. Sometimes it can be frustrating if either the child cannot get the word across to you or the child cannot guess the word you are acting out. It is OK and helpful in that situation to use hints—you can either give a hint or ask the child to give you a hint, such as "What letter does it start with?" "How often do people feel this feeling?" If children do not understand the word they picked, you can give them the choice of picking another feeling or asking you to explain it. If you need to read it to them or to explain it, do this in a whisper so that you can later guess the word after the child acts it out.

Once the feeling has been guessed, the person who acted it out is asked to tell a time when they felt that way. If the child goes first, say "When is a time you felt ________?" (feeling word they just acted out). Encourage the child as needed. Respond to the child's feeling disclosure with understanding and empathy. For example, "I can see why losing your cat would make you so sad," or "How wonderful that you came in first place—that's amazing, you deserve to feel lots of pride."

When you act out a feeling and you tell a time you felt that way, make a meaningful disclosure that you are comfortable making, as that sets the stage for the child to continue developing trust in you. Examples of genuine disclosures that hopefully don't seem unduly revealing might be, "I felt sad when my dog (or my grandmother) died," "I felt mad when someone cut in front of me in line at the store." If you can pick genuine examples from your life that relate to things in the child's life, you can further open up lines of communication and model appropriate sharing of feelings. If a discussion about an incident stimulated by the feeling goes on, that is great.

However, do not get completely sidetracked so that you don't ever get past one feeling for Feelings Grab Bag.

My Feelings Poster

The goal of My Feelings Poster is similar to those for Feelings Flashcards and Feelings Grab Bag—to engage children in identifying what feelings they have (and what terminology they use for certain feelings) and in discussing examples of when they have recently felt each of those feelings. Because it is a drawing and art activity, it is especially useful for children who like art.

For the My Feelings Poster, offer the child poster or construction paper and crayons, markers, etc. Say,

> You can make a My Feelings Poster. You can draw pictures of faces showing different feelings. If you'd like me to guess what feeling I think the face is showing, I'd be glad to do that, or if you want, you can write the feeling word under the face (or ask me to write it).

Children can draw simple faces with words underneath depicting each feeling, or choose to draw faces in more detail, or only write the words. Ask children to tell a time they felt each feeling as you go along. The poster can be used in later sessions to assist with feelings identification.

If you prefer, you can use other feelings identification activities you felt were effective in the past. These activities must meet the criteria of (a) having the child identify feelings based on people's faces and/or body postures and (b) having the child talk about times they felt each of the feelings.

FEELINGS THERMOMETER

Introduce the Feelings Thermometer as a way of recognizing when your temperature is rising and your feelings are getting bigger. Ask the child if they have seen how the red line in a thermometer goes up when the weather gets hot, and elicit the child's experiences with thermometers. Say,

> See this thermometer? (Point to the Feelings Thermometer, Handout 11.) It shows how our feelings can get hotter and more intense when your feelings temperature rises, like when you get very sad or very mad. At the top here, we can feel like we're at the boiling point and about to explode. Let's see if we can figure out what things might make you a little bit upset (like a 2–4), really upset (6–8), and overwhelmed by strong feelings/the very most upset (10).

Work with the child to identify situations that fit these numbers and write them down next to the appropriate number on the Feelings Thermometer. Next, use the thermometer to help the child identify triggers for upsetting feelings, focusing on anger if the child's issues are mostly impulsivity, defiance, and/or aggression. If the child's main issues revolve around depression or anxiety, focus mostly on feelings of sadness or worry, as appropriate. Also, attempt to help the child identify where in their body they feel the increase in temperature when getting hotter and hotter. For example, one child said he gets a slight funny feeling in his stomach when he starts getting mad (at a rating of about 3); as he gets more furious (at about a 6), his hands start clenching into fists, and when he's ready to explode (at a 9 or 10), he feels like his heart is beating really fast, he feels sweaty, and he thinks his fists will make him lash out without him being able to stop it.

For younger children, this is the last activity of the session. But for all children, sum up by noting that you have spent time today identifying feelings and talking about how they can notice what they are feeling before they get out of control. Say,

> I'm really glad we worked today on recognizing different kinds of feelings and also on knowing when our temperature is rising out of control. Over the next couple of weeks, we will be doing some activities to learn ways to cope with feelings that are painful or scary.

ADOPTION FILL-IN-THE-BLANK (CHILDREN 8 AND OLDER)

For this activity, use Handout 12: Adoption Fill-in-the-Blank. Although this activity is mainly for children over 8, if you have a slightly younger child with lots of concerns about adoption, feel free to try it. To some degree, the child's cognitive ability limits the use of this activity; if younger children cannot easily identify what words regarding adoption might start with each of the letters below, this activity will not be a good choice for them.

Ask the child to think of something related to their adoption experience that starts with each of the letters in *adoption*. After the child fills in the blanks, talk about what they noticed about the words used to describe the adoption experience. Provide empathy and reflection to let the child know you accept all their different feelings expressed.

CASE EXAMPLE: THE SPRINGFIELDS

The therapist decided to do Feelings Grab Bag as the feeling identification activity with Carlos because he doesn't really like to draw and told the therapist in the first session that he liked to make up stories and act them out. Before the session, the therapist had put only the feeling words in the left column of Handout 10: Feelings for Feelings Grab Bag (for younger children) in a bag with a superhero design and asked if Carlos wanted to go first. He wanted the therapist to go first. The therapist drew the feeling "mad" from the bag and began stomping around the room with an angry face. Carlos very excitedly and quickly said "mad" and was very pleased with himself for guessing so quickly. When asked about a time he felt mad, Carlos said he feels mad when Maria won't let him come into her room or play with him. The therapist thanked him for sharing, and then said that the therapist feels mad when friends agree to do something together and then change their mind and back out.

When it was Carlos's turn, he drew "scared" from the bag and opened his eyes and mouth very wide and ran as if trying to escape from something. The therapist had a few errant guesses but then guessed "scared." The therapist noted what Carlos did that helped the therapist figure out the feeling and said that the therapist felt scared when the therapist had to go to a meeting for work where all the people there would be strangers. This was completely true and also overlapped with Carlos's fears of being left alone at a birthday party or play date. He said "that happened to me when I went to Jonah's birthday party at the gymnastics place. I knew Jonah and another kid but nobody else, and I didn't know how to do gymnastics and was scared to try. I had a bad time." Later, Carlos was frustrated when the therapist couldn't guess when he acted out "brave" and said he didn't want to play anymore.

Maria enjoyed acting out feelings in Feelings Grab Bag. She then approached the Adoption Fill-in-the-Blank activity with enthusiasm and came up with answers very quickly. Here are her answers:

A—Awful
D—Dreadful
O—Odd
P—Painful
T—Terrible
I—Idiotic
O—(she had a hard time coming up with anything for this)
N—Nightmare

The therapist reflected that Maria had a lot of strong and negative feelings about being adopted and noted that it must be very painful for her. Maria began crying, and between sobs she described how she had thought it was a good idea to be adopted and that at first she really liked Rachel and Lewis. They seemed to understand some of her past, and they did fun activities. But since the finalization, she has been hit by waves and waves of sadness, longing for her birth mom and finding Rachel especially annoying. She said Rachel wanted to know everything she thought about, and she had stuff that was private and that she shared with no one. The therapist first encouraged Maria to talk freely by listening intently, and later reflected her feelings, noting that it sounded as if finalization felt like a door closing on her connection to her birth mother, which must feel like a huge loss for Maria. Maria asked that the therapist not to share her feelings with the adoptive parents, and the therapist agreed, also mentioning that they would be spending a lot of time over the course of ADAPT processing and talking about all of the many feelings she has about her birth and adoptive families.

Parent Session 3: Focusing on the Positive

In this session, we continue the focus on helping parents increase positivity in the parent–child relationship. There are four goals for this session. First, the homework to do child-led play at least three times per week (and hopefully every day) is reviewed, and any barriers to success in the play are explored. Second, the strategy of preteaching (contingency management) is discussed with the parents, including doing a role play to increase skills development. This strategy, which involves anticipating possible problem situations and proactively developing a plan, helps parents to give appropriate choices when family members are calm and not aroused, increasing positivity. Third, positive parenting strategies to increase desired child behaviors are reviewed, with the emphasis on positive reinforcement in a variety of formats. Fourth, the adoption-specific behavioral plan developed last week is reviewed. Problems that may have emerged are discussed, and the plan is revised accordingly for use in the coming week.

Materials for this session include

- Handout 13: Positive Parenting Strategies,
- Handout 14: 101 Ways to Praise a Child,
- Handout 15: Model Reward Chart,
- Handout 16: Praise and Encouragement Records, and
- Handout 17: Reinforcers for My Child.

REVIEW SESSION 2 PARENT HOMEWORK: CHILD-LED PLAY

Ask the parents: "How did it go with doing child-led play each day?" First get parents' general impressions of what it was like to do child-led play and ask how they felt about it. If parents did not do any or very little child-led play, explore what interfered with doing it. Frequently, families report that they did not have time to spend 10–15 minutes per day in play. First, empathize with how busy life is and note the many demands on families, especially with working parents and many child activities. Do not shame the parents for not doing it, but also work through barriers to help them be successful with child-led play. This type of play builds connection and attachment, helping the child feel heard and important, and this positivity is a reserve that may need to be drawn on when limit setting and discipline are necessary.

In exploring why no or little play happened, begin with logistical barriers. Explore what small time samples might be available for such play, for example, right after school before beginning homework or right before bath time after dinner. Sometimes looking at the family's schedule helps parents see that neither they nor the child have any breathing room, and this is a great time to try to build in the play time. For families who insist there is just no time for daily play, try to have the family commit to doing child-led play a few specific times per week, for example, both days of the weekend.

If any child-led play happened, go over the Child-Led Play Record Sheets (Handout 9) from Session 2, saying, "Let's go over the sheets you filled out." Praise parents for keeping records, and collaboratively review the sheets. Be sure to note successes where ratings were positive, and examine what went wrong when the ratings were not good. Review Handout 7: Child-Led Play Skills, from Session 2 to help identify what the issues were.

DISCUSSION OF POSITIVE PARENTING STRATEGIES

Use Handout 13: Positive Parenting Strategies, to discuss various strategies. Note that these strategies are effective in increasing behaviors the parent would like to see more of.

Preteaching

Tell parents that a good way to develop new behaviors or increase the frequency of desired behaviors is to use preteaching and positive feedback. In preteaching, the parent lets the child know ahead of time what behavior is desired in a certain situation and what will happen if the desired behavior does occur as well as what will happen if the desired behavior does not occur. The idea is to anticipate possible problem situations and then offer the child an informed choice about what will happen in the different scenarios. Elicit from the parent possible problematic situations where this could be useful. Say, "What is a time or situation that you dread because you think the child is quite likely to misbehave?"

If the parent cannot come up with an example, you can use the example of going to the grocery store where the child runs up and down the aisles and has a tantrum if not allowed to buy what is desired. Note that this situation has a high likelihood of disaster, and ask parents what preteaching they might do, noting choices for behavior for the child and what the consequences of these choices might be. If they are not able to come up with ideas or if you feel it would be more helpful, describe preteaching yourself. For example, suggest the following:

> Robbie, when we go to the store today, I'd like you to stay with the cart at all times, and don't ask me to buy you any particular thing at the store. I'll let you know you are doing a nice job by giving you a thumbs up sign when you stay by the cart and help me get what's on our list without asking for extra things. If you can stay with the cart and not ask me to buy things, then you can pick out a treat at the checkout stand. So if you want a treat at the checkout stand, what do you need to do?

In many of the adoption-specific behavioral plans that the parents are working on, preteaching would be very helpful. Work with the parents to specify how this might occur in their situation as part of their behavioral plan, and ask the parents to role play preteaching with their child. You can take the child's role and respond appropriately. If the behavior of concern has resolved by this session, ask parents to pick another of the three concerning behaviors chosen in Session 1 to examine how this behavior is related to the child's past history, and develop a preteaching and reward plan to be carried out this week, role playing the specific preteaching plan.

Praise

Ask parents what sorts of behaviors they generally praise, and ask for an example of what they say when they praise the child. Note that praise and encouragement have been shown to motivate positive behavior change and help children feel good about themselves. When praising, we want to catch the child being good, doing something that is positive. So often, we do not really notice when the child is doing well; our attention is often grabbed only when the child misbehaves. With praise, we note the child's accomplishments rather than their mistakes. Examples include "What a beautiful picture you made" and "You played so nicely with your sister." Praise is most effective if it occurs immediately after the positive action and works best when the behavior being praised is specifically labeled. So, rather than just saying "Great job," encourage parents to say instead, "Great job cleaning up those toys," "I loved how you used your imagination in making up that song." Ask each parent to think of something positive that happened today that they were pleased with and to state a labeled praise for that behavior. If it is not a specific labeled praise or is damning with "faint praise," help the parent reshape what they would say. Make sure to use labeled praise to compliment the parents' example of the praise, for example, "Excellent work in using labeled praise for Johnny getting his own cereal and milk." Be enthusiastic and upbeat when giving examples of labeled praise.

Encouragement

Help parents learn that praise involves commenting on the child's accomplishments, whereas encouragement involves commenting on the effort of the child, regardless of whether they accomplish the goal. Examples are, "You are trying so hard on that assignment," "You must feel so proud of yourself," "You never gave up on getting those pieces to fit together." Like praise, encouragement is most effective when specifically labeled, given enthusiastically, and given in real time (though discussing it again later can also be helpful). Encouragement is especially meaningful in building the child's self-esteem. When attention is paid to the children's effort or there is acknowledgment of how they must feel about themselves, their sense of self-esteem becomes internalized and focused on who they are, rather than what they did. Especially stress the importance of giving positives such as praise and encouragement for children being adopted past infancy, because many have experienced adverse events such as abuse and neglect and may have received little positive reinforcement, praise, or encouragement in their previous lives. Also note how building the child's positive sense of self in this way facilitates attachment as well.

Suggest each parent use a ratio of eight positive praising or encouraging statements to every one critical statement. Ask them to reflect on their current ratio, and note that generally most parents find that they give considerably more critical feedback than positive feedback. For example, it's so much easier to say, "you left your jacket on the floor again" than "thank you for hanging up your jacket" and how much more likely parents are to say, "you didn't finish your homework" rather than "I see how hard you're working to figure out those word problems." Also encourage parents to use nonverbal praise and encouragement as well, through use of high fives, thumbs up, smiles and laughs, clapping, whistling, or hooting to show appreciation for the child's accomplishments or efforts. Although Handout 14: 101 Ways to Praise a Child does not always use labeled praise, suggest that parents put it up in their home where they can see it frequently to remind them to praise and encourage the child often.

Be sure to emphasize the need to praise and encourage the child in many areas of life. It is important that academic achievement not become the main focus of praise and encouragement so that all aspects of the child's strengths and interests are positively reinforced. Help parents also focus on other aspects of the child, such as kindness to others, swimming ability, LEGO-building, etc., especially because for some children, academic achievement may not necessarily be a strength over time. Throughout this and all sessions, model by giving generous specific labeled and immediate praise and encouragement to the parent.

Physical Affection

Inquire about how parents may use physical affection to show positivity to the child, in what situations they use it, and how the child responds. Note that warm hugs and kisses encourage a positive parent–child relationship, and that a hug is worth many many words (though maybe not quite a thousand). It is a wonderful nonverbal way to show caring, whether or not accompanied by verbal praise or encouragement.

Children who have experienced trauma may have unusual reactions to physical affection, so be sensitive to this issue when discussing it with parents. If they express concern, discuss what in the child's history they associate with the concern, and brainstorm comfortable ways that they may help the child with these issues. For example, sexually abused children may have one of several reactions to physical affection from adoptive parents. Some children are frightened of physical contact and may need a long while before they can even allow the adoptive parent to hold their hand, put an arm around their shoulder, or hug them. Empathize with parent's reaction to this (which may be a combination of sadness, disappointment, and frustration), normalize it, and help parents respect the child's need for physical distance. Note that at times when the child feels vulnerable and needy, for example, when hurt or sick, the child may be more open to physical comforting. If the child is older, ask if it would be OK to give a hug.

On the other hand, if a child has become sexualized from an abuse history, the child may initiate physical contact that feels uncomfortable for the parent and push for physical contact to become more intimate, and the parent may need to set a limit. For example, the parent might say, "I want to be close to you too, but why don't we hold hands instead?" For these children, use of physical affection to build positivity must be done slowly and sensitively.

Tangible Reinforcers

Introduce the idea of using tangible reinforcers, noting that these are things that can be used to increase desired behaviors, particularly in situations where praise and encouragement may not be enough. Sometimes an incentive is needed to help children learn new behaviors, perform tasks that are necessary but possibly not fun, or try something scary or intimidating. Sometimes parents do not want to use tangible reinforcers because they feel they are bribing their child. If parents bring this up, note that a bribe is typically given *before* an activity in hopes that the child will then do what is asked; in contrast, a reward is given *after* the activity has been successfully completed. Note that incentives are used in all walks of life, for example, as payment for work, and that we use them with children to help get a new positive behavior started. Discuss the various types of tangible reinforcers, including things, privileges, and special time or activities using the Positive Parenting Strategies (Handout 13) and what parents think might be most useful for their child. Introduce the Model Reward Chart (Handout 15) as a good way to track progress, emphasizing that it both helps parents keep track of the child's progress toward the goal and helps keep children motivated.

Note that for younger children, a daily reward is usually most helpful and can be something like a sticker or a small treat to eat. Children older than 7 or 8 usually are able to work for a more distant reward but benefit from daily notice of their progress, such as a point or sticker on a chart or a token; for example, if they get 10 points, they might earn a small toy or a special playdate. Remind parents that tangible rewards should be accompanied by verbal and/or nonverbal praise and encouragement.

REVIEW AND MODIFICATION OF ADOPTION-SPECIFIC BEHAVIOR PLAN

Go over the adoption-specific behavior plan worked out in the last session with the parent and talk about how the plan worked (or didn't work). Say, "How did it go last week with the behavioral plan we worked out for (child's name)? Let's discuss how we might revise it, based on what you have learned this week." Ask to see the Adoption-Specific Behavior Record (Handout 8), process what worked and what didn't, and collaboratively modify the plan. Be sure to incorporate preteaching, praise and encouragement, and reward charts, as appropriate. If using an incentive, work out the specific incentive to be used as well as details of what the child must do to earn the incentive. Give the parent more copies of the Adoption-Specific Behavior Record to fill out for the next week. If the parent has not filled out the Behavior Record for this week, stress how important it is to do so, noting that details written down at the time are often crucial to figuring out the best and most effective revisions of the plan.

HOMEWORK: PRAISE AND ENCOURAGEMENT RECORDS; REINFORCER LIST

Ask each parent to review the Positive Parenting Strategies (Handout 13) and try to use all of the positive parenting strategies during the week. Ask each parent to fill out the Praise and Encouragement Records (Handout 16), using the ratio of eight praising/encouraging statements to one critical statement.

Ask each parent to reflect on what is reinforcing to the child and to fill out Handout 17: Reinforcers for My Child. Remind them to think of privileges and special activities as well as "things" that would be rewarding for the child. Remind parents also to fill out the Adoption-Specific Behavior Record (Handout 8), using the revised plan that was worked out in the session.

CASE EXAMPLE: THE SPRINGFIELDS

The therapist inquired about child-led play. Lewis responded that play with Carlos had gone very well. He and Carlos had played with LEGOs about 10–15 minutes four times over the week; they were working together on building a garage for fixing cars. Rachel reported similar positive outcomes of play with Carlos, though she noticed that she had asked some questions and once or twice found herself trying to make the play go in a certain direction. The therapist praised them for finding a way to do successful child-led play and particularly noted Rachel's insights about her difficulties keeping the play child led.

With Maria, it had been a different story. She thought the whole idea was stupid and said she wasn't interested in spending any regular time with her parents—if she had free time, she wanted to spend it with her friends. She flatly turned down the ideas the parents had developed in their last session. Lewis was frustrated with her and did not try again over the week, and the therapist empathized with his frustration.

Rachel reported that when she and Maria were in a bookstore, Maria asked if she would buy her an adult coloring book. Rachel said she would buy Maria one and also buy herself one if Maria would agree to spend 10 minutes a day coloring together. Maria really wanted the coloring book and the 90-piece colored pencil set with it, so she agreed. Rachel reported that for the first 3 days, they colored in silence because the rules of child-led play prohibited Rachel from asking questions. On the fourth day, Maria asked Rachel: "Did you ever have a crush on a boy when you were 12 years old?" Rachel answered honestly, and they had a good discussion about Maria's teenage crush on Herbie Stoll, a baseball player, all while coloring and never making eye contact. Rachel was extremely happy with the outcome.

The therapist introduced the idea of preteaching and asked if the parents could think of a situation where it might help. Lewis brought up the behavior they had been working on, Maria's aggression toward Carlos. Last week, they had tentatively talked in session about setting up a point system so Maria could earn points toward clothing. This had not really worked well; they had no way of noting whether she earned the points and also had not set up how many points were required or what type of clothing. When they had asked Maria if she would like a "Carlos-free hour" after dinner, she said no, because she didn't want him in her room anytime.

The therapist and the parents brainstormed how they might preteach about Maria's aggression toward Carlos and the consequence of earning clothing points. Lewis suggested the following and then role played it, with Rachel acting as Maria.

> Maria, you know we have all been struggling with you and Carlos fighting after dinner. I know he can be a pain, but it is not OK to hit him or physically

> throw him out of your room. We understand that you want alone time and are fine with you telling Carlos that he can't come into your room after 7 p.m. If he doesn't comply, please ask us for help instead of hitting him. You can earn new clothes when you keep your hands and feet off him. What do you think?

Rachel as Maria responded, "Great! I'll tell you, you'll get him out of my room, and I'll get a new outfit every day."

Lewis looked stumped, and the therapist helped him refine the preteaching statement to say, "For every day you are not physically aggressive to Carlos, you can earn $1 toward new clothes. When you have earned $25, your mom will take you to the mall if you want." The therapist wondered whether it would be helpful to make a chart to track progress. They decided to put a dollar sign ($) on the chart each day that Maria kept her hands and feet off Carlos. The therapist praised their work on refining the adoption-specific behavioral plan and noted that they might in the future want to consider a reward plan for Carlos about staying out of Maria's room after 7 p.m.

Child Session 3: Coping Strategies of Deep Breathing and Muscle Relaxation

In this session, we continue the focus on helping children develop coping strategies for dealing with stressful situations and emotionally fraught material. Many children with complex histories have difficulties with emotion regulation in a variety of situations as a result of trauma and lack of adequate caregiving. The common coping strategies taught in this session, deep breathing and muscle relaxation, are helpful for everyone and are especially needed when processing the issues of adoption, trauma, and loss in the modules that follow. The children learn that these strategies are useful when they find their temperature rising, referring back to the Feelings Thermometer used in Session 2.

Materials for this session include

- a script for deep breathing (in text),
- a small stuffed animal (for younger children for deep breathing),
- a script for muscle relaxation (in text),
- Handout 18: Muscle Relaxation Pictures, and
- markers or crayons for coloring the muscle relaxation animal pictures.

TEACHING COPING STRATEGIES

Begin by asking whether the child noticed their temperature rising any time over the week when they felt angry, sad, or upset. If the child gives an example, explore the situation and the child's feelings, providing validation for those feelings. Regardless of whether the child can come up with an example, say, "Today we're going to learn some coping strategies, things we can do when our temperature is rising and we're angry or upset. Do you know what coping means?" If the child gives a reasonable explanation, enthusiastically praise the answer. If not, say, "Coping involves doing something to help ourselves calm down and feel better and less upset."

Deep Breathing

For the deep breathing exercise (adapted from Waterman & Walker, 2009)[2] ask the child to get comfortable either in a chair or on the floor. Make sure that the child's arms and legs are relaxed, not crossed or tight. Once the child is comfortable, follow the deep breathing script below. Say,

> One way to relax yourself quickly when you're mad or upset without anyone knowing what you're doing is through deep breathing. It's a different kind of breathing and not how we usually breathe when we're upset. When we're upset, usually we breathe fast and shallow, like a dog panting. [*Exaggerate fast shallow breathing with an angry face so it's funny.*] Deep breathing is deep and slow and it lowers our emotional temperature. It's often used by basketball players at the free-throw line or baseball players if they're being teased.

Ask if the child is comfortable closing eyes, and if so, suggest they do it. If the child does not want to close eyes, let the child know that is fine. For some children with trauma backgrounds, closing eyes makes them feel vulnerable, and they should not be forced to do so. Dim the lights in the room if possible.

> Let's try it. We're going to breathe from our stomachs (you can use *tummy* instead of *stomach* for younger children if you think that is more appropriate) so put your hand on your stomach; some people call this *tummy breathing.* (For younger children, putting a small stuffed animal on their stomach that can rise or fall with breath can help children get the idea.) Take a very slow deep breath, so deep that you can see your stomach (or the stuffed animal) rise with your breath. Now slowly let out your breath and watch your stomach (or the stuffed animal) fall. Watching your stomach is a good way to make sure you're taking deep breaths. A good way to make sure you're taking slow breaths is to count. Each breath in should take four counts and each breath out should take another four counts. Keep your hand on your stomach and let your breath follow my count: Breathe in, two, three, four. Breathe out, two, three, four (repeat this about 10 times). Think about nothing but your breathing, let it flow in and out of your body.

Ask the child whether they feel relaxed and whether they felt they were able to make their breaths deep (raising stomach or stuffed animal) and slow (count to four

---

[2]From *Helping At-Risk Students: A Group Counseling Approach for Grades 6–9* (pp. 45–46), by J. Waterman and E. Walker, 2009, New York, NY: Guilford Press. Copyright 2009 by Guilford Press. Adapted with permission.

on the in breath, count to four on the out breath). If a child brings up any problems, work with the child to clarify how to do the breathing, continuing to practice it. Sometimes younger children have difficulties sitting still for deep breathing. In this case, challenge them to see how still they can hold the rest of their body while they make their tummy move up and down. Occasionally younger children breathe very fast, and you can suggest that they count slowly to four as they breathe (in addition to you counting as well). Remind children 8 and older that the great thing about deep breathing as a coping strategy is that they can do it anywhere at any time without anyone even noticing. Suggest that children try using deep breathing (tummy breathing) this week at least twice when they feel they are getting angry or upset and their temperature is rising.

Muscle Relaxation

For the muscle relaxation exercise (adapted from Ollendick & Cerny, 1981)[3] say, "Another good way to relax and calm down when we are angry or upset is through muscle relaxation. When we tense and then relax our muscles, it helps us calm down, take a break, and feel less emotional."

Make sure the child is still sitting comfortably, and suggest the child close his or her eyes if comfortable. When reading the script, speak in a soft, even tone. Pause between sentences. Demonstrate tensing and relaxing each appropriate muscle set as you read the script, and feel free to exaggerate the movement. If the child is young and gets restless, you can stop between the different body parts and allow the child to color in the Muscle Relaxation Pictures (Handout 18) that you just practiced from the handout (e.g., lemon, furry cat).

For relaxing hands and arms, say the following:

> Pretend you have a whole lemon in your left hand. Now squeeze all the juice out. Feel the tightness in your hand and arm as you squeeze. Now drop the lemon. Notice how your muscles feel when they are relaxed. Take another lemon and squeeze it. Try to squeeze it harder than you did the first one. That's right. Real hard. Now drop your lemon and relax. See how much better your hand and arm feel when they are relaxed? Once again, take a lemon in your left hand and squeeze all the juice out. Don't leave a single drop. Squeeze hard. Now relax and let the lemon fall from your hand. (Repeat this process with the right hand and arm.)

For relaxing arms and shoulders, say the following:

> Pretend you are a furry, lazy cat. You want to stretch. Stretch your arms out in front of you. Place them up high over your head, way back. Feel the pull

---

[3]From *Clinical Behavior Therapy With Children* (pp. 67–70), by T. H. Ollendick and J. A. Cerny, 1981, New York, NY: Plenum Press. Copyright 1981 by Plenum Press. Adapted with permission.

in your shoulders. Stretch higher. Now just let your arms drop back to your side. OK, kitten, let's stretch again. Stretch your arms out in front of you. Raise them over your head. Put them back, way back. Pull hard. Now let them drop quickly. This time let's have a great big stretch. Try to touch the ceiling. Stretch your arms way out in front of you. Raise them way up high over your head. Push them way, way back. Notice the tension and pull in your arms and shoulders. Hold tight now. Great. Let them drop very quickly and feel how good it is to be relaxed. It feels good and warm and lazy.

For relaxing shoulders and neck, say:

Now pretend you are a turtle. You're sitting on a rock by a lake or a peaceful pond just relaxing in the warm sun. It feels nice and warm and safe here. Uh-oh! You sense danger. Pull your head into your house. Try to pull your shoulders up to your ears and push your head down into your shoulders. Hold in tight. It isn't easy to be a turtle in a shell.

The danger is past now. You can come out into the warm sunshine and once again you can relax and feel the warm sunshine. Watch out now! More danger. Hurry, pull your head back into your house and hold it tight. You have to be closed in tight to protect yourself.

OK, you can relax now. Bring your head out and let your shoulders relax. Notice how much better it feels to be relaxed than to be all tight. One more time now! Danger! Pull your head in. Push your shoulders way up to your ears and hold tight. Don't let even a tiny piece of your head show outside your shell. Hold it. Feel the tenseness in your neck and shoulders.

OK. You can come out now. It's safe again. Relax and feel comfortable in your safety. There's no more danger. Nothing to worry about. Nothing to be afraid of. You feel good.

For relaxing the jaw, say the following:

You have a giant jawbreaker bubble gum in your mouth. It's very hard to chew. Bite down on it. Hard! Let your neck muscles help you. Now relax. Just let your jaw hang loose. Notice how good it feels just to let your jaw drop. OK, let's tackle that jawbreaker again now. Bite down. Hard! Try to squeeze it out between your teeth. That's good. You're really tearing that gum up. Now relax again.

Just let your jaw drop off your face. It feels so good just to let go and not have to fight that bubble gum. OK, one more time. We're really going to tear it up this time. Bite down. Hard as you can. Harder. Oh, you're really working hard. Good. Now relax. Try to relax your whole body. You've beaten the bubble gum. Let yourself go as loose as you can.

For relaxing the stomach, say the following:

This time imagine that you want to squeeze through a narrow fence and the boards have splinters on them. You'll have to make yourself very skinny if you're going to make it through. Suck your stomach in. Try to squeeze it

> up against your backbone. Try to be as skinny as you can. You've got to get through. Now relax. You don't have to be skinny now.
>
> Just relax and feel your stomach being warm and loose. OK, let's try to get through that fence now. Squeeze up your stomach. Make it touch your backbone. Get it real small and tight. Get as skinny as you can. Hold tight, now. You've got to squeeze through. You got through that skinny little fence and no splinters. You can relax now. Settle back and let your stomach come back out where it belongs. You can feel really good now. You've done fine.

For relaxing legs and feet, say the following:

> Now pretend that you are standing barefoot in a big, fat mud puddle. Squish your toes down deep into the mud. Try to get your feet down to the bottom of the mud puddle. You'll probably need your legs to help you push. Push down, spread your toes apart, and feel the mud squish up between your toes. Now step out of the mud puddle. Relax your feet. Let your toes go loose and feel how nice that is.
>
> It feels good to be relaxed. Back into the mud puddle. Squish your toes down. Let your leg muscles help push your feet down. Push your feet. Hard. Try to squeeze that mud puddle dry. OK. Come back out now. Relax your feet, relax your legs, relax your toes. It feels so good to be relaxed. No tenseness anywhere. You feel kind of warm and tingly.

To conclude this exercise, say the following:

> Stay as relaxed as you can. Let your whole body go limp and feel all your muscles relax. In a few minutes I will ask you to open your eyes (if child has closed them).
>
> As you go through the day, remember how good it feels to be relaxed. Sometimes you have to make yourself tighter before you can be relaxed, just as we did in these exercises.
>
> Practice these exercises every day to get more and more relaxed. A good time to practice is at night, after you have gone to bed and the lights are out and you won't be disturbed. It will help you get to sleep.
>
> Just remember the turtle, or the jawbreaker, or the mud puddle, and you can do these exercises at school or anywhere and nobody will know. Very slowly, now, open your eyes and wiggle your muscles around a little. Very good. You've done a good job. You're going to be a super relaxer.

Ask the child how it felt to relax their muscles. Elicit which of the animal relaxations they liked the best and, if possible, what they liked about that task. If the child did not need to stop between muscle groups to color in the Muscle Relaxation Pictures handout, introduce it now and give the child the handout and the crayons or markers.

Sometimes there may be time left over at the end of this session. Therefore, it is useful to have a game or ball or other activity that the child can choose to play with available if there is time. Allow the child to choose from a couple of age-appropriate activities.

HOMEWORK: PRACTICE DEEP BREATHING AND MUSCLE RELAXATION

Brainstorm with the child about situations in which it would be helpful to use deep breathing and in which the child might use muscle relaxation. Stress the fact that deep breathing is quick and can be used anywhere, as the child thinks about either emotions or situations when each strategy would be useful. Ask the child to practice deep breathing at least two times over the next week.

Before ending the session, review the Muscle Relaxation Pictures (Handout 18) with the child and encourage the child to practice these exercises every day to get more and more relaxed. Remind the child that a good time to practice is at night, when in bed and the lights are out.

CASE EXAMPLE: THE SPRINGFIELDS

Carlos had some difficulty understanding the concept of deep and slow breathing. The therapist gave him a small stuffed rabbit to use to help him understand tummy breathing. Carlos put it on his stomach and at first breathed very fast and laughed, saying, "Look, the bunny is dancing." The therapist asked him to breathe in rhythm with the numbers said, and then the therapist counted breaths in, one, two, three, four, and breaths out, one, two, three, four. After several tries, Carlos seemed to get the idea. The therapist stressed that he would know he was taking *deep* breaths if the bunny moved up and down on his tummy when he breathed, and that he would know he was taking *slow* breaths when he counted to four slowly as he breathed in and counted again slowly to four when he breathed out. In contrast to deep breathing, he easily got the concept of muscle relaxation and enjoyed doing the activities. He got restless quickly, though, so the therapist suggested coloring in the pictures, and he enjoyed coloring each one after practicing the associated activity. The therapist had to take the paper away after Carlos drew each picture because he wanted to color in one that hadn't yet been practiced. At the end of the session, there were a few minutes left before the end of the session, and Carlos chose to play Candyland for that time period.

Maria easily understood the rationale behind learning the coping strategies and said she felt both deep breathing and muscle relaxation would be helpful to her. Specifically, she thought deep breathing would help her when Rachel's questions to her were annoying and that muscle relaxation would be useful as she as trying to fall asleep, because this is often a time when she starts thinking about her birth mother and feels sad. At the end of the session, Maria did not want to color in the animals and instead used the time to talk with the therapist about an issue she was having at school with two of her friends. The therapist listened, asked clarifying questions, and empathized with Maria's feelings.

The therapist reminded both children to try to use deep breathing at least two times during the week when their temperature was rising and they were starting to become upset or angry, and to practice muscle relaxation every day. They were given the Muscle Relaxation Pictures handout to remind them about relaxing the different parts of their body.

Parent Session 4: Developing Adoption-Specific Discipline Strategies

The purpose of this session is to help parents understand that children who have been traumatized need appropriate discipline strategies that take into account their specific trauma history. First, parents are helped to understand why typical popular strategies used with nonadopted children, such as time-out, might be completely inappropriate for their child. Next, parents learn that effective discipline may require them to adjust their attitudes, expectations, and responses to their children as they develop appropriate, effective, and creative approaches to handling specific types of behavior, looking through the lens of the child's past history. Finally, positive discipline strategies are discussed, with the focus of individualizing them for the particular child.

Materials for this session include

- Handout 19: Positive Discipline Strategies, and
- Handout 20: Behavioral Strategies for Common Difficult Child Behaviors Using Adoption-Specific Lens.

REVIEW SESSION 3 PARENT HOMEWORK: KEEP REVISED REWARD CHART

Review homework from Parent Session 3 about the reward chart. Make sure that parents have clearly stated an observable desired behavior, what the reward is, and exactly what the child needs to do to achieve it, and then revise the reward chart as necessary.

PRESENTATION OF DE-ESCALATION

A major principle for reducing a child's emotional dysregulation/intensity is de-escalation. In doing so, the parent helps to coregulate the child's feelings as a step toward the child learning to calm down without parental assistance as children get older. Say,

> One way parents can help their kids when they are out of control is through de-escalation to bring down the overall intensity of the child. To de-escalate a situation, the parent becomes calmer, quieter, and less reactive as the child's intensity/reactivity increases. As the child increases in intensity (e.g., screaming, stomping, etc.), the parent works to decrease their own intensity to help the child regulate their strong emotions.

Ask parents if they remember a situation where they used de-escalation or if they can point to situations with the child where de-escalation was needed. Point out that generally, de-escalation means that parents lower their voice as the child's voice rises, the parent walks away or goes to another room as the child gets more out of control, and the parent's words are few and said very calmly. Although this may seem counterintuitive, talk about people's natural instinct to get more aroused and upset when loved ones get more intense and shrill. De-escalation is a way to counter this destructive and upward spiral of intensity.

POSITIVE DISCIPLINE STRATEGIES

To have positive discipline, you want to help each parent develop clear and consistent limits with clearly stated and applied consequences, being mindful of adoption-related issues that must be taken into account. Help the parent to recognize that discipline is not about revenge or winning; it's about teaching appropriate behavior and discouraging problem behavior.

Go over the following basics with the parent:

1. Anticipate potential problems.
2. Whenever possible, give the child a choice between options that are acceptable to you.
3. Be contingent, using preteaching.
4. Be consistent and follow through every time with the consequences you set.
5. Use de-escalation—become calmer and quieter when your child's intensity rises.
6. When it's over, let it go and move on.

Tell the parent that "everyday" kids mind about 70% to 80% of the time and often take 10 to 15 seconds to respond to a parental request to help the parent not set the bar for the child's obedience impossibly high.

Discuss Handout 19: Positive Discipline Strategies, emphasizing that it is best to use the least restrictive strategy whenever possible. Note that these are to be used when wanting to decrease a behavior; when wanting to increase a behavior, refer back to Positive Parenting Strategies (Handout 13) from Session 3. These discipline strategies are for purposes of behavior change, not as punishment. As you discuss the strategies discussed next, ask parents for an example of what behaviors their child exhibits that might be appropriate for each category of strategy.

DEVELOPING A STRATEGY FOR DIFFICULT CHILD BEHAVIOR

Using information from the PPR (Handout 4) and the Adoption-Specific Behavior Record (Handout 8) that the parents have been working on, ask parents to identify an important child behavior that is a still a problem for the family. Help the family develop a clear behavioral plan that is consistent with the child's adoption history for this behavior, including both rewards and consequences. This may relate to the same behavior they identified earlier and have been working on, in which case you will want to spend considerable time going over the behavior records in detail and discussing with the parents to have a very detailed plan going forward. If that problem has resolved, ask parents to pick another behavior of concern and develop a detailed plan with a preteaching plan, consequences, and rewards. Reemphasize the importance of verbal praise and encouragement for the child, as well as of reflecting the child's feelings. In parallel, be lavish in your praise and encouragement of the parent for developing the program and later carrying it out.

Some of the most common behavioral difficulties of children with traumatic and neglectful histories include lying, stealing, hoarding food, and running away. These behaviors have a different meaning in traumatized children with multiple placements or institutionalization than they do in children without these adverse histories and, therefore, require different approaches. In fact, standard strategies for dealing with these problems are frequently ineffective in children with difficult histories. It is really important to understand what the behavior may represent for a traumatized child so specialized strategies can be used for handling these behaviors in the context of the child's adoption history. It is also important to understand what meaning the behavior has for the adoptive parent. Next, we outline some adoption-specific strategies for these behaviors that take into account the child's past history. Give parents a copy of Handout 20: Behavioral Strategies for Common Difficult Child Behaviors Using Adoption-Specific Lens, that summarizes the following issues.

Stealing

Stealing in children with difficult histories usually relates to early deprivation. The child may have had to steal to survive or to have something to trade with others to get their needs met when, for example, homeless or living in a neglectful, drug-involved environment or an orphanage. Stealing also helps a child who has not had needs met by caregivers feel self-reliant and can create predictability in an uncertain environment. Therefore, it was probably adaptive in a former context.

To handle stealing behavior, encourage parents to do the following:

1. *Acknowledge stealing behavior in the context of the child's life story.* For example, say something like "I know that you had to steal things when you lived on the street so you could eat, and you knew you could depend on yourself [Or I know you had no toys of your own to play with in the orphanage and the older kids would take anything you had from you]. So it's totally understandable that you would feel you need to steal things. But now we can talk about what you need, and we can find a way for you to get it without having to take it."
2. *Provide an outlet for the need to steal that is acceptable to you.* For example, parents might put a basket of things the child tends to steal, adjusted for the particular child (e.g., soaps or lotions, little toys), in a closet and let the child know if they feel like stealing something, it is OK to take something from the basket.
3. *If the child steals from others outside of home, note that you understand why they would feel the need to steal, given this was how they got their needs.* Have the child return

the stolen item(s) to the other person or to the store and apologize to the relevant people, either verbally or in writing. Be calm and matter-of-fact, and do not shame the child.

Eventually as the child feels more secure in the home and develops a solid history of having needs consistently met, the stealing behaviors will decrease.

Hoarding

Note that although the following examples relate to hoarding food, the same principles apply to other types of hoarding as well. Hoarding in children with difficult histories also often reflects deprivation and unpredictability. If a child is in a neglectful environment where the basic needs of life such as food are not guaranteed, it would be adaptive to hoard things and especially food to make sure you had some at times when none was provided. It may also represent an attempt to bring order to the chaos that surrounds the child and increases the child's sense of control. Additionally, for some children who have not had much emotional nurturance, food may have served as an alternative way of soothing themselves.

To handle hoarding behavior, encourage parents to do the following:

1. *Acknowledge hoarding behavior in the context of the child's life story.* For example, the parent could say something like, "When you and your sister didn't have enough to eat, it was useful to gather and hold onto any food you could find since I know there wasn't enough to go around [OR I know you didn't get enough to eat in the orphanage and you are still afraid of being hungry]. Now we have plenty of food, and you can always get some, so there's no need to keep candy and fruit and string cheese under your bed."
2. *Keep some food the child likes or tends to hoard available and accessible at all times.* This might involve leaving a bowl of fruit on the kitchen table or having a special snack drawer with items the child likes, such as peanut butter crackers, chips, fruit roll-ups, and boxed juices, that can be accessed freely when the child feels the need to have food or keep it in their room or backpack. A parent can say something like, "It may take a while for you to trust that you will have food to eat in our home when you need it. Until then, maybe we can get some packaged snacks that you can get at any time and keep them in a drawer in the kitchen. If you feel like you need to keep some with you, you can put some extra in your room or your backpack as long as they are sealed and won't attract ants." If it is a fairly recent adoptive placement, allow the types of snacks the child is used to as well as potentially healthier alternatives. Changing the child's diet all at once makes the transition adjustment harder.
3. *Do not lock up food or restrict hours for eating.* If children feel the need to hoard food and are denied access, it will increase their sense of deprivation, and they will feel very stressed and deprived in the first months or year after placement. Their eating will almost certainly self-regulate over time as they realize they are now in a safe, secure, and plentiful environment.

4. *Make gradual changes to the child's diet over a period of time in a way that does not lead to a sense of restriction.* Slowly add more of what you would like the child to eat and then decrease the frequency of unhealthy foods the child may love. There is no need to completely ban your child's favorite foods, but such foods may eventually be mostly for special occasions. Sometimes it may be hard not to personalize the child's food preferences, for example, "He knows how much I hate him to have sugary sodas—he's doing this to spite me," or "I worked so hard on this great three-course meal and all she wants is chicken nuggets from McDonald's." Think about what the child has been accustomed to. It is really hard to get used to new tastes and foods, and this often has nothing to do with rejecting caregivers or their efforts. It is important to reflect on what the psychological meaning of familiar foods may be. Acknowledge this to the child, perhaps saying something like, "I bet you love to have Cheetos because you and your mom used to have them every day after school, and it reminds you of her," or "I know you never got to have soda pop in the orphanage and you feel deprived without it."
5. *Include the child in snack and meal planning, shopping, and preparation.* If the child is part of choosing what is available to eat and helping to cook it, this will increase their sense of control and investment in the meals and also help them feel effective and good about themselves.

Lying

Lying among children with difficult histories generally relates to protection and survival in a previous dangerous and unpredictable situation. Children without a stable base of attachment do not trust in the parent's unconditional love or feel safe enough that they won't be rejected at a deep emotional level if they tell the truth. Particularly for children who were verbally and physically abused, lying may have helped them avoid punishment or trauma. If children have been moved or lost caregivers unpredictably, they may feel that lying will prevent these caregivers from feeling that they are bad and rejecting them, causing further loss. Lying may also represent fantasy wish fulfillment; for example, the child may wish that their father was flying combat missions in a war zone, rather than languishing in prison. In all of these scenarios, lying could be seen as an adaptive response to a scary and unpredictable situation. Lying is a very difficult behavior to change, and it is important to recognize that it may take considerable time as well as effort in building trust to resolve.

To handle lying behavior, encourage parents to do the following:

1. *Acknowledge the lying behavior in the context of the child's life history.* For example, say something like "I know when you lived in the orphanage, you needed to lie in order to avoid being punished," or "I know when you lived with momma and Harvey, you needed to lie to avoid getting beaten by Harvey, so it makes sense that you would lie now when you are worried you will get in trouble. But I will never beat or hit you, no matter what you have done. And I know you are also worried that somehow we will send you away if

you have any problems like your foster mother did. But we are your forever family and whatever you do, we will want you and keep you in our family. So it isn't dangerous to tell the truth here."

2. *Avoid labeling behaviors as lying when it serves another purpose.* For example, children may say they'll do their homework or take out the trash, and when you check, they have not done it, this is not lying. Use the label "lying" only for deliberate misleading and use the label very sparingly.
3. *Do not corner child in a lie or try to catch them in a lie.* For example, if you saw the child take a sibling's possession, do not ask, "Did you take Jake's LEGOs?" Children with difficult histories may have an almost automatic adaptation to lie for protection and will lie when emotionally aroused. Simply ask the child to give the LEGOs back to Jake, and if necessary, institute a contingency if the child does not comply. Trying to catch the child lying turns the situation into an adversarial confrontation when this is not helpful and can be avoided.
4. *Do not ask children why they lied.* Especially for traumatized children, lying can be an almost automatic impulsive response, and they most often do not know why they lied. If cornered about why they lied, their anxiety will be raised, they may not understand why they did so, and therefore they will confabulate a response under pressure—a further lie. Even when faced directly with evidence that they lied, children with these difficult histories often are unable to back down. Acknowledge that the child lied but do not try to force the child to admit it.
5. *Give lots of praise when children are honest and forthcoming.* Especially when acknowledging something they were not supposed to do, be effusive in praise, and say something like, "High five! I'm so glad you told me the truth when you could have lied. I hope you will learn that it is safe to be honest with me." It is very easy to only notice negative behavior, but it is extremely important to acknowledge and highlight positive behaviors and to give lots of praise and encouragement.
6. *Reflect confabulation as a wish and do not label it a lie.* For example, if the child says their birth mom took them to Disneyland for their birthday last year and you know their mom was in jail at that time, say something like, "You wish your mom had taken you to Disneyland. That would have been a very special day."

Eventually as the attachment becomes secure and children feel safe and comfortable in a home they perceive as permanent, they will feel more comfortable telling the truth.

Running Away

Running away among children with difficult histories usually relates to a survival or exit strategy that was adaptive in the past. For some children, it may have been necessary to avoid abuse. For others who have had multiple placements, it may feel safer to be the one who leaves rather than risk being rejected and forced to leave again. It also may be a coping strategy to take off and avoid a situation when feeling overwhelmed or emotionally dysregulated. And sometimes children may run away to test whether the parent cares enough and they are worthwhile enough for the parents to try to find them and bring them back.

To handle running away behavior, encourage parents to do the following:

1. *Acknowledge the running away behavior in the context of the child's life story.* Say something like, "I know when you have big feelings, you feel like you need to run away to get some space. And if you run away from us, you're leaving us before we can leave you like those other families did. But we love you and want you to always be part of our family, so we won't just let you go. We want you with us and we are not going to leave you."
2. *Help the child develop and use other ways of dealing with strong feelings.* Possibilities are labeling feelings and using words to communicate need; having a time-out word or space to go to for calming down; relaxation techniques such as deep breathing, muscle relaxation, and calming image; cognitive coping; and problem solving.
3. *Recognize triggers for running away and help the child recognize them. Predict that the child might want to run away in certain situations, and make plans in advance with the child to use coping strategies or distraction, etc.* For example, you might say, "Last time you weren't allowed to sleep over at your birth brother's house, you ran away. I'm concerned that the situation now is kind of like that, and you may feel the need to run away. Let's figure out what we can do to help you feel safe enough to stay."
4. *Remind the child of their worth, of how special they are to you, and how sad you would be if they were not with you.*

Note that if there are still many concerning behaviors on the PPR, this session may need to be extended to two to four sessions to help the parent with behavioral control in an atmosphere of love, praise, and encouragement.

HOMEWORK: TRYING A BEHAVIORAL PLAN

Ask parents to try out the behavioral plan discussed in detail in this session and to keep notes on the Adoption-Specific Behavior Record (Handout 8 in Parent Session 2) about the occurrence, parameters, and outcome of the work on the behavior of concern.

CASE EXAMPLE: THE SPRINGFIELDS

The therapist asked the parents how the reward plan they had developed for Maria's aggression to Carlos had gone last week. Rachel had presented the plan to Maria, and at first she was suspicious that the parents would not actually give her money to buy clothes. However, Maria said she would try it, noting that she'd love to have these awesome sandals she saw at the mall. Rachel started to make a chart, and Maria belittled her poor drawing skills. Rachel then said, "Well then, why don't you make the chart since you're so artistic?" Maria made a lovely chart, which parents had brought to session.

The chart showed that Maria had been nonaggressive to Carlos on 6 of 7 days, and the therapist asked how the parents felt it was going. Lewis said that they were trying to give Carlos a lot of attention after dinner to lessen his need to go into Maria's room and that he was pretty pleased with how it was going. Rachel noted that the one night she didn't earn her dollar was pretty rough. Maria had a paper due the next day in a class in which she wasn't doing well, and when Carlos came in and wanted to show her his LEGO creation, she yelled at him to get out and shoved him out of her room. Carlos began crying, and Lewis yelled to Maria, "Now see what you've done!" Maria then slammed the door. Maria was happy about earning $6 toward the sandals but bemoaned that it would take a long time to earn them (they cost $37). The therapist praised the parents for instituting the reward system and noted that often a plan may need a bit of revision. The parents decided to add in a bonus of $5 per week if Maria was nonaggressive to Carlos after dinner each night of the week. The therapist checked to make sure that they were putting a $ sign on the chart before bed for each day Maria earned it and were accompanying this with verbal praise for keeping her hands and feet to herself.

The therapist and parents then reviewed the Positive Discipline Strategies (Handout 19). Rachel felt they were not doing a good job of ignoring Carlos's whining when he didn't get his way or when he was anxious about separation, and they wanted to work on a plan to help him be less whiny and clingy. In discussing this, Rachel said this happens in many different situations and she wasn't sure where to start. The therapist noted that it's best to work on a behavior that happens very frequently in one situation first and then generalize it to other situations. The therapist said the behavior should be something easily observable by others and should occur at least three times per week so there would be instances in which to try out the plan. Rachel said that almost every day when she takes Carlos to school, he whines that he doesn't want to go, that he wants to stay with her, that he's scared, etc. Several days a week, he ends up crying in the car, and it is very hard for Rachel to get him to go into his classroom. When the therapist asked why they thought Carlos was acting this way, Lewis remembered back to the first ADAPT session and said he was pretty sure it was because Carlos had had so many placement changes and was worried that he might have to leave their family too. Maybe he was afraid that Rachel would not come back to pick him up after school.

The therapist praised his insight, and asked how they might help Carlos feel safer and more secure about this. Rachel thought it might help to remind Carlos in the morning that she would see him after school was over, to tell him she loved him and that they would always be together, and to note concretely what they would be doing after school (e.g., "then we'll go to the park with the big swings," "then we'll stop and pick up chicken for dinner"). Lewis thought that was a good idea. They decided to make a reward chart for Carlos for going to school as a brave boy (no fussing, whining, or crying) but weren't sure what he would like to work toward. They decided he could earn a "brave point" every day and that they would put a superhero sticker on his reward chart each day he was successful. Further, they worked out that if he got brave points on 4 out of 5 days, he would earn a reward. The parents decided to work out the reward in collaboration with Carlos.

Child Session 4: Problem-Solving Strategies

In this session, we continue work with the child on building coping strategies in preparation for the remainder of the ADAPT curriculum. The previous session focused on coping strategies to calm oneself; this session focuses on development of problem-solving strategies. The goal is to develop a repertoire of coping skills to apply when faced with a variety of problems, but mainly interpersonal issues. The last coping skill, using a calming image, will be presented when the family meets together in the next session.

Materials for this session include

- feelings cards/poster/thermometer (see Child Session 2);
- poster board, markers, etc.;
- Handout 21: Kids' Coping Solutions; and
- Handout 22: Coping With My Problem.

REVIEW HOMEWORK TO PRACTICE COPING STRATEGIES

Review Homework from Child Session 3 about using the coping strategies discussed previously. Ask the child how it went using deep breathing and muscle relaxation to calm down when upset. Praise the child enthusiastically for using the strategies and encourage the child to continue doing so. If the child used the strategies inappropriately (i.e., in the wrong situation, or wrong strategy for the situation), ask the child about how the strategy worked and brainstorm other ways to use that strategy or other strategies in that situation if the child did not feel it was helpful. If the child has not used the strategies at all, practice deep breathing and muscle relaxation briefly at the beginning of this session and also ask again when each of the strategies might be useful.

IDENTIFYING A PROBLEM AREA WITH THE CHILD

Note that the child has learned coping strategies to deal with strong feelings already, and let the child know you are going to work on learning other ways to solve problems today. Ask the child to identify an area they are concerned about. This area may or may not overlap with parent's concern (e.g., fear, anxiety around something specific, anger outbursts, interpersonal conflicts, etc.). We want to work with something that is an issue from the child's perspective. If the child cannot identify an area of concern after thorough discussion with you, ask the child what their mom or dad would say if they were asked about what they wish the child would work on. Explore whether this issue is something the child would like to work on. The issue need not be major; mostly, we want to work with something of concern from the child's point of view. Discuss and elaborate the child's feelings about the issue, using feelings cards/thermometer, etc., and review the coping strategies already learned to see which would be helpful.

TEACHING OF PROBLEM-SOLVING STRATEGIES

Note that the coping strategies (deep breathing and muscle relaxation) are very helpful in dealing with a person's own strong feelings, but that they may not solve the problem. Ask the child for other ideas about how to solve the problem, and shape the child's answers to meet the following three problem-solving constructs. If the child cannot come up with ideas (more common with the younger children), then bring up the following ideas:

1. Talk it out. Bring up the issue with the other person involved and try to give a little, take a little (e.g., negotiate).
2. Look at options. Generate various options and then look at the consequence of each of the options.
3. Seek out help. Talk to a friend (most common for older children) or ask a trusted parent, teacher, or other adult to get involved (most common for younger children).

Go over Handout 21: Kids' Coping Solutions, noting that children can do things themselves to cope with their feelings and also do things to work on the problem with other people. Discuss what solutions might work for the child's problem, and look at the consequences of the various solutions and what alternative solutions might look like. Write down all possible solutions on poster board or paper. After the child chooses one of the solutions, role play it with the child and revise as needed, role playing the other possible solutions the child thinks might be helpful. Give the handout to the child to take home.

HOMEWORK: COPING WITH MY PROBLEM

Confirm with the child what problem they plan to work on this week and what strategies they think might be helpful. Ask the child to keep a record of how things went with using strategies discussed for the problem behavior. Look at Handout 22: Coping With My Problem, discuss it with the child, and remind the child to bring back their problem-solving sheet next week. Note that the child can try out another strategy if the first one is not working.

CASE EXAMPLE: THE SPRINGFIELDS

Carlos reported that he liked muscle relaxation best, that he had used it before sleep and also once when Maria was mad at him. He used deep breathing when he was sad about going to school and leaving his mom. Maria continued to find deep breathing helpful when her parents were bugging her.

Carlos had difficulty coming up with a problem to work on, but finally settled on not wanting to go to school and crying in the morning. He felt like he could learn more by staying home with mom. In going over the Kids' Coping Solutions handout, the therapist asked what problems there would be with staying home with mom. Carlos thought and then said that he would miss playing with his friends and also couldn't go on field trips. The therapist praised him for his answers and then asked how staying home with mom would work with her job. He paused and then said, "Oh yeah, she goes to work after she drops me off, so she couldn't stay home with me." As noted previously, he said he could use deep breathing when he is sad and also thought he could seek help from his mom. He thought it would help if she told him on the car ride to school exactly what time she would pick him up. The therapist and Carlos role played asking his mom to do this. The therapist also wondered whether taking one of his stuffed animals in the car with him to hold might help, and Carlos thought it might help to bring his stuffed lion to help him be brave.

Maria easily came up with two problems areas—her annoyance at Rachel's nagging and conflict with a friend at school who she felt was avoiding her. Although the therapist would have preferred the issue with Rachel, Maria decided to work on the conflict with her friend. She was very responsive to the problem-solving solutions and decided she would talk with her friend and share her feelings using "I" statements, that she would walk away when she felt angry at the other girl, and that she would use deep breathing to deal with her feelings.

Joint Session: Sharing Positives and Coping Strategies

The purpose of joint sessions, which occur at the end of most modules, is to consolidate the material from individual parent and child sessions, promote sharing among family members, and facilitate positive interactions and family closeness. In the joint session for Module 1, there are two goals. First, families participate in an activity to increase positivity among family members (What I Like About You). Second, families develop a shared set of coping strategies that are appropriate for children and parents alike (deep breathing, muscle relaxation, calming image) and that will be helpful in dealing with emotionally powerful content in the following modules.

Materials for this session include

- Handout 23: What I Like About You (one copy for each family member);
- scripts for deep breathing and muscle relaxation (in text from Child Session 3);
- small stuffed animals for demonstrating tummy breathing for young children;
- Handout 18: Muscle Relaxation Pictures (from Child Session 3);
- a script for guided imagery (in text);
- paper, markers, etc., for the calming image activity; and
- Handout 24: Coping Strategies Log (copies for child and each parent).

WHAT I LIKE ABOUT YOU ACTIVITY

For the What I Like About You activity, ask each family member to share what they find wonderful and special about each other. You will write these down, using Handout 23, What I Like About You, with a separate sheet for each family member.

Especially for younger children, you might copy the What I Like About You sheets onto different colors of paper and ask the child to choose a color. Say,

> We are going to do an activity called What I Like About You. Each person will say two things they really like about each other family member. I will write them down on these sheets and then each person can take home their sheet so they can remember all the positive things said about them. Say only positive things, no "buts" or anything negative. The person who is hearing what others like about them can only say, "Thank you." Who would like to start?

Ask each family member to share two things that they find wonderful and special or really like about each other family member. Write down the answers on each person's sheet. If there is more than one child in the family participating in ADAPT, make sure that each child also says two things they like about each other child as well as about the parents. Accept and write down *any* positive statement, even if quite limited (e.g., she is good at brushing my hair, I like her corndogs). However, if the statement is not completely positive, ask the person to say something they really like and is positive about that person. Only positive statements should be written on each person's sheet.

If someone says they cannot think of anything positive to say (most likely with teens), express incredulity and ask the person to think of anything positive, even if it's very small. If the person still refuses to give something positive, ask other family members what they think that person could find positive about the family member being discussed. When all the sheets have been filled out, ask how it felt to say positive things to the family members and what it felt like to hear the positive statements about themselves. Then give the What I Like About You sheets to the appropriate family members to take home. If the family has great difficulty expressing positives, you might want to make copies for yourself before handing the sheets out to the family members or make notes immediately after the session about what positives were given for later use.

DEEP BREATHING AND MUSCLE RELAXATION

In the second activity, emotion regulation coping strategies are taught to parents to give family members skills to deal with the difficult and painful feelings that will inevitably arise as they later talk about adoption issues that may have previously been dealt with by avoidance. This also lets parents know what coping strategies the child is learning so they can encourage the child to use them at home and school.

Both to help the child have a sense of control and to reinforce the coping skills of deep breathing and muscle relaxation, enlist the child's help in teaching the strategies to the parents. Say,

> (child's name), you learned some ways to be calm and relax—deep breathing and muscle relaxation. Let's teach them to your parents to help them calm down when they are upset or angry and their emotional temperature is rising. Can you start by telling them about deep breathing (tummy breathing)?

If the child used the stuffed animal to practice deep breathing previously (to watch stomach raise and lower the stuffed animal), ask the child if they'd like to use the stuffed animal in teaching the parents. Have the deep breathing script from Child Session 3 available to help fill in gaps in the child's explanation. The most important part is that the breathing be *deep* (tummy rising) and *slow* (breathe in on count of four, out on count of four). If the child does not want to teach the parent, then proceed to use the deep breathing script in its entirety.

Next, ask the child (or a different child if there is more than one child in the family) to teach muscle relaxation to the parents. Remind them that they can start with squeezing a lemon, and have the Muscle Relaxation Pictures (Handout 18) available to help the child remember the different metaphors used. If the child does not want to do the teaching, or does not remember, then read the script for muscle relaxation from Child Session 3. Because it is really important to get to the final activity, do not spend too much time on these coping strategies, which should be a review for the child.

GUIDED IMAGERY

Tell the family,

> Another way to calm down when you are upset or angry is to use a calming image. First, I'm going to guide you in experiencing a calming image, and then I'm going to ask each of you to think of your own calming image and to draw it with the paper and markers.

Lead the following guided imagery exercise or you may substitute another you like better. Say,

> I know you are relaxed from the muscle relaxation we just did. Close your eyes if you are comfortable with that. Scan your body for any tension. If you find tension, release it. Let it go and relax. Experience a peaceful, pleasant, and comfortable feeling of being relaxed as you prepare to take an imaginary trip to a beautiful place. Take a deep breath, and breathe out slowly and easily. Take a second deep breath, and slowly breathe out.
>
> Picture yourself on a a beautiful white, sandy beach. As you look out, you see crystal clear, brilliant blue water ahead of you and hear the waves lapping at the shore. When you look up, you see a fluffy white cloud drifting in the gentle breeze.
>
> Watching the cloud brings a feeling of peace, of deep relaxation. You feel no cares or concerns in the world but are focused completely on the relaxed feeling you experience. You can hear sea gulls, the sound of the gentle breeze through the trees, and the roar of the waves. As you take a deep breath, you enjoy the smell of the salty ocean air.
>
> You see yourself walking slowly on the beach and lying down, and enjoying the warmth and softness of the sand. As you listen to the waves and the sea gulls and feel the warmth of the sun and the sand through the cool breeze, you realize that you are calm, relaxed, and at peace.
>
> You are aware that you can return to this special place any time you want to. Feeling very relaxed, you come slowly back to this room, knowing that you

> will bring these peaceful and relaxed feelings with you. Your body and mind are relaxed and refreshed, so now slowly open your eyes.

Ask family members how they felt about the activity and process any feelings that family members bring up.

DEVELOPING OWN CALMING IMAGE

In this activity, the parents and child each develop a calming image of their own. Say,

> Now you each have a chance to develop your own special calming image that you can use when you are upset or sad or angry and your temperature is getting very high. It should be a place where you feel safe and secure, calm and peaceful. For many people, this image is somewhere in nature. Like in the example we just heard, try to notice all your senses in your calming image. What do you see? Hear? Smell? Feel?

Give each family member paper and markers and/or crayons with which to draw their calming image. If a family member objects to drawing the image, suggest describing the image in writing, although because it's a visual image, a drawing may give more information. If family members decide to write about their image, again remind them to use all their senses and note what is seen, heard, smelled, and felt. Sometimes children want to draw exciting rather than calming images, such as a roller coaster or exciting videogame; ask them if this is a place where they would feel calm and relaxed. If they say "no," then ask them to draw a calm, peaceful place and brainstorm possible ideas. Accept whatever they give as long as they endorse that it is calm and peaceful—some previous drawings have been of the child's bed, swimming underwater, in a tree house, watching TV.

Allow up to 10 minutes for drawing or writing. After they are finished, invite family members to share their image with other family members. Ask about senses the person does not mention and that are relevant to the image, for example, "What do you hear in your image? What smells do you notice?"

Ask all family members when they think it would be helpful to use their calming image, as well as when deep breathing and/or muscle relaxation might be helpful.

HOMEWORK: USING THE CALMING IMAGE

Ask parents and children to use their calming image one or two times in the next week. Give each family member Handout 24: Coping Strategies Log, on which to record their experiences using the three emotion regulation strategies discussed in the session.

CASE EXAMPLE: THE SPRINGFIELDS

During the What I Like About You activity, both parents easily came up with two things they each liked about Carlos and struggled a bit with things for Maria.

However, Rachel pretty quickly noted that Maria had wonderful fashion sense and was a good friend to her friends, and Lewis said that she was a fabulous artist and that underneath all the animosity, she really loved her brother. The therapist noted that the second thing was not all positive and asked Lewis to either restate what he was saying in a totally positive way or find something else. He then said that Maria was very sensitive to the pain of others and tried to make them feel better. The therapist praised his efforts. Carlos had no trouble coming up with positives for both parents and his sister, though some of his were quite concrete but developmentally appropriate (e.g., he liked his mother's pancakes and that his dad played soccer with him). Maria paused quite a bit before answering but then gave positive comments about each parent. However, she said she could think of nothing positive about Carlos. The therapist jokingly said, "There must be something, even very small, that you like about him!" Carlos looked like he might cry at this point, and Maria finally said that he was good at learning his letters and had nice eyes.

During the coping strategies portion, Carlos was eager to teach his parents muscle relaxation and did so with much animation as he went through squeezing lemons and being a lazy cat and a turtle. Maria rolled her eyes during this but was ignored by everyone. She reluctantly explained how to do deep breathing, giving a very clear explanation and practice, which the therapist enthusiastically praised.

The family members seemed to enjoy the guided imagery (though Carlos was quite wiggly), as well as drawing their calming image. Rachel drew a beach scene with waves, soft sand, and warm sun. Lewis drew a rushing stream in the forest with lots of fish jumping out of it, noting that he finds fishing very relaxing. Maria, who is very artistic, drew a beautiful picture of magnolia trees and a multitude of different types of flowers with birds flying around. When she described her image, she said that this was a place on the edge of the town where she lived with her birth mother. She used to leave the house and go there when her mother had arguments with her boyfriend. Carlos drew the backyard of the Springfield's house with a soccer ball and a basketball. He said it was cool and windy out there, and it helped him feel calm to kick the soccer ball.

4 Module 2
Developmental Understanding of Adoption Experience

The parent component of Module 2 includes four overall goals. First, it aims to assess where the parent(s) are in their comfort with, awareness of, and understanding of the adoption experience for themselves and for their child. Second, it provides the opportunity for the parents to tell or cocreate the child's adoption story. This module also helps the parents develop comfort with and skill in talking with their child about difficult information in their past at a developmentally appropriate level. Finally, it will assist the parents in processing feelings about their child's birth parents and in understanding their child's feelings of divided loyalties, as well as enable the opportunity for the child and parents to communicate about such feelings.

The child component of Module 2 includes three overall goals. The first goal is to ascertain children's comfort with and awareness of how and why they came to be placed for adoption and to clarify information about their adoption story. The second is to facilitate children's ability to tell their story at an appropriate developmental level, to understand the meaning of adoption, to ask questions they may still have about their adoption story, and to validate adoption as a valued form of family. Finally, the child sessions aim to help children share their feelings about birth parents with their adoptive

http://dx.doi.org/10.1037/0000096-005
Adoption-Specific Therapy: A Guide to Helping Adopted Children and Their Families Thrive, by J. Waterman, A. K. Langley, J. Miranda, and D. B. Riley

parents and to have the opportunity to process and normalize potential feelings of divided loyalties.

Module 2 consists of three separate parent and child sessions and one joint session for the sharing of the separately created narratives and discussion around the child's unanswered questions.

Parent Session 1: Parental Path to Adoption

The goals of the first parent session in Module 2 are to check in about progress toward the goals identified at the beginning of treatment, which is done at the beginning of each new module; to explore in depth the parents' path to adoption; to discuss books about adoption appropriate for the developmental level of the child; and to prepare parents to write their version of the child's adoption story.

Materials for this session include

- Path to Adoption Questions (section in text),
- Handout 25: Suggested Adoption Books by Age Group, and
- Handout 26: Child's Adoption Story.

REVIEW PROBLEM AREAS AND PROGRESS (DONE AT THE BEGINNING OF EACH MODULE)

Check in with parents to assess the progress the family is making on the problem areas that were noted at the beginning of treatment. It can be helpful to have a graphic representation of their ratings of these problem areas week to week to present to the parents to serve as a springboard for discussion on how things are going and a visual representation of potential progress.

REVIEW MODULE 1 SESSION 5 HOMEWORK: TRYING A BEHAVIORAL PLAN

Spend some time reviewing the current adoption-specific behavioral plan and how the strategy has worked with the child. Revise the plan as necessary on the basis of the family's progress and needs.

REVIEW USE OF COPING STRATEGIES

Check in with the parents about situations in which they have noticed their child using the coping strategies learned in Module 1 or times when the parents have been able to cue the child to use such strategies. Also, inquire about an example of when parents have been able to use the techniques of deep breathing, muscle relaxation, and/or calming image themselves as a coping strategy.

PARENT'S PATH TO ADOPTION

Spend the remainder of the session allowing the parents to discuss their path to adoption. Encourage the parents to tell their story spontaneously in their own words. The next section, Path to Adoption Questions, will enable you to fill in any gaps in information to help the parents explore the reasons that led them to choose adoption as a way to build their family. This discussion often includes issues related to a history of infertility and possible pregnancies and miscarriages, each with its own potentially powerful emotions. It is important to provide empathic listening and reflective commenting to encourage parents as they recount their story. Use the questions below to guide discussion of issues if they do not come up spontaneously. Discuss special issues that may arise for single or same-sex parents; possible issues that may arise are listed below.

Path to Adoption Questions

1. *Why did you choose adoption as a way to build your family?* (may include discussion about infertility, possible pregnancies, and the emotional sequelae; altruistic aims; kinship issues; how long they have been trying to build a family)
2. *How did you choose the type of adoption?* (e.g., international, domestic, private, foster care)
3. *What child characteristics did you consider? Why?* (e.g., age, gender, particular characteristics they wanted or did not want such as substance exposure, mental illness in birth parent, average IQ)
4. *Do you have a personal connection to adoption? Have you had previous experience with adoption?* (e.g., being adopted or having an adopted sibling, adopting previous children, friends who were adopted or who adopted children)
5. *What has been your experience with preparing for adoption, placement of the child in your family, and pre- and postadoption support?*
6. *What was the reaction of your family and friends to your decision to adopt?*
7. *Special issues for single parents may include:*
    - development of support systems, both informal (friends and family) and formal (support groups, therapists, social workers)
    - providing input from an adult of the other gender
    - child care, after-school care, and work/home life balance concerns
    - burdens of carrying all the responsibility alone for the child
8. *Special issues for same-sex parents may include:*
    - concerns about talking to child about parents' sexuality
    - providing input from adult of other gender (particularly if parents' gender does not match child gender)
    - fears about discrimination from social services, school, peers
    - issues with family members

ADOPTION BOOKS TO READ WITH CHILDREN

Provide the parent with Handout 25: Suggested Adoption Books by Age Group which they may want to purchase and read with the child. Elicit questions that the parent may have about which books may be most appropriate, given the child's age and developmental level.

HOMEWORK: WRITING THE ADOPTION STORY; ADOPTION-SPECIFIC BEHAVIOR RECORD; PRACTICE OF PRAISE AND ENCOURAGEMENT

Ask the parents to write out a draft of the child's adoption story in a developmentally appropriate manner, either using Handout 26: Child's Adoption Story or using a computer if they prefer for ease of editing. Ask, "Do you have questions about what you think you might want to put in or leave out of your story? Is there anything you think may be challenging?" Discuss these issues and let parents know that you will be reviewing their draft story during the next session and helping them edit it before it is shared with the child so there is no pressure to get everything right in the first draft. Provide reassurance that you can help guide them in this process.

Review the adoption-specific behavioral strategy discussed at the beginning of the session and any modifications that were made to it. Finalize the plan to have the parent implement it over the next week, keeping track of progress on Handout 8: Adoption-Specific Behavior Record. If parents do not still have the Adoption-Specific Behavior Record in their folder, or if they need more copies, give them copies to take home.

In each parent session after Module 1, one of four parenting strategies discussed in Module 1 will be highlighted at the end of the session, and parents will be reminded to continue practicing it. Review the concepts of praise and encouragement and why they are important strategies for all children, and particularly for adopted children. Ask parents how they are doing with providing praise to their child at least five to eight times per day and help them problem solve things that may be getting in the way of their doing so. Emphasize "encouragement" and praising a child's efforts rather than only the end product. For example, "I can see how hard you are working on your math problems" (even if they are not all correct). If needed, role play everyday situations in which a parent could find ways to intervene with praise or encouragement to provide a model for the parents (i.e., at the dinner table, playing outside, during homework time, getting ready in the morning), and then have the parents practice as you role play as the child and note their progress even if the product is not in line with the full goal just yet. It is important for you to also model this behavior with the parents, making sure to praise and encourage them throughout the session. Remind parents of Handout 14: 101 Ways to Praise a Child from Module 1 Parent Session 3. If they have not yet put it up somewhere in their home, discuss where parents can keep it visible as a helpful tool and reminder.

CASE EXAMPLE: THE SPRINGFIELDS

The therapist checked in with Rachel and Lewis about how things were going with the children's behavior plans. They noted that Maria's behavior plan had been a bit confusing, and in talking things through with the therapist, they decided to make it more specific and easier to succeed with. Specifically, they modified it so that Maria received $1 in clothing points for each school day that she got a positive report (participating, no stealing) and another $1 each afternoon/evening that she interacted with Carlos without aggressive behavior, and they decided to provide a reinforcer at the end of each day when she earned both points (watch a 30-minute TV show or stay up 30 minutes later). Carlos's plan to earn "brave points" was going well as they were having him practice age-appropriate independence skills (getting the mail by himself, following all the steps in the shower alone) and social activities (playing with peers in a separate area from mom at the park or someone's home), as well as continuing to earn brave points for going to school without whining or a fuss.

In discussing the use of coping strategies, Rachel described noticing that Maria had come to her with some ideas of how to problem solve a peer issue that was bothering her that week, which she praised her for, and when the parents were feeling stressed out by a traffic jam, that Carlos had reminded them all to use the "calming images" they had come up with in the first joint session. Rachel said that she also had used the muscle relaxation script with the children when they had a hard time falling asleep. The therapist provided a great deal of praise and encouragement for these efforts and outcomes, which was repeated at the end of the session and was a nice segue into a review of praise and encouragement for the children.

Rachel and Lewis jointly described their path to adopting Maria and Carlos. They talked about their struggles to conceive a child biologically and their sense of frustration when fertility treatments were not successful. They both found the experiences very painful and described the toll it took on their relationship. Rachel expressed feeling guilty and angry at herself at times for not having tried to have children when they were younger. Because their financial situation did not allow them to proceed with in vitro fertilization or to afford international or domestic private adoption, they attended a foster/adoption orientation with their neighbors who had grown children and were interested in potentially fostering/adopting another child.

During their preadoption training in their county, they decided that they were open to a child of any age beyond infancy and any gender. Given that they are in an interracial marriage and live in a multiethnic community, they were also open to a child of any ethnicity as they felt they were savvy to issues of building a multiracial family and would be committed to helping a child from any background maintain connections to their cultural identity. Whereas Lewis was more emphatic about wanting to eventually adopt a second child, Rachel didn't have strong feelings one way or the other about having one or two children. Because of their own histories of loss related to infertility and their desire to be parents, they emphasized to their social worker that they were only interested in having children placed with them who needed an adoptive placement and did not have current visits with their birth family.

Rachel had a close friend in high school who was adopted, and Lewis had an "uncle" who he had found out as an adult was actually a friend of his father who was "taken in" by his grandmother as a teenager and remained part of the family. Lewis stated that his family for the most part has been very accepting of the children from the outset, making well-intentioned jokes about how the kids looked like they could be their biological kids as their skin color was about halfway between Rachel and Lewis's. Rachel's family had been less accepting when they first presented the idea of adoption to them, but after the children came into their home, her parents had quickly become attached to their new grandchildren. Although Rachel had never had a great relationship with her sister, her nieces and nephew seemed to embrace their new cousins, and having parenting in common with her sister now has led to an easing in their own relationship. They noted that being parents has reconnected them with some of their old friends who have children of similar ages and also helped them establish new relationships with families in their neighborhood and school, including a Latino family from the same country the children's birth mother was originally from, about which they felt very positive.

Near the close of the session, Lewis and Rachel made a plan to work together to type up an initial draft of their developmentally appropriate adoption story after the kids had gone to bed one night this week and to make revisions back and forth during their lunch breaks at work. Lewis said he would then e-mail it to the therapist prior to the next session.

When reminded about practicing giving praise and encouragement, both parents noted that given their hectic after school and evening schedules, they had slacked off on their focus on providing praise to the children for what they were doing well. The therapist led parents in a role play of homework time and modeled how praise and encouragement could be easily integrated even when the children were just doing small things well. For example, as the parents role played being the children, the therapist noted, "I like the way you are sitting still and focusing on your work," and "I am proud of you for sticking with that problem." When they switched roles to practice a family car ride, Rachel and Lewis were able to come up with several ways to praise the children even if everything wasn't going according to plan. They provided praise and encouragement in that situation by stating, "I like how you are both staying on your own sides of the car," "thank you for answering your sister so nicely," "I know it's a long drive and I appreciate you telling me about it without shouting or whining." The therapist encouraged the parents to come up with a signal to remind one another to provide praise and encouragement in every possible setting with the children that week and to praise each other for following through on these efforts. They decided to place the 101 Ways to Praise a Child (Handout 14) on their refrigerator to remind them during mealtimes and homework, which was often completed in the kitchen.

Child Session 1: Normalizing and Understanding Adoption

The goals of the first child session in Module 2 are: (a) to normalize adoption as a valued family form, (b) to assist children in becoming comfortable discussing their past history and feelings about adoption, and (c) to help children develop a greater understanding of their own adoption story. Materials for this session include an age-appropriate book on adoption (see Handout 25: Suggested Adoption Books by Age Group from Parent Session 1).

REVIEW MODULE 1 SESSION 5 HOMEWORK: COPING WITH MY PROBLEM

Spend some time reviewing the child's recordings of how things went when the child used the problem-solving strategies discussed in the last session, using Handout 22: Coping With My Problem and Handout 24: Coping Strategies Log. Assist the child in talking through what they tried and how they think things went. If the strategy they used was not successful and the problem is ongoing, help them make a revised plan to try additional strategies that may be more appropriate or helpful to the situation.

READING AN AGE-APPROPRIATE BOOK ON ADOPTION AND DEVELOPING A GREATER UNDERSTANDING OF THE CHILD'S OWN ADOPTION STORY

The therapist must obtain affirmation that the parent has told the child or the child knows that they are adopted. Do not engage in this module unless child has been told. It is equally important to have some level of understanding from the parent as to what the child has been told about their story before you proceed. Also proceed cautiously in this module if it is not clear that the adoption will be finalized.

Engage the child in an exploratory process to gain a greater understanding of the child's ideas about why they were placed for adoption. Be prepared to offer suggestions if the child needs help getting started. Sometimes it can be helpful to begin the discussion by saying something like, "This is a place where kids can talk about adoption and what it is like to be adopted."

Before the age of 7, most adopted children, while enjoying the "story" of how they joined their families, have little cognitive understanding of the complexities as to why they are not with their birth families. About age 7, children begin to realize that to be in the family they are with, someone had given birth to them but could not or chose not to parent them. It is important to emphasize to all children that they were not responsible for the decisions surrounding their placement and that adoption occurs because of adult decisions.

Read a book about adoption aloud with the child, noting the child's nonverbal and verbal reactions, and discuss what you have just read. A list of appropriate books is provided in Handout 25: Suggested Adoption Books by Age Group. One favorite of children of all ages is *Murphy's Three Homes: A Story for Children in Foster Care* (Gilman, 2009). Ask the child to tell you what they think *adoption* means: how adoption occurs, the professionals involved (i.e., social workers, judges, attorneys, therapists), and the legal underpinnings of adoption (if the child is old enough to understand). This includes their understanding of the permanence of adoption (forever family, same rights and responsibilities as a biological parent) and their thoughts about why they are not with their birth family, former foster families (if applicable), or other relatives. Your increased understanding of what the child already knows and doesn't know and how they perceive adoption will guide the remainder of this module.

NORMALIZATION OF ADOPTION

Within your discussion, offer some of the following information to the child to help normalize and destigmatize the experience of adoption.
What is adoption?

- Adoption is a way of providing a new forever family when your birth family could not take care of you.
- Adoption is a legal process.
- Each adoptive family is unique and has many different people who love them. Children are adopted in many ways. Explain the different ways that adoption can occur, individualized for the child's own story.

Adoption is common.

- More than 127,000 kids are adopted in the United States each year.
- There are over 1.5 million adopted children in the United States—that is over 2% of all the children living in America.
- Close to 10,000 children are adopted each year from foster care.
- About 5,000 children are adopted from other countries each year.
- Children can join their families at birth or even as teenagers. Before being adopted, they may have lived with their birth families, other adults chosen by their birth parents to raise them temporarily, foster families, or in orphanages.
- Kids can be adopted by a relative, foster family, or a new family, which may be a couple, a family who has other children by birth and/or adoption, or a single parent.
- Over 58% of people know someone who has been adopted or has an adopted child.
- Did you know that families are formed in many ways? Adoption is just one of many ways to be in a family. Can you tell me other kinds of families?
- Children are adopted for many different reasons and everyone's story is different too.
- Did you know that Steve Jobs, founder of Apple Computers that makes iPhones and iPads, was adopted, as well as Simone Biles from the U.S. Olympic Gymnastics team, Miss USA, some of Angelina Jolie and Brad Pitt's children, the founder of Wendy's, Superman, Spiderman, etc.
- Add in other adoptees or adopted parents that might be of special interest to the particular child.

HOMEWORK: BRING AN ADOPTION-RELATED OBJECT AND PRACTICE DEEP BREATHING

Ask the child to bring something to the next session that has something to do with their adoption story. It could be a video (e.g., of their birth or their adoption day in court, or their orphanage), pictures (e.g., of birth family, foster family, or orphanage staff or the first day they spent time with their adoptive family), their Lifebook (or other memory book or scrapbook), stuffed animals (e.g., something they brought with them from their previous family or that was given to them by the judge on adoption day), clothing (e.g., that they brought with them from a previous placement or that their birth or foster parent gifted to them or they wore in the orphanage where they first met their parents), etc. In each child session after Module 1, one of four coping and problem-solving strategies discussed in Module 1 will be highlighted at the end of the session, and children will be reminded to continue practicing it. Also ask the child to practice their deep breathing at least two times during the week and to record this on Handout 24: Coping Strategies Log.

CASE EXAMPLE: THE SPRINGFIELDS

First, the therapist checked in with Maria about how things were going with the problem she planned to use for her Coping With My Problem (Handout 22). Maria said that her friend rolled her eyes at her and she immediately felt angry, but instead of pushing her friend or saying something mean, she took a deep breath and said, "What did I do?" and she felt like it worked well because her friend stopped rolling her eyes and said she hadn't meant to and they went on talking. The therapist gave Maria a lot of praise for trying this out and for sharing it in the session.

The therapist engaged Carlos in a discussion about adoption, beginning with, "Let's talk for a few minutes about adoption. What does 'adoption' mean to you?" Carlos hesitated and then said that adoption means that you move to a new family. The therapist gently queried further, and Carlos shared that he felt afraid of adoption because it means he might move. The therapist asked Carlos if it would be OK with him if the therapist read Carlos a book about adoption and showed him the book *Murphy's Three Homes: A Story for Children in Foster Care* (Gilman, 2009). Carlos agreed and was really engaged in the book; at the end of the story he asked if he could read it again, so the therapist sat with him and they read it through again. This spurred a discussion around the difference between foster care and adoption, and the therapist addressed some of Carlos's confusion by clarifying that adoption meant that he would *not* be moving to a different family and that Rachel and Lewis will be his forever family. Carlos said that everyone talked about adoption with him but he was never quite sure what that meant exactly. Referring to the feelings chart, Carlos pointed to "calm" and said that it made him feel more calm to know he wasn't going to be moving, and he also pointed to "sad" because he said he realized he could not go back to living with his foster family. The therapist acknowledged Carlos's mixed feelings and shared that many other kids who are adopted like him feel the same way. The therapist reiterated to Carlos that "this is a place where kids can talk about adoption and what it is like to be adopted so you can talk with me at any time about all of these different thoughts and feelings," and Carlos responded with a quiet smile.

The therapist engaged Maria in a discussion about adoption by starting with some of their previous conversations around the topic in Module 1. Maria responded right away with great affect, shouting: "I told you—adoption is my nightmare. It means I can hardly remember what my birth mom looks like." The therapist remained calm and empathic (instead of responding to Maria's loud voice and negative tone), acknowledging both the strong feelings Maria had about adoption and Maria's statement about missing her mom and feeling like her memory of her was fading. The therapist's calm reaction seemed to keep Maria engaged and unashamed of her strong outburst. The therapist normalized Maria's feelings, stating that many children who have been adopted have mixed-up feelings about adoption, some of which can be confusing or seem to conflict with one another.

By referring to the feelings chart used in Module 1, the therapist and Maria were able to identify different feelings that Maria has about adoption and why. For example, she shared that she feels sad when she thinks about her birth mom because she doesn't really understand why they can't be with her and because she worries about her mom and wants to know she is OK. She feels confused because she likes Rachel and Lewis and how they take care of her and Carlos, but she feels like if she lets them love her, then she is betraying her birth mom, whom she still loves and misses very much. She feels worried about settling into their home and getting too "used to them" because this is about the time that she usually gets moved to a new home. She still misses her last foster family and her foster brother, and she doesn't want to get those feelings again if Rachel or Lewis get mad at her. The therapist praised Maria for talking so openly about this and reflected how difficult it must be for her to carry around all of these feelings and worries.

The therapist reminded Maria that she had mentioned earlier that she wasn't sure why she didn't live with her birth mom and gently queried about what Maria's understanding of these events were. Maria said she knew that her mom used drugs and alcohol because she used to see it but she didn't know there was anything wrong with it. She remembered that they used to have to move from one hotel room to another and that some of the grown-ups that came around scared her and made her feel nervous. She recalled that she and Carlos used to be hungry and not have food to eat, and her aunt told her that was because her mom used their money to buy drugs. When she and Carlos were removed from their mom and placed with their aunt, their aunt told Maria that they couldn't be with their mom because she loved drugs more than them. Maria always thought if she could see her mom again she would find a way to be better so that her mom could love her more than drugs. The therapist praised Maria for all the things she remembered and shared, and normalized that a lot of kids whose parents use drugs and alcohol feel like it is somehow their fault. The therapist then spent some time reinforcing the idea that there was nothing Maria ever did to make her mom use drugs and that there is nothing that Maria could have done or do now to make her mom stop using drugs. The therapist and Maria started a list of questions that she has about her adoption story including details about why she was removed from her mother's care and why she had to leave her aunt's house and then the two foster homes.

The therapist guided a discussion with both Maria and Carlos about people they might know or know of who are adopted, presenting the facts around the prevalence of adoption. The therapist wondered out loud with them about the different feelings that Spiderman's and Madonna's children may also have about being adopted. Might they have had feelings similar to Maria's and Carlos's? How might they have handled them?

At the close of the session with each child, the therapist again provided praise for their work in the session and let them know that the next week they would be able to create a book of their life story, including all of their families. The therapist asked them each to bring something into the next session that has something to do with their adoption story. Maria said she had a couple of things in mind. The therapist asked if it would be OK to let Rachel know about this so she could help remind the kids to bring it for the next meeting, and they agreed. The therapist also asked each of them to practice deep breathing at least two times during the week and reviewed how to record this on the Coping Strategies Log (Handout 24).

Parent Session 2: Understanding the Child's Path to Adoption

The purpose of this session is to hear about the parents' understanding of their child's journey to adoption. It is helpful for parents to reflect on the mixed feelings inherent in being adopted. Sometimes parents only consider the joyous occasion that finalizing an adoption was for them without also being aware of the tremendous losses that occur from the perspective of the child for adoption to take place. These may include losing birth family and/or foster families or previous caregivers, as well as biological or foster siblings and extended family, schools, teachers, friends, culture/country, religious practice, language, pets, teammates, etc. Parents who understand the complexity of the mixed feelings that can coexist for children—happiness at being adopted and sadness at losing loved ones—are better able to empathize with the child and not take these feelings as personal rejection. Similarly, in creating a timeline of the child's experience, parents often expand their understanding of and empathy for their child and all they have been through as a context for who they are today—their reactions, behaviors, and resilience. Finally, this session aims to equip parents with developmentally appropriate language to use to answer difficult questions their children have about their history and reasons for not being with their birth parents.

Materials for this session include

- Handout 27: Child's Placement History Timeline,
- Handout 28: Sample Scripts for Discussing Difficult History With Children, and
- Handout 29: Children's Questions About Adoption at Different Developmental Stages.

REVIEW MODULE 2 SESSION 1 HOMEWORK: WRITING THE ADOPTION STORY; ADOPTION-SPECIFIC BEHAVIOR RECORD; PRACTICE OF PRAISE AND ENCOURAGEMENT

Spend some time reviewing the homework from the previous session. Check in with the parents as to their progress on the draft of the adoption narrative they are creating to eventually share with their child and let them know you will be working on this further in today's session. Review any modifications that were discussed last week for the adoption-specific strategy on the Adoption-Specific Behavior Record (Handout 8) to ascertain how the new plan is working and to troubleshoot any areas of concern. Finally, discuss the family's progress in incorporating praise and encouragement into their daily parenting skills and help them identify ways of making this practice sustainable for their family.

DISCUSSION OF CHILD'S PAST HISTORY AND THE ADOPTION STORY

Ask the parents to share their child's "adoption story" in an open-ended fashion. As they are telling the story, take note of what parts of the child's history or the adoption story may not be included, what parts bring smiles or particular emotions to the parents, or anything else notable. Once the story has been shared, if it has not already been volunteered, be sure to inquire in detail about the circumstances of their meeting the child, the child's past history, including losses and possible abuse/ neglect or other trauma, medical history, etc. Point out that although the adoption is often a joyous time for the adoptive parents, there may be mixed feelings for the child. For example, children may have intense feelings of sadness and loss about losing their birth family and/or foster families/previous caregivers, as well as biological or foster siblings and extended family, schools, teachers, friends, pets, teammates, culture/country/ religion, etc., along with excitement/anxiety about their new family and forever home.

COMPLETE CHILD'S PLACEMENT HISTORY TIMELINE

Assist the parents in using Handout 27: Child's Placement History Timeline, to plot a detailed placement history for their child, including possible gaps in knowledge of where the child was at any given time. Inquire about what the child already knows about their history and at what age the child learned of certain facts, events, losses, etc. Encourage expression of feelings about notable aspects of the timeline—for example, the child had 13 previous placements or there is a gap of 2 years during which no one knows where the child was—and provide empathy and compassion for parental feelings about these difficult past events.

UNDERSTANDING THE CHILD'S CONNECTIONS TO BIRTH PARENTS

Open up a discussion about the parent's feelings about the child's birth parents, acknowledging that there are often a lot of feelings present and all of them are acceptable. Make an effort to reinterpret any negative attributes that the parents bring up to develop empathy for the birth parent, and help parents to be able to share positive aspects of birth family history that they have or could obtain. For example, you may help the family frame substance abuse as a chronic disease and addiction rather than a moral failing.

Discuss the deep connection that the child has to their birth family, with the goal that the adoptive parents can allow and honor the special place in their child's life of the birth family, without diminishing the importance of the attachment of the child to the adoptive family. Spend time clarifying for the parents what "divided loyalties" means and explore the complexity of this for children who are adopted and especially for those who spent time with their birth parents. Assist the parents in understanding that although it can feel like the child's care for the birth parents and care for the adoptive parents are opposing, it is possible for the child and the family to hold both beliefs at the same time. That is, children can love and feel a deep connection to their birth family at the same time that they also love and feel a deep connection to their adoptive family.

Emphasize that just because the child may not be talking to their parents about the birth parents, it does not mean that they are not thinking about them. In fact, most children think very intently about their birth parents but often are afraid to talk about them in fear of hurting their adoptive parents. Thus, urge the parents to take the lead in starting conversations about the birth parents to give permission for the child to talk about them and to have positive feelings about the birth parents in front of their adoptive family.

ROLE PLAY SHARING DIFFICULT INFORMATION WITH THE CHILD

Assess the parents' comfort with discussing difficult issues in the child's history (e.g., birth parent's drug use, criminal history, abuse/neglect, mental illness, issues with foster parents/previous caregivers, poverty). Inquire about what questions the child has already asked about their history and/or why they are not with their birth parents. Help the parents role play how they may share difficult information with the child in a manner that is appropriate to the child's developmental level. It is important to convey to the parents that all children deserve to know the truth of their own story. The goal of this process is to help the parents feel comfortable in understanding that their child should be provided with all information about their life history and knowing how to do so in a developmentally appropriate manner.

It can be particularly difficult for parents to contemplate discussing birth family histories of criminality, substance abuse, mental illness, abuse/neglect, and domestic violence with their child. Refer to Handout 28: Sample Scripts for Discussing Difficult History With Children. Make sure to have a copy for the parents to take home, as this handout can be valuable later on at different developmental stages.

Reassure parents that it is OK if they do not know the answer to a question that may be asked by the child. If that is the case, encourage them to say something like, "That's a really good question. I don't know the answer, which must be frustrating for you. Let me see if I can look into that for you and find the answer." Likewise, even if a parent knows part of an answer but doesn't feel prepared for the best way to respond or the question comes up in a setting that may not be appropriate for discussing these personal issues, encourage them to say something like "That's a really good question. I'm so glad you asked me. Let's make some time to talk about that later (after the party, soccer game, when we are back at home together, etc.)."

Explore parental concerns about talking with their child about their birth parents' substance abuse. Help the parents to view addiction as an illness rather than a moral failing, noting that it is very difficult to stop using, rather than a simple choice to stop. The goal is to help the adoptive parents develop empathy for factors that may have led to the birth parents' addiction problems; examples are mental illness, depression and sadness, their own traumatic history or abuse, neglect or experiencing domestic violence, and possibly inadequate parenting they experienced.

One common concern is that if the child knows about the birth parent's substance use, they will be more likely to use and abuse drugs or alcohol. Note that predisposition is not predetermination, and encourage parents to discuss with the child that the fact that their birth parent used drugs does not mean that they themselves will become addicted. Parents can point out the resources and options that their children have that their birth parents may not have had and reassure the child that they have the family support necessary to avoid substance use and get appropriate help with any issues that arise.

Discuss with the parents whether it is appropriate to disclose birth parent substance exposure and especially prenatal exposure at the child's current development level. Children under about 8 years of age are generally satisfied with the explanation that they could not remain with their birth parents because they were not able to take care of them. However, after about 8 years of age or so, children begin to wonder why their birth parents couldn't take care of them (even if they do not tell their adoptive parents about their questions). Whether the child is ready to hear this information depends on age and level of maturity. If after discussion, it appears the child is too young to understand and process information about birth parent substance use at the current time, help the parents decide on a more appropriate time, noting signals their child may send that are indicators of their developmental readiness. Given many parents' reluctance to deal with this sensitive topic, share your opinion about the child's developmental readiness. As a general rule, we consider the majority of children 10 and up old enough to consider their parent's addiction.

Discuss the child's developmental and emotional status to help determine what information the child may be ready to deal with. Have the parents role play sharing a difficult piece of the child's history that the child does not know about their past in a developmentally appropriate manner. Explore their feelings about both the difficult information and the process of sharing it with the child. Emphasize the importance of giving physical affection as well as positive acceptance while sharing difficult information with their child. When children feel heard and supported, and they are told the truth with empathy for the birth parents and themselves, they are more likely to approach their parent with questions again in the future. This can reinforce the child–parent bond and trust, even though the information shared is difficult.

Provide the parents with Handout 29: Children's Questions About Adoption at Different Developmental Stages and ask if they have particular questions about what might be appropriate to disclose currently.

HOMEWORK: REFLECTION ON A DIFFICULT PAST

Ask the parents to reflect on the difficult parts of the child's story and history and what they may feel comfortable sharing, if appropriate, in the joint session. Let them know that their child may be identifying questions about birth family or history that you will share with them and help them prepare answers in case they come up in the joint session.

Ask the parents to continue with Praise and Encouragement Records (Handout 16) and Adoption-Specific Behavior Records (Handout 8), troubleshooting and modifying as needed.

CASE EXAMPLE: THE SPRINGFIELDS

The therapist asked Rachel and Lewis how their progress on the draft of the adoption narrative for the children was going. They replied that they had spent some time working on the narratives but had some questions about the best way of sharing some of the details of their story in the separate narratives for the two children. The therapist said they would be discussing this during the session.

In reviewing how things were going with the adoption-specific behavioral plan to address Maria's aggression toward her brother, the family revealed with some surprise that Maria seemed very receptive to their verbalizing ideas about how her behavior may be related to feelings she has about no longer being Carlos's primary caretaker and also being at an age at which she wants to have her privacy and time away from her little brother. Although she was at first dismissive when Rachel or Lewis noted these things, now she seems to calm down quickly when they approach it with understanding in this way instead of just complaining about the behavior or responding with a lost privilege or other punishment. This week, in fact, Maria was close to earning enough points to buy the new pair of sandals she had been working toward. Lewis said he was actually surprised to realize that there had been very little aggression in the last couple of days. Rachel reflected that this has helped her understand Maria's behavior in a different way and because of that she feels less angry in those moments and more able to stay calm and de-escalate the situation, which helps Maria also become calmer.

In discussing the family's progress with incorporating praise and encouragement into their daily parenting skills, Rachel and Lewis both laughed a bit as they shared that they kept a tally sheet one Saturday to see if they could actually provide the eight praises for every criticism or negative statement. Although they couldn't quite reach that ratio, Lewis talked about how just being aware of it helped them to provide far more praise and encouragement than they had been doing. Lewis tended to prefer nonverbal social praise and had gotten very comfortable giving the kids a thumbs up or a high five in different settings, and the children both seemed to like it, although sometimes Maria would roll her eyes (as she smiled). Rachel agreed that the kids no longer looked at them strangely when they provided praise and positive reinforcement, so Rachel figured that they must be becoming more natural at it. The therapist provided a lot of praise and encouragement to Rachel and Lewis for their efforts in this regard and explored the impact this has had on the general atmosphere at home, which Rachel readily stated had become more positive and less serious.

As Lewis and Rachel were sharing Maria and Carlos's adoption stories, the therapist noted that both parents became tearful when talking about the neglect that both children had suffered and about the circumstances of the day they were detained when Carlos was found on the streets alone and Maria was looking for him frantically. When the therapist probed, Rachel said that it was painful for her to think about Carlos as a 3-year-old being on the streets defenseless and frightening to think about what could have happened to "her boy." Lewis added that it struck him just how much responsibility Maria had on her shoulders at a very young age and how frightened and guilty she must have felt that day. He also reflected that it makes sense that Maria would be aggressive at times as she was in the position of having to defend herself and her brother from people and dangers that they may never even know about. In contrast, when Lewis was talking about the first time they met the children, both parents smiled widely as they recalled how nervous they had been and how they had barely slept the previous night. The therapist assisted Rachel and Lewis in plotting the information that they had for each child on separate timelines. They agreed that Carlos may not have much memory about his early years and initial placements, and it may be important to go through it all with him so he has a cohesive story about where he has been since birth. Rachel also noted that Maria was with her mother for many more years and feels a more powerful sense of loss of her mother than Carlos. Both parents wondered aloud if Maria knew about all the reasons for changes in placements or not. They realized that they did not have many details about the children's first foster home.

The therapist helped Rachel and Lewis explore what adoption has meant to them and all of the things it might mean to Maria and Carlos, pointing out that although the adoption is often a joyous time for the adoptive parents, there may be mixed feelings for the child. Lewis acknowledged that they sometimes forget that adoption also comes with loss of the birth family and for his children also their former foster parents and foster siblings. Rachel again became tearful when she and Lewis thought through all of the people and things that Carlos and Maria had been separated from over the course of their lives. Rachel realized that she could relate to these feelings in a small way as she recalled sitting in the rear of the courtroom during the termination of parental rights hearing and that she felt elated that this meant they would be moving forward with the adoption, but she also found herself crying as she realized what a devastating day this was for the birth mother and also for Maria and Carlos—having lost a connection with their mother.

The therapist helped Lewis and Rachel process some of their own mixed feelings about the children's birth mother. They each expressed empathy for the birth mother from what they knew of her struggles with addiction and her own likely history of trauma and abuse and the loss of her children. Lewis said, "At the same time I am angry at her for putting the kids through this, for the pain they suffered and maybe still do. It wasn't fair to them. They were just babies and they had no say in it." The therapist validated that they can feel both empathy and understanding for the birth mom at the very same time that they are angry at her for what the children have been through and that all of these feelings are acceptable and can coexist. The therapist went on to draw a similarity between these seemingly incompatible feelings and those of the children's feelings of divided loyalties or coexisting connections with both birth family and adoptive family. Lewis said that he could understand how deep the connection is to a parent even if the parent has not treated the child well, as he found himself seeking a relationship with his own father even though he had not always treated Lewis's mother well and had basically abandoned the family for some period of time. The therapist emphasized that allowing space for the child to honor the birth family can be easier said than done, but that it can be helpful to recognize that allowing this does not diminish the importance of the child's connection with the adoptive family. Children truly can love both families, and being connected to one does not take any love away from the other. Because especially Maria may have similar fears—that she cannot have love and a deep connection for birth and adoptive families at the same time—the therapist urged Rachel and Lewis to take the lead in starting conversations about the birth family and the most recent foster family so that the children feel like there is an open line of communication on this topic and that Rachel and Lewis are comfortable with them talking about their birth and foster families and interested in knowing their thoughts and feelings.

The therapist reviewed the scripts for discussing difficult information, and Rachel and Lewis role played answering questions in developmentally appropriate ways with each of the children. They decided to talk with Carlos about his mother's substance use and not being able to properly take care of the children. They decided that because Maria had further questions, they would practice answering questions about abuse/neglect, domestic violence, and not knowing who her father is in case she brought it up in session and/or to be prepared for future inquiries. The therapist guided them through this practice.

Child Sessions 2 and 3: Child's Adoption Story and Unanswered Questions

The overall goal of Module 2 Sessions 2 and 3 is to allow the child to create an adoption narrative via the creation of a Lifebook. The Lifebook provides a way for the child to integrate a cohesive story of their life and who has cared for them, including biological parents, foster families, other relatives, or orphanage caregivers, and their adoptive family. The process of creating the Lifebook enables the child to reflect on questions that they have about their life story thus far, any missing information they wish to understand better, as well as the opportunity to draw and/or write about their memories or understanding of themselves and their various caregivers and families over time. This cohesive narrative is critical for the child's understanding of who they are and where they come from. If the child already has a Lifebook, ask the child to bring it in so that the therapist can review it with the child and see if there may be anything that the child would like to add or learn more about, such as missing information.

Materials for these sessions include

- child's adoption object (pictures, etc., that the child brings to session),
- Handout 30: My Adoption Story: A Lifebook (for children ages 10 and under),
- markers and crayons,
- art supplies for collage project for children over 10 years (construction paper, glue, glitter, magazines, etc.), and
- Handout 31: Questions for My Parents.

REVIEW SESSION 1 CHILD HOMEWORK: BRING AN ADOPTION-RELATED OBJECT AND PRACTICE DEEP BREATHING

Take a few minutes to review the content of last session, including what adoption is and some famous adoptees, and discuss the fact that all children have a story about when they were born and how they joined their families, letting the child know that today the focus will be on the child's story.

Ask children to share about the item or items they brought in that are connected to their adoption story as a way to initiate this discussion. Inquire about the meaning of the object to the child and their understanding of where it came from. Also ask about where this "special item" is kept in the house. Often, special pictures of the birth family or birth records or a special outfit or toy that the child brought when joining the family are put in a safe deposit box or hidden away. It can be helpful to explore with children the possibility of integrating the item into their everyday life and whether they may like to see it more often—for example, to keep the stuffed animal in their bedroom or to have one of the pictures framed and placed in their bedroom or living room. This sends the message that all of these things are part of their story and of who they are in a way that is integrated into their identity and not split into separate life pieces. This sense of a cohesive narrative is critical as children develop an integrated story of their life. (Note: if the child wants photographs to be kept out, parents are encouraged to display copies and keep the originals or have an electronic record of the pictures made for safekeeping.)

TELLING OF THE CHILD'S ADOPTION STORY: A LIFEBOOK

Begin by explaining that their "adoption story" is about how they came to join their forever family. Use age-appropriate language to inquire about different aspects of the child's story. Include questions such as the following:

- How old were you when you were adopted?
- If children were placed at an older age, ask whom did you live with/where did you live before being placed with your adoptive family; who was in that family

or those families; who took care of you; what were the names of foster parents, birth or foster siblings, other relatives, orphanage staff, and others you may have been close to?

- What do you remember about the day you met your forever family (or if they were very young at placement, what have people told you about that day)?
- Why were you adopted? (This question should help to assess children's understanding as to why they are not with their birth family and the depth of the information shared by the adoptive parents.)

Collect unanswered questions children may have. Suggest that they can ask their parents about these questions during the family session in a couple of weeks. Common questions are the following:

- Why was I given or taken away?
- Why was I adopted?
- Was there something wrong with me?
- Who are my birthparents?
- What do they look like? Do I look like them?
- Do I have any brothers or sisters? Where are they?
- Why couldn't they keep me? Why did they hurt me?

Many children who are adopted may have to deal with difficult information about the birth family and/or the circumstances of their detainment from their birth family or their adoption, and they also may have to face the harsh realities that information may not be available and/or it is not attainable because of legal barriers. This is particularly problematic for children adopted internationally from orphanages where there may be no information at all about their origins. Therefore, it is important to let the child know that it may be that they cannot get answers to all their questions and empathize with how difficult this may be.

Although there is no set time for telling the story, each child's temperament and emotional and intellectual maturity will influence the readiness for processing. This is often a gradual process, with more information or more detail being shared as is developmentally appropriate. It is essential and best practice for children to grow up from the time of placement knowing they are adopted, even if they are too young to really understand the concept for some time. Even during infancy or toddlerhood, parents can mention adoption so it is always in the child's vocabulary; examples might be "When we adopted you, we lived in our other house," "Today is your adoption day and we'll celebrate it every year." Although no two adoption experiences are the same, most children do move through a clearly defined developmental staging of their adoption experience and often hold similar feelings and thoughts about adoption and what it means to them. Acknowledge these similarities and provide a forum for sharing to help normalize the experience.

The younger children (ages 5–10) complete the My Adoption Story: A Lifebook (Handout 30). This booklet contains pages on the adoptive (forever) family, the foster family(ies), the orphanage (if applicable), and the birth family. If you are working with mature 9- and 10-year-olds, they can do the older children's activity described next instead if they wish. Start the Lifebook by first bringing out the pages for the adoptive family to have the child work through, using the questions previously discussed regarding their knowledge and understanding of how they joined the adoptive family. Once this section is completed, next work with the child to fill in the foster family(ies) section if placed from foster care or the orphanage section if applicable. Finally, assist the child in working through the pages related to their birth family. Be sure to process all feelings that arise with the child. Obviously, working through these Lifebook pages may take several sessions and may arouse strong affect in the child. It is very important to process the child's feelings along the way and recognize that some children may need to do just a few pages at a time, then take a break to play a game or use play material before returning to work on the Lifebook.

For older children (ages 11–14), you may assist them in creating a collage that reflects their story. Be sure to have plenty of art materials, scissors, and glue or tape as well as many magazines of different types from which the child can cut out pages or pictures. Alternatively, the child may choose to write out their story and add images.

If children have an already completed Lifebook, they may bring it to the session and review it with the therapist to express their story. If appropriate, the child may add some of the pages from the current Lifebook into a previously completed Lifebook if it adds important information.

PROCESSING FEELINGS ABOUT BIRTH PARENTS

Thoughts about birth parents and birth family members can cause the child to feel disloyal to their adoptive family, and conversely, love for one's adoptive parents can cause the child to feel disloyal to birth parents. These divided loyalties may cause a great deal of conflict for children who are adopted, and it is essential that therapists understand the delicate balance between children's love for their adoptive family and their often intense preoccupation with thoughts about their birth families. Children who did spend time living with their birth parents have very strong emotional ties that cannot be severed and should not be forgotten.

When working on the Lifebook or during the collage activity, include discussion with children about how often they think about the birth family, what are they thinking and when, as well as fantasies of where their birth families might currently be and what they imagine about them. Later placed children will have vivid memories of their birth families and may still request and desire connections. It is important to ascertain whether the child has an open adoption and if the child actually has visits with the birth family, and take this into account when discussing feelings about the birth family. If the child has contact with the birth family, issues of divided loyalties may be stronger and need to be discussed in greater detail.

Assess the child's comfort with discussing their adoption story and the feelings associated with the story with the adoptive parents, and then ascertain what information may be missing that the child wishes to know and is developmentally appropriate to obtain. Help the child with feeling identification throughout the story according to skills learned in Module 1.

LISTING CHILD'S UNANSWERED QUESTIONS

Assist the child in developing a list of questions they have about the adoption story on Handout 31: Questions for My Parents to be asked with parents in the next session. Provide the parents with a copy of the list of unanswered questions in preparation for the upcoming joint session. Hold a discussion with the parents to see what information they have that they have not yet shared, and encourage parents to contact the placement agency or extended birth family if they are comfortable to obtain more information if available in response to the child's queries.

HOMEWORK: REVIEW AND PRACTICE OF MUSCLE RELAXATION

Ask the child to practice muscle relaxation at least two times during the week and to record this on their Coping Strategies Log (Handout 24). Reinforce the homework assignment with the parents so that they can support the child's muscle relaxation practice at home or even practice as a family.

CASE EXAMPLE: THE SPRINGFIELDS

Carlos was eager to share the teddy bear that he got on his adoption day in court. The bear seemed to have taken on new meaning now that Carlos understood that adoption means he doesn't have to move again and that Rachel and Lewis are his forever family. Carlos said that he recently started putting the teddy bear on his bed and sleeping with him at night.

Maria shared a picture of herself and her birth mother in front of someone's house. She said she didn't remember where it was but that it was one of the only pictures she has of her mom. She also brought a picture of her blowing out candles at her last birthday party with Rachel, Lewis, Carlos, and some friends and neighbors behind her. She said it was her first birthday party and it meant a lot to her, and she remembered thinking to herself, "maybe things will be different here." Maria said she would like to frame both pictures and have them in her room so she can look at them and have both memories.

Both children worked on their adoption stories during Sessions 2 and 3. Carlos started his Lifebook with his adoptive family and drew pictures of what he remembered about first meeting them, what they like to do together, extended family who have become part of his life, etc. He also had a fair amount to add about his most recent foster family but little information to offer about his early life in the care of his mother, aunt, or first foster placement. His list of questions included: Why was I taken away? Why did I live with so many different people? Why did this happen to us and not other kids?

Maria chose to create a poster collage with drawings and images from magazines and asked the therapist to write in some words to describe some of the images. She said she wanted to order it to "start at the beginning." She was able to come up with several memories of her birth mother, some positive and some that she realized were negative (involving her mom's substance use and neglect), and she added drawings and magazine images reflecting food, feelings, and places she associated with that time in her life. She wrote the word *tranquilita* as she remembered that her mother used to repeat this word in a soothing voice to help Maria feel calm and get to sleep when she was very young and crying. She also shared some memories about Carlos's father and other boyfriends of her mother's but she was not sure who her birth father was or if he might be one of those men she had memories about. She added question marks and words like *curious, confused,* and *nervous* to these images. She also spent some time talking about bad feelings regarding the first foster care placement. She recalled that she and Carlos were fed different food and sat at a different table than the rest of the family and that they were not included in outings with the family but stayed behind with a neighbor who was boring and not very nice to them. She drew an image of them at a small table looking small and sad. She created images reflecting a sense of sadness, rejection, and isolation.

Maria had a lot of memories about her recent foster family and was able to generate information about her adoptive family and write in memories of their first meeting and images of things they like to do together. Her questions remained about reasons for all of her changes in placement, if anyone knew the whereabouts of her birth mom, and if she would ever see her again. She also wondered if she would ever know who her birth father is. Maria and the therapist reflected on how many different types of images and feelings are included in Maria's story and how the question marks make it hard for her to feel like she can put it all together. She said that she couldn't remember a time when she has really felt *tranquilita* and she didn't think she ever would. The therapist acknowledged the burden it has been for Maria to carry around so many different pieces and questions that do not feel connected or resolved.

Maria wasn't sure how comfortable she would feel in talking about all the elements of her poster with her adoptive parents in the upcoming joint session, but she agreed to start with talking about one thing from each placement in her life and to ask the therapist to help her explain certain things if she felt she couldn't. Maria agreed to have the therapist share her list of questions with her adoptive parents. She mentioned that Rachel had told her earlier in the week that they really want to know about Maria's thoughts and feelings about her birth mom and foster family, and that she was OK with Maria talking about this and that they would try to help her find answers to any questions that she had if they could. Maria was surprised by this and did not respond at the time. She wanted to see what they said during the joint session before she decided exactly what questions she would bring up in the session herself.

The therapist spent a fair amount of time with Maria during these sessions normalizing her sense of conflict around divided loyalties, affirming her strong emotional ties to her birth mother and her need to know if her birth mother is OK and where she is. The therapist helped Maria try to understand that she can hold deep connections and feelings with both her birth and adoptive families as well as feelings for her foster family and that having multiple connections does not diminish or cancel out the connections with the others.

Parent Session 3: Parental Fears About Birth Parent Contact

The goal of this session is to assist the parents in processing their feelings about their child's birth parents and about their child's connections to birth family members. This session allows parents to understand their child's feelings of divided loyalties, reiterating the important concept that children are able to love and feel connected to their adoptive family at the same time that they love and feel connected to their birth family. Parents need to have a grasp of this to help reassure their children that loving one family does not diminish their love for the other and that these two sets of feelings can coexist simultaneously. At the same time, parents are given the opportunity to discuss their own feelings and concerns and to have the therapist recognize that this process is not always comfortable and easy and, in fact, is more complex than families may have anticipated when they started the process of adoption. In addition, this session aims to equip the parents with an understanding of the importance of, and a concrete plan for, finding ways in which they can let their child know that the lines of communication are open about discussing birth parents and how they can provide opportunities for their child to communicate about such feelings with them. This type of open communication about birth families can actually enhance a child's sense of trust and connection with adoptive families who are willing to share this with their child.

There are no materials for this session.

REVIEW HOMEWORK FROM PARENT SESSION 2: REFLECTION ON A DIFFICULT PAST

Ask the parents to reflect on the difficult parts of their child's history and what they feel comfortable sharing if appropriate in the following week's joint session. Emphasize the importance of the information being delivered in a manner that is developmentally appropriate for the child, and role play this practice to increase parental comfort in talking about the information that is to be shared.

Check in on the family's progress with Praise and Encouragement Records (Handout 16) and the Adoption-Specific Behavior Records (Handout 8), and make modifications as needed.

PARENTAL FEELINGS ABOUT BIRTH PARENTS

Help the parents explore their concerns about their child's birth parents. Questions you may want to ask include the following:

- Does the child or adoptive family have contact with any birth family members?
- Do they have safety concerns due to previous lifestyle issues of birth parents?
- Do they know how to contact the birth parents if desired or necessary?
- Are there birth siblings, does the child know about them, and where are they?

If there is no current contact with the birth family, discuss parental thoughts and feelings about possible future contacts. Validate all feelings that they may have about the reconnection with the birth family, fears of the child wanting to live with birth parents, any potential safety concerns related to contact with the birth parents, etc. If there is ongoing contact with birth family members, including siblings, explore the parameters of the contact and parental feelings about it. Encourage parents to be open to the possibilities of contact within limits of safety and what is developmentally appropriate. Denying children who wish contact to have any connection, even if just sending pictures at holidays or meeting on a birthday, makes them feel unheard and decreases trust. Discuss the impact of divided loyalties on their sense of family and security with the child.

CHILD'S CURRENT AND FUTURE REQUESTS FOR BIRTH PARENT VISITS

Ask the parents about what thoughts they have about the child potentially wishing to search for and/or reconnect with their birth parents or other birth family members. Provide psychoeducation about various methods of handling the child's possible future requests for birth parent contact, taking into account the child's age and developmental stage. Often parents may interpret the child's wish to visit with birth parents as a rejection of them or their parenting, which may not be true. This is a sensitive area for adoptive parents, and it is important to explore the parents' feelings, which are often mixed.

Discuss the complexities of birth parent contact, both the benefits of maintaining connections and concerns in situations where a birth parent may be continuing to struggle with substance use and/or mental health issues. Note that when adoptive parents avoid the issue of birth family connections or give children messages that they are not open to listening to and empathizing with the children's wishes or longing for birth parent contact, trust is diminished and there will be less family closeness. In these cases, the Internet and social media become attractive vehicles for opening connections with the birth family, with or without the adoptive parents' knowledge and support. Process this information and what it might mean for their child and family. For example, children may have connected with their birth parents through finding them on Facebook, and birth parents may have also located their children through Facebook or other social networking sites. Stress with the parents that they need to talk with their children about working together if contact is desired and how they can help their child feel comfortable to share with them if they are contacted by a birth family member.

Help the parents think through a variety of issues regarding birth parent contact. Also clarify that wanting to know information about the birth family does not necessarily mean children are wanting or ready for contact at that time. If contact with birth parents is to be established or reestablished, it is recommended that the adoptive parents meet with the birth parents before involving the child to assess safety issues and clarify the adults' roles and boundaries. This can help manage the child's expectations of what the birth parent may be like. Also, contact can be made gradually and does not have to happen with an in-person meeting right away. For example, the adoptive parents and birth family could exchange e-mails, phone calls, or text messages; the child could write a letter to the birth parents; or a phone call could be arranged. Sometimes the child or birth or adoptive parent may choose not to proceed with an in-person meeting after having some contact, and other times such contact can establish a nice foundation for the in-person meeting. In international adoptions, communication via letters or Skype may be the only type of contact that is possible.

Sometimes young children may want to establish or reestablish contact with birth parents when they may not be developmentally ready. You can help parents discuss and process their own feelings about this and work out whether their reservations are based on the child's developmental lack of readiness or their own issues. Often, we suggest a time gap between first contact and a face-to-face meeting to allow parents and child to carefully consider all aspects of initiating contact. You can be helpful to the parents in sorting out these issues.

ROLE PLAY RESPONDING TO CHILD'S REQUESTS FOR BIRTH PARENT VISITS

Have the parents role play the child asking to visit or make contact with the birth parents, with the therapist taking the role of the child and the parents responding to the child's request. Encourage the parents to role play responding at the child's current age and also as if the child were 16 years old. Stress the importance of understanding and reflecting the child's feelings and setting parameters during the role play, and encourage the parents to make space to process their own feelings away from the child with their therapist or social support system.

PREPARING TO SHARE ADOPTION STORY AND UNANSWERED QUESTIONS IN JOINT SESSION

Discuss any changes parents have made to their version of the adoption story to be shared in the next session with the child. Fine-tune the story with the parents as needed. Ask the parents which of the child's unanswered questions they feel they can answer, and use the Sample Scripts for Discussing Difficult History With Children (Handout 28) from Session 2 if needed to help the parent practice their responses. Check in with the parents about their feelings about sharing the adoption story and process those feelings so that they can focus on the child and what comes up for the child during the joint session.

HOMEWORK: PRACTICE ONE-ON-ONE CHILD-LED PLAY

Check in with the parents to see how they have been able to incorporate one-on-one time while following child's lead in play. Spend a few minutes troubleshooting and refining the practice as needed. It can be helpful to engage in a short role play during which the therapist is the child to get a sense for how well the parent is able to put the child-led play skills into action and to assist in knowing what areas to help the parent refine. Always provide a lot of praise for parental efforts and what the parents are doing well.

CASE EXAMPLE: THE SPRINGFIELDS

At the outset of the session, Rachel and Lewis shared that in writing their narratives for the kids, they had really gained a lot of understanding of their children's perspectives, losses, and connections, particularly for Maria. Lewis was able to reflect on the fact that Maria was with her birth mom for 8 years, which is a majority of her life, and of course those connections and feelings cannot just disappear no matter the circumstances of their separation. Rachel shared that she told Maria during the week that she and Lewis cared about Maria's thoughts and feelings about her birth mom and about her foster family and were OK with her talking with them about that. She reported that Maria looked taken aback and didn't say much, but Rachel felt good about putting it into words and knew that Maria heard it. She realized in saying it aloud that of course she did want to know about anything important to Maria and was committed to trying to see things from Maria's perspective and not let her own feelings interfere. She and Lewis agreed that they still had some work to do on understanding the concept that their kids could love other people/sets of parents as much as they love Lewis and Rachel and that feelings for one doesn't diminish their feelings for the other. Lewis said that although he understands it intellectually, he can't help the twinge of hurt that he felt when he read Maria's question about whether she would ever know who her father is. "I'm her father," Lewis said, "so that hurt to hear. I want to be the only father, but I'm not." The therapist acknowledged this reality and how hard it can be to understand. Rachel reminded Lewis that he is the only father she will likely know and reflected that she feels similarly when Maria talks about her birth mom or acts rejecting of Rachel's "mothering." They agreed to provide each other with space to talk about this together away from the children so they could both feel heard and be reminded of their goals for open communication and bonding with their children despite the complexities of being an adoptive family that others may not understand. They were able to empathize with how Maria would also be struggling with the idea of dual love and loyalties and did some problem solving about messages of openness they could give to Maria to make the process easier as they all figured out the best way to communicate about these emotionally charged issues.

The therapist engaged Lewis and Rachel in a discussion about their own feelings toward the children's birth mom. Rachel shared that she would be more worried about the birth mom or Maria eventually reaching out to one another and her not knowing about it. She would hope that at that point, Maria would feel comfortable asking Rachel and Lewis to support her in that process, which would help them feel safer about it. Lewis said that he wants his kids to know that they were removed from their mother and from their aunt for a reason—more than one—that meant that their mother or aunt could not safely care for Maria and Carlos so it is important if they ever want to reach out to birth family that Rachel and Lewis be involved because they always want to keep them safe. The therapist validated all of their concerns and worries and praised them for their goal of keeping open communication so that they can be part of Maria's and/or Carlos's team if their journey leads them to contact their birth family at some point in time. The therapist also provided education around the wide spectrum of potential connections that children may have with their birth family, ranging from exchanging letters or phone calls once a year, to the adoptive and birth parents or other extended family talking or meeting first, to an in-person visit or visits with any given extended family member.

Lewis and Rachel agreed that at this point, the children were not asking for contact with their birth family, but Maria was questioning her mother's whereabouts more because she was worried about her and wanted to know if she was OK. They agreed that if the question came up they would let her know that they could potentially reach out to the previous foster family who had contact with one of the children's relatives at some point to see if they could find any information out about her mother's current well-being. The therapist acknowledged how much it might mean to Maria to have them help her find an answer to something so important to her, and to support her no matter what the answer is or if any information at all can be gathered.

The therapist role played with Rachel and Lewis the delivery of the adoption stories for each of the children. Rachel explained that they had gathered pictures from the children's county file and the previous foster family of each of the children at different times in their lives, and they planned to incorporate them in the joint session sharing of the narratives. Next they role played responding to the list of questions that the children had come up with, and it was clear that both parents had used the language in the helpful scripts for sharing difficult information. They agreed that before answering any questions the children asked, the parents would first respond with something like "That is a really good question" or "I am so glad you asked me that." If the children asked a question in the joint session that they were not prepared for, they agreed to say, "That is such an important question and I'm really glad you asked me that. I'm not sure of the answer right now, but I will look into it and get back to you." The therapist reinforced the supportiveness of this statement and how it maintains open communication and emphasized the importance of actually getting back to the child once information is gathered or to let them know they are still looking into it. For Maria's question about who her birth father is, there was no information in any of Maria's record to provide this. Through role play they practiced helping Maria to sit with this difficult reality and to support her in how painful it must be to not be able to know who her father was, and to let her know that she can talk about those feelings with them anytime she needs to.

Finally, the therapist checked in to see how child-led play practice was going. Lewis was happy to report that Carlos-led LEGO projects had continued, and he felt that they both looked forward to it. He also stated that he and Maria had taken a couple of walks to the convenience store and chatted along the way and that during car rides he would not turn on the radio and allowed her to guide the conversation if there was any. He even said that she had engaged him in a brief game of handball against the garage one day, and he let her take the lead on how the game went. Rachel shared that she made time for one-on-one play with Carlos after dinner before bedtime, which also kept him from bothering Maria during the evening hours when she tended to want her privacy. The coloring book activity that she and Maria had started had evolved into "girl time" a couple of times per week, during which Maria chose the activity, and it had on different occasions included coloring, drawing, painting, hair braiding, and nail polish.

Joint Session: Sharing Adoption Story and Unanswered Questions

The purpose of the Module 2 joint session is to enable the joint sharing and processing of the parents' story of the child's adoption as well as the child's Lifebook. The session allows for any remaining questions that the child has about their history to be answered or at least heard as well as providing space for the family to acknowledge any divided loyalties the child may be feeling and to open up communication within the family so that the child is given permission to share their thoughts and questions and speak about their birth family with their adoptive parents. If there is more than one adopted child in the family, we strongly recommend that each child have a separate session with the parents so that the focus can be on that child's unique adoption story.

Materials for this session include

- Handout 26: Child's Adoption Story (written by parents),
- Handout 30: My Adoption Story: A Lifebook (or collage done by child),
- Handout 31: Questions for My Parents (filled out by child), and
- art material (e.g., construction paper, markers, and crayons, glue, glitter, etc.) if child wants to add new information into their project.

REVIEW MODULE 1 SESSION 4 JOINT HOMEWORK: USING THE CALMING IMAGE

Ask the parents and child about using their calming images developed in the last joint session, when they are using them, and how it has worked. Encourage the family to continue using the calming images and discuss situations where they may find it to be useful.

SHARING THE ADOPTION STORY

Introduce the parents and child to the idea of presenting their adoption stories by saying something like, "You have all been working on telling your family's adoption story in the last two sessions. And today we're going to share the stories with each other."

Encourage the child and parents to share their writing and artwork to discuss their understanding of the adoption story. It may be helpful to ask the child who should go first. Allow both parents and child adequate time to read or show their story. Encourage the parents to accept all the child's feelings and to provide further information about the child's past if developmentally appropriate. Make sure to create sufficient time to check in with the child as the stories are shared to process any feelings or questions that may come up. Encourage physical affection between parents and child if appropriate.

DISCUSSING UNANSWERED QUESTIONS CHILD MAY HAVE

Assist children in asking the parents the questions that were developed last week about their history. If children are reluctant to share the questions, ask if they would like you to help read the unanswered questions. If some of this information has been provided during the sharing of the adoption story, acknowledge the new information and allow time for the child and parents to process it together. The parents then provide answers to what is known and developmentally appropriate to share. If the information is not available, model for the parents how to acknowledge the disappointment and frustration the child may feel about not having access to the information.

For example, the therapist might say or encourage the parents to say, "I know it feels really sad not to know information about your birth parents, and it's very frustrating; I don't have the information now, but we can try to find out the answers to some of your questions," or alternatively, "I'm really glad that you shared your questions with us—let me think about them and we can talk about them soon" (if parents hadn't considered the question or are not sure how to present the information). Cue the parents to provide support and reassurance to the child throughout this process, including letting the child know how much they love the child, if they do not naturally do so.

This session often elicits a great deal of strong emotion for parents and children, which you will validate. Note that this session also often elicits strong emotion for therapists. Do not be concerned if you are deeply touched by the content and affect of the session, and give yourself permission to express it, in ways that augment rather than take away from the genuine connection that often occurs between parents and child.

(OPTIONAL) INTEGRATING NEW INFORMATION GAINED INTO CHILD'S PROJECT

The child and parents may wish to add to the child's adoption story, using drawing or other forms of art material, the media described previously, or a preorganized project such as using family figures to play out the story on the basis of parental answers to the child's questions. If there is time and the family is willing, this can be a nice way to assimilate any new information into their understanding of their adoption story and Lifebook.

DISCUSSION OF DIVIDED LOYALTIES

Begin a discussion of divided loyalties by normalizing and reaffirming that children may continue to have feelings for and loyalties to birth families. Ask the children, if they are comfortable, to share any concerns they may have about bringing up their birth parents in front of their adoptive family. Encourage them to share any mixed messages they may feel coming from their adoptive parents regarding their birth parents, such as fears of making their adoptive family feel uncomfortable or feel that they don't love them as much. These messages may either be about whether it is OK to talk about the birth parents or about negative messages about the birth parents coming from the adoptive parents.

Discuss the fact that having divided loyalties is both common and normal. Encourage the parents to reinforce the message that they understand and support the child's connection to their birth family and that they understand it does not mean the child does not love and care for the adoptive parents.

Reinforce the need for the child to hold positive feelings about the birth family despite issues and problems birth parents may experience, and mention that these issues will be discussed in more detail later in Module 5 on identity and self-esteem.

DISCUSSION OF SEARCH AND REUNION (IF APPROPRIATE)

Prior to this session it is important that parents have been prepared for a discussion with their child around their potential interest in locating or reaching out to their birth family or potentially meeting them. If the issue of search and reunion has come up in the individual child sessions with older children, assist the child in discussing this with the adoptive parents.

CASE EXAMPLE: THE SPRINGFIELDS

At the outset of the joint session for Carlos, the therapist reminded the family of their calming images and how they had fun trying to remember each others' images. Everyone agreed that Carlos was the best at using the calming image and also reminding them when to use it to stay calm. The therapist reminded the family that they would be sharing their adoption stories with one another and asked Carlos who he would like to go first. He said he wanted to share his Lifebook first and did so with some assistance from the therapist. Rachel and Lewis were both engaged in looking at the Lifebook and hearing what Carlos had to say about it. They all became teary-eyed when they talked about the first day they met one another. The therapist provided an opportunity to acknowledge what feelings the children may be having and the meaning of their tears. Carlos asked some of his questions as he was going through his Lifebook, and Rachel and Lewis were able to provide answers to some of them and to let him know that they would look further into some of the questions they did not have answers for.

Lewis and Rachel then read their adoption narrative to Carlos, and both were physically affectionate with him as they spoke, and he sat right between the two of them. Rachel and Lewis also shared a photo book they had put together for Carlos with pictures of him they got from his Department of Children and Family Services (DCFS) file and recently gathered from the previous foster family. They also shared with him the information they gathered for the timeline they had put together about Carlos's life to help fill in some of the information that was missing from his Lifebook. Carlos seemed to visibly relax as he was able to fill in some of the information he was unaware of and see himself at different ages with Maria and with his former foster family, as well as with Rachel and Lewis. Carlos said he was happy that he was always with Maria as he reflected on that constant throughout his timeline of placements. When Carlos said, "I don't really know why I am not with my mom and why I had to leave my aunt's house," Rachel was able to say that his mom and his aunt weren't able to take care of him and keep him safe. When he asked why not, Lewis responded, "Your mom had a problem with drugs that made it hard for her to take care of herself or you and Maria. It wasn't your fault that she used drugs or that she couldn't stop being addicted to drugs. It was a grown-up problem. Your aunt's boyfriend did not treat her well, either, and that was scary for you and Maria so the judge decided that you and Maria deserved to be cared for and in a family where you would be safe and loved." Rachel chimed in, adding "I'm sad that you couldn't stay with your birth family and that they couldn't take care of you, but I am also so happy that you are part of the Springfields' forever family. We love you so much!"

In Maria's joint session with her parents, she seemed tense and anxious, and she asked to hear her parents' story first. She seemed to relax a little in her seat as they were talking, and Lewis reached out and touched Maria's shoulder as he shared one of his favorite memories of the day the kids moved into their home. Throughout their story, they repeated how much they loved Maria and what they loved about her. Rachel specifically said that she loved Maria for who she was and not just because she always wanted to have a daughter. Maria teared up when Rachel said this, and both parents gave her a hug.

When Maria brought out her poster to share with Rachel and Lewis, she described her feelings and images from when she was with her mom, taking care of Carlos, with her aunt, and with her two foster families, but she stopped short of talking about her adoptive family. The therapist asked Maria if her parents could ask questions about her poster, and she nodded that they could. Lewis asked Maria what it was like to have to take care of her brother when she was so young, and Rachel noted all the question marks on the poster and wondered what some of her questions about those things might be. After some back-and-forth discussion, validating Maria's feelings, Rachel asked her if she could share something she had for Maria. She presented Maria with a decorated manila folder with her name on it. Inside were pictures she had gathered from the adoption file and the former foster family recently, as well as pictures of the children with Rachel and Lewis. She told Maria that she had copies made in a separate folder so that Maria could do whatever she liked with these and wondered if she might want to add them to her poster or to create a new photobook or Lifebook with them. At one point Maria asked why Rachel hadn't shared the pictures before and appeared angry. The parents were careful to explain their recent contact with the foster family and acquisition of the photos.

On seeing some of the pictures, Maria began to cry, and Rachel and Lewis moved next to her and put their arms around her. Maria eventually was able to talk about some of the pictures that she had never seen and what was happening in them. There was a picture of her birth mother when she was not much older than a teenager and tears streamed down Maria's face as she noted that she looked like her. All three cried and shared stories of the pictures, and Maria gave Rachel a hug and stayed sitting close to her.

The therapist brought up the issue of divided loyalties and helped Maria and her parents explore this difficult concept and how it can be hard to understand that you can have coexisting feelings and connections to both birth and adoptive families. Maria was able to say that she feels bad about thinking about her birth mom when she knows she didn't take care of her like parents are supposed to, but she just can't help it. Rachel and Maria were both crying at this point, and Lewis told Maria that he and Rachel loved Maria no matter what or whom she thought about and that they wanted to know about feelings she had and what was important to her, including being able to talk about her birth family, her foster family, or even boys she might be interested in. Rachel added that they were all on the Springfield team, and Maria was part of it. Maria was able to go back to her poster and share some of the feelings and images she had included about her adoptive family. With a sense of humor, she described some of their early days getting to know each other and some of her favorite things that they now do together. The therapist urged the family to have another look at Maria's pictures together later that day and that week and for Maria to let them know the next time they met how she may plan to compile them. The therapist also asked if Maria might want a copy of the adoption story that Rachel and Lewis had written about her, and she said that she wanted to put it in the folder too. Because Maria did not ask all the questions she had originally listed, Rachel let her know that they could go through those questions any time that Maria wanted to.

Module 3

Loss and Grief Issues in Adoption

5

The purpose of the parent sessions for Module 3 is to facilitate the parent(s)' understanding of the losses their child has suffered, to help parents learn ways to assist children through the grieving process, to help parents deal with their own adoption-related losses, and to assist parents in dealing with feelings of rejection they may experience as a result of their children's grief process.

The purpose of the child sessions for Module 3 is to help children identify and acknowledge their previous losses, to assist children in understanding the circumstances surrounding their losses and support the exploration of their feelings, and to assist the children with their grieving process. Module 3 consists of two separate parent and child sessions and one joint session with parents and child together.

Parent Session 1: Understanding the Child's Losses and Grief Reactions

The goal of this session is to encourage parents to understand, embrace, and honor the many overwhelming losses that their child may have endured prior to joining their adoptive family. This task may be particularly challenging

http://dx.doi.org/10.1037/0000096-006
Adoption-Specific Therapy: A Guide to Helping Adopted Children and Their Families Thrive, by J. Waterman, A. K. Langley, J. Miranda, and D. B. Riley

and confusing for parents whose feeling of joy around adopting children into their family—especially first-time parents—is likely at odds with what their adopted child is feeling, especially children adopted at older ages. Although the child may be happy to join the adoptive family, the child is likely grieving the loss of birth and foster family members or other previous caregivers such as orphanage staff. Although parents are eager to love and attach to their child, the child's unresolved grief and loss can often compromise the child's ability to attach to the parents. When parents interpret their child's behavior as rejection, a range of feelings can be elicited including disappointment, sadness, hurt, and anger.

Materials for this session include

- Handout 32: Loss Chart,
- Handout 33: Understanding My Child's Losses, and
- Handout 34: My Child's Grief Reactions.

REVIEW PROBLEM AREAS AND PROGRESS

Check in with the parents to review and assess the progress made, if any, on the three problem areas regarding their child's behavior identified at the beginning of treatment, as is done in the first session of every module. Ask parents to rate the current degree of concern in each area. If giving the weekly behavioral measure (Parent Progress Report from Module 1), review prior to the session and share a graphic representation of the weekly ratings on each of the problem areas (up to three), allowing the parent to view the progress made. Review the relationship between the problem area and the current adoption-specific behavioral plan, and revise the behavioral plan as needed.

Check in with the parents to determine if and how the parents have been able to complete the homework assignment to practice one-on-one child-led play with their child. If any difficulties have arisen with this activity, explore these difficulties with parents and help them identify possible solutions to encourage continuing practice of one-on-one child-led play with their child. For example, a mother may say that it was a very busy week and there was no time, or she couldn't quite think of something else to do other than what was done in the session. Empathize with all the demands on a parents' time, and suggest adjusting the expectation to just 10–15 minutes or just three times during the week. Suggest possible activities including breaking a longer activity into smaller chunks of time, and brainstorm with the parents about what activities might be enticing to their particular child.

THE GOOD GRIEF FRAMEWORK

Provide the parents with grief education using author Maria Trozzi's (1999) Good Grief Framework. Ms. Trozzi outlines four tasks of the grieving process for children. The four tasks are: *understanding, grieving, commemorating,* and *going on*. This module is about these tasks; the tasks of understanding and grieving are covered in the first individual child and parent sessions, and the task of commemorating is covered in the joint session. The remainder of the modules deal with the task of going on.

UNDERSTANDING THE CHILD'S LOSSES AND THE PARENT'S LOSSES

Help the parents to reflect deeply and completely on the losses they know and/or imagine their child may have suffered. Ask, "What are the various losses that your child has suffered?" In addition to birth families, foster families, and caregivers in orphanages, help parents recognize that their child very likely also suffered losses related to extended family members, teachers, schools, coaches, friends, clergy, pets, country/language, culture, religion or ways of religious observance, neighborhood, favorite foods, clothes, and other personal possessions.

Use Handout 32: Loss Chart to help facilitate awareness of all the losses both the parent and the child have suffered. After talking about the child's losses, ask each parent to fill out a Loss Chart for the child, detailing all the losses the child has experienced or likely has experienced, covering the areas indicated in the previous paragraph.

It is very important for parents to be able to put themselves in their children's shoes. To facilitate this, encourage the parents to reflect on and share the losses they may have experienced in their own adoption journey—for example, infertility, miscarriages, foster children returned to birth parents, failed adoptions, the hope of parenting with a partner, and hope for a child who looked like them, as well as all significant losses they have experienced in their lives—loss of a parent, friend, pet, and other relationships. Then ask each parent to complete their own Loss Chart.

In discussion of losses listed on the Loss Chart, talk with the parents about the importance of helping children understand the circumstances related to the losses. This involves knowing what situation caused the loss and knowing what happened to the person, place, or thing that was lost (if known).

It is also important to help parents understand the unique nature of loss in adoption, known as "ambiguous loss" (Boss, 1999). While children are grieving the ability to be raised in their birth families ("physically absent"), their birth family members may certainly remain very much on the minds of the children ("psychologically present"). This is true in both closed and open adoptions. The experience of ambiguous loss will be impacted by the degree of postplacement contact with birth family. Although there are many benefits with open adoption, it is important that parents understand that their children are still coping with loss and grief.

HOW CHILDREN GRIEVE

Parents need to understand how the grief process applies to their particular child. Ask the parents to explore their thinking and observations of how they think their child expresses grief, specifically, "How does (child's name) show his/her grief?" Parents may be unaware that some of the child's difficult behaviors are in fact manifestations of grief. If appropriate, reinterpret these behaviors as indications of grief. Examples include punching a hole in a wall, crying inconsolably when a play date ends, tantrums during winter break from school, and temperamental and oppositional behavior at birthdays and/or holidays because they elicit memories of their life with previous families or in the orphanage.

Parents also need to have an understanding of how grief is processed from a developmental perspective. Especially emphasize that children do not grieve in the same manner that adults do. Children are usually less likely to verbalize their feelings of grief but rather demonstrate grief in their dysregulated behavior as suggested in the previous paragraph. Children can also be sad and distressed one minute and then return to happily playing in the next minute. In other words, they are more inclined to grieve in small chunks of time.

Discuss with parents that even though their child may not talk about missing loved ones or previous caregivers, or missing the neighborhood or orphanage they grew up in or food or traditions they were accustomed to, this does not mean that they are not grieving. In fact, sometimes older children do not share their feelings about previous losses for fear of upsetting or hurting their adoptive parents. They may feel intensely disloyal to acknowledge to their adoptive parents their feelings of grief regarding birth or previous foster parents or caregivers. Parents may also need assistance to comprehend and process their feelings about how their child can deeply miss a previous caregiver who was abusive or neglectful.

METHODS TO HELP CHILDREN WITH THE GRIEVING PROCESS

In this part of the session, empower parents to assist their children with the second task of Trozzi's grief process—the task of grieving. Discuss methods (listed next) by which the parents can help their child to grieve previous losses of caregivers and other important things and people in their lives and how they can support their child in experiencing the painful feelings associated with these losses. As you discuss the child's grief and losses, parents can become very emotional, so be sure to validate and accept the parents' feelings, just as you are aiming to help them validate and accept the child's feelings. This process can be especially challenging for parents who tend to avoid their child's grief, feeling more comfortable reassuring their child that everything is fine now that they are with their "forever family." Help parents to understand how these well-meaning statements invalidate what their child is experiencing, while also acknowledging how painful it can be for parents when the child discusses their love or longing for a previous family or situation. Emphasize how important it is for the child to feel that their parents are really there for them and that the parents completely accept the child's pain. Model how parents can express empathy for how difficult this can be when the child is hurting. A hug or kiss may be more helpful at times than any actual words spoken by the parent.

Next, discuss with the parent the following methods for assisting the grieving process. Individualize the methods for their particular child, according to their developmental stage:

- Giving permission for the child to be sad: "It is OK to be sad. Come to me when you need a hug."
- Bringing up past losses to discuss: "Gee, it's your birthday tomorrow. I know you loved the chocolate cake Miss Irene (former foster mother) baked for you so I made one just like it."

- Accepting the child's feelings rather than trying to make them go away: "I understand that you miss your birth mother" instead of "It's OK. You have me now."
- Having pictures or objects from birth families, foster families, or the orphanage around the house.
- Looking at Lifebooks or family photos with the child; you can use the Lifebook made by the child in Module 2.

HOMEWORK: UNDERSTANDING YOUR CHILD'S LOSSES AND GRIEF REACTIONS; PRACTICE DE-ESCALATION

For homework, ask the parent to fill out Handout 33: Understanding My Child's Losses, discussing what losses the child may be aware of, as well as the child's understanding of why each loss occurred.

Using Handout 34: My Child's Grief Reactions, ask parents to notice the child's behaviors that may be indicators of their child's unique expressions of grief. Request that parents list these behaviors on the handout and reflect on and note what specific strategies they can use to help with the child's grief reactions.

Remind parents to continue with their Praise and Encouragement Record and their Adoption-Specific Behavior Record. If a previous behavior problem has resolved, make sure to work with the parents to choose a new behavior, examine how the problem is related to the child's past history, and develop an adoption-specific behavior plan for this week.

Also remind parents about using de-escalation when their child's intensity escalates, and ask them to focus on practicing this important skill throughout the week. If parents report that they are continuing to struggle with this concept, practice de-escalating behavior in the session.

CASE EXAMPLE: THE SPRINGFIELDS

After checking in about behavioral progress, the therapist asked about the practice of one-on-one child-led play. Rachel shared that she had played with Carlos using his many dinosaur figures and had followed his lead as he made up a story about them, while Lewis reported he and Carlos both value their time together building with LEGOs. Following Maria's instructions, Lewis and Maria created a house with Sculpey, a soft type of clay. Both parents noted that the children now look forward to the one-on-one time with parents. Even though they may not be able to do it every day, Rachel and Lewis said they are learning to really enjoy the child-led play.

The therapist then explored with the couple the many losses that Maria and Carlos have suffered. Rachel noted the loss of their birth mother, the aunt they lived with, and likely other birth family members, as well as the two foster homes they were placed in before coming to live with Rachel and Lewis, which include three foster parents and the 14-year-old son of the couple they had lived with. Lewis noted that both had lost their birth fathers—Maria never even knew hers. He also mentioned that the children may miss living in Latino neighborhoods and possibly miss speaking Spanish.

Rachel and Lewis came in aware of the enormous grief that Maria is experiencing about her birth mother because she had expressed it more openly, and the therapist helped them to understand that Carlos is grieving as well, mostly in relation to his last foster family to whom he was quite attached. When Rachel shared how deeply sad she feels about Maria's rejection of her, the therapist normalized both Maria's conflicted feelings and how hard it is to experience rejection from a child you are trying to attach to. The therapist encouraged the parents to try really hard not to take it personally and that the more they are able to not respond negatively to the rejection, the more it will help Maria to attach to them.

Discussion then moved into the losses Rachel and Lewis had experienced on their road to parenthood surrounding their infertility. Rachel shared that for the most part, she felt she had moved on but that sometimes when the couple is fighting about the children, she goes back into wondering what could have/should have been. However, she is usually able to recover and tries to feel hopeful. The therapist acknowledged her pain and how very hard their job is while also providing support and encouragement to keep trying and learning. The therapist moved the discussion back to the losses the children experienced that may not have occurred to the parents—losses related to all the moves and changes the children had experienced, including other important people and things such as their teachers, friends, neighbors, and pets. Rachel and Lewis filled out the Loss Chart (Handout 32) for their children and for themselves. In addition to more common losses such as loss of a child who might look like him, Lewis noted that he had lost his two-seater sports car since they now needed to have a sedan. Rachel and Lewis were asked to think about their children's behavior through the lens of loss and grief. The therapist suggested that while Maria may have attention-deficit/hyperactivity disorder, it is also possible that some of her difficulties in school—inattentiveness, impulsive, aggressive behavior, and stealing—may also be manifestations of grief, which the parents acknowledged. They shared that they believe Maria may have felt guilty and torn by some of the success and happiness she has experienced in her new school and family, and so was reverting back to old behaviors, as they suspect that Maria may have taken some money from Rachel's purse. The therapist affirmed the couple's attempts to talk with Maria about her grief, but reminded them that it may be difficult for Maria to do that for fear of feeling disloyal to them. The therapist also emphasized Rachel's observation that grief is a back-and-forth process—not linear.

In talking about how the couple can assist both children through the grieving process, the therapist highlighted again the importance of accepting and validating their children's feelings. The therapist reassured the parents that in the children's sessions, Maria and Carlos will be looking at their losses and their grief and will be helped to also understand how their behaviors relate to their experience of loss and grief. Rachel noted that in addition to doing the homework this week, she will try to think about Maria's loss and grief when Maria says things like "you're not my real mother." Although acknowledging how painful this was for her, Rachel wanted to attempt to say something like "I know how much you miss your birth mom." The therapist praised Rachel's attempt to let Maria know she understood her painful feelings, despite how difficult it is for Rachel to hear Maria's statement.

Child Session 1: My Losses and Loss Box Activity

The purpose of this session is to assist children in their grieving process by helping them identify and acknowledge all of their previous losses, helping children to understand the circumstances surrounding their losses, and supporting the exploration of their feelings around these losses.

Materials for this session include

- a shoe box;
- art materials to decorate box and artistically express losses: construction paper, glitter, glue, paint, jewels, fabric, clay, markers, etc.; and
- Handout 35: What Children May Lose.

REVIEW MODULE 2 SESSIONS 2 AND 3 CHILD HOMEWORK: REVIEW AND PRACTICE MUSCLE RELAXATION

Check in with the child on the previous homework to practice muscle relaxation at least two times during the week and to record this on their Coping Strategies Log (Handout 24), troubleshooting any problems the child may have in using this coping strategy. Children may need parental support to practice this skill, as it is sequential and progresses through the muscle groups of the body. The therapist may need to reinforce with parents the benefit of scheduling a specific time each day when they can be present and support the child in their practice. Ideally, the parent and child participate in this practice together.

IDENTIFICATION AND DISCUSSION OF CHILD'S LOSSES AND LOSS BOX ACTIVITY

Loss in adoption is a complicated and profound experience. As in all adoptions, children who enter foster care or are placed in an orphanage in another country have experienced the devastating loss of not being able to live with their birth families. Children moving into foster care may experience further losses because of multiple moves and continued separation from birth parents and siblings. Children who do not appropriately grieve their past losses may not be able to successfully attach in future relationships, so it is very important to assist children in processing their past losses. The work with the child as well as the parent is based on the four stages of grief work developed by Dr. Maria Trozzi (1999) as discussed in Parent Session 1 of this module.

To work through the first task, the task of understanding, tell the child that you have a very helpful project called the Loss Box to help them remember, express their feelings, and celebrate the important people and things that they have lost. Instruct the child to choose a shoebox from a supply you have in the office and encourage them to decorate the box with the available art materials. If the shoebox has writing or designs on it, cover it with white paper prior to the child session. As the child begins to decorate the box, review the child's adoption story with them and ask them about the losses they experienced connected to their story. Provide the child with Handout 35: What Children May Lose, a list of common losses children adopted from foster care or internationally often experience, to stimulate discussion of the child's own losses.

Ask the child to think about the people, places, and things that are no longer in their lives. Examples of questions to ask the child include the following:

- Who were you close to? (adults, caregivers, friends, teachers, coaches, neighbors, relatives) Who do you miss the most? What do you miss about them?
- Where did you live? (houses, apartments, group homes, homeless shelters, institution, etc.) Can you describe your room? Who shared your room? How many places do you remember living?
- What do you remember about your neighborhood—the sights and sound and smells? The food? The music? The language(s) spoken?
- Where did you go to school? How many schools? Who were your best friends there? Did you have a favorite teacher?
- Did you have pets, and if so, what happened to them?
- Did you lose any favorite toys? Clothing?

Remember that the child may have conflicting feelings about identified losses. For example, children may be grieving for a parent, yet also remember incidents of neglect, abuse, domestic violence, or parental drug use that are not happy memories. Adults in their world may be puzzled by and not understand why they still love and miss a parent who traumatized them. Support the child in identifying all of the feelings represented in the loss, noting that we can have several possibly conflicting feelings at the same time. The child can feel angry at their birth father for the maltreatment but also still love him.

When the decorating is completed, help the child create a representation of each loss through artistic expression—for example, drawing, writing, clay work, and collage. As the child draws, writes, or sculpts the representation of the loss, encourage the child to talk about their understanding of why this loss occurred. You may ask, "Why do you think the social worker brought you to live with the Jones family? I wonder why you couldn't stay with the Jones family?" or "What did your social worker, foster parent, parent tell you about why you were being moved?" or "Why do you think you came to live in the orphanage?"

During the creation process, help the child explore what was significant about the identified loss and what does it feel like to have the loss. Ask, "I can imagine how frightened you must have been. What was that experience like for you?" If the child expresses feelings of guilt about the losses (e.g., feeling they caused the loss by negative behavior, not living up to expectations, sharing information with authorities, etc.), validate the child's feeling while reassuring the child that it was not the child's fault. You can say,

> Many children worry that being separated from their birth family was their fault—they might think something is wrong with them, that they aren't lovable, or that they should have helped their birth parent. Or, they may think they caused their removal by being "bad" or by telling family secrets to a teacher, social worker, or the police.

Respond to the child's perception with compassion:

> How hard that must be for you to believe that it was your fault. The truth is, it is always the parents' responsibility to take care of and protect their children. I'm so sorry your birth mother could not take care of you because she was having trouble taking care of herself.

The Loss Box activity will likely extend over several sessions and should not be rushed. This work must proceed at the child's pace, respecting that the child may not be able to deal with too many losses at one sitting. If the child appears to become overwhelmed with the task of grieving—perhaps by asking for the session to end, bringing up new topics, putting head down and not responding—you can take a break and play a game or do guided imagery or whatever else will feel soothing to the child.

HOMEWORK: REVIEW AND PRACTICE OF CALMING IMAGE

Ask the child to practice using their calming image at least two times during the week when they are feeling angry, sad, or worried and to record this on their Coping Strategies Log (Handout 24). Be sure to reinforce this homework assignment with the parent.

CASE EXAMPLE: THE SPRINGFIELDS

The therapist asked Maria how she was doing with practicing the muscle relaxation exercise. Maria laughed and admitted she only did this one time because it felt silly—specifically doing her upper body. The therapist explored what seemed silly, explained the benefit of the exercise to Maria, and then reinforced that it will most likely feel less silly with practice. She encouraged Maria to try again to practice this exercise during the coming week.

The therapist told Maria that in today's session, they are going to talk about the people and things she has lost in being removed from her birth family and other caregivers. The therapist gave her Handout 35: What Children May Lose. Maria teared up as she said, "Of course, my mother." She expressed that she misses her and worries about her every day. Additionally, Maria identified missing her previous foster family and the family dog, a guidance counselor from a previous school she attended, a neighborhood friend from that same time, and her aunt. The therapist asked Maria if she knew why she had to leave her birth mother, her aunt, and her two foster families, her school, her neighborhood, etc. Maria replied that her mother was using drugs, which made her sick and left Maria to care for Carlos, and they were hungry a lot. Regarding her aunt, she said it was because her aunt's boyfriend had a bad temper and they were not safe there. She said she's glad she didn't get adopted by her first foster mother who was "so mean." She wished her second foster family could have adopted them—"They were really nice," but they just wanted to be foster parents.

The therapist remarked on how many important people (and the dog) that Maria had lost and provided empathy about how painful that must be. Maria said she missed some things about her old neighborhood, like being able to see her aunt and eat good Mexican food, but that she did not miss the loud noises at the motels they stayed in and not feeling safe after dark.

The therapist described the Loss Box activity to Maria. Maria chose a big box and decorated it with aluminum foil and stickers and used glue to attach various items. When she was finished, she took the Model Magic clay and made figures of her birth mother and her aunt. Maria continued this activity over the following session to make models for her neighbor friend, the guidance counselor, her foster parents and their son, and their dog Lucy.

As she created each figure, the therapist asked her to share her memories and feelings associated with each loss. Beginning with her birth mother, Maria stated that she misses the way her mother used to sing to her before bed when she was little, before her mother stayed out at night. The therapist validated her feelings and asked Maria if she ever blames herself for her mother's troubles. Maria admitted that she sometimes got angry with her mother when she was hungry and for making her take care of Carlos when she wanted to play with her friends. She reported that she wishes she had tried harder to do what she was told. The therapist mentioned that many children who are removed from their birth families feel responsible for the move. The therapist acknowledged knowing how much Maria loves and misses her birth mother—and of course she would—and that it is very sad that her mother suffered from drug addiction, which made it impossible for her to properly care for herself or her children. The therapist underscored that understanding this doesn't make Maria's pain of her loss and her sadness any less, but it hopefully will help her understand she was not responsible for her mother's substance abuse.

The therapist asked Maria to talk about her feelings about her aunt and the experience of living there and having to leave her aunt as well. Maria stated that her aunt was OK but was always arguing with her boyfriend, who was really scary. She was relieved to leave her aunt's home but didn't much care for the foster mother she lived with for a year. Maria noted that this foster mother favored Carlos, and she got blamed for his misbehavior, so she doesn't want to include her in the Loss Box. Although she wasn't sad to leave this foster mother, she had become close with the guidance counselor at that school because she was always being sent there for her difficult behavior. This guidance counselor seemed to understand her and would often eat lunch with her. Maria also had a neighbor friend who was a few years older who was very kind to her.

Maria teared up again as she made the figures for the foster family she lived with before coming to live with her adoptive family. These foster parents were very patient and sweet, and their son played video games with her and gave her treats. She shared that the whole family would go to watch his baseball games and then have ice cream afterward. She and her foster brother often walked the family dog together. Her foster mother let her decorate her room with posters of her favorite singer and gave her arts and crafts sets that they could do together. Maria expressed anger that she doesn't understand why she cannot visit them, and the therapist reflected her anger and also wondered if there wasn't a great deal of sadness as well. When Maria completed her Loss Box, the therapist enthusiastically acknowledged her beautiful, hard work—both artistically and for her ability to explore and express her memories and her feelings.

At the beginning of the therapist's session with Carlos, he proudly shared that he practiced muscle relaxation three times that week. The therapist gave Carlos a high five and encouraged him to keep up the good work.

The therapist told Carlos that they were going to talk about the people and things that he misses since no longer living with his birth mother. The therapist gave him What Children May Lose (Handout 35) and read it to him; this seemed confusing to Carlos, so the therapist asked him about who he remembers living with before his adoptive parents. He said that he can only remember his last foster parents and their son. He remembered he liked his preschool teacher, Mrs. Rosen. He also remembered that his room in the foster parents' house had bright blue walls. He has a vague memory of being scared of someone but he cannot remember where or whom. The therapist wondered if it might be his aunt's boyfriend who wasn't very nice to her when he and Maria lived there briefly. As he talked about these people, the therapist asked Carlos why he thought he couldn't remain living with the foster family that he really liked. He said his adoptive parents have told him that foster parents are not forever parents and that they help take care of children who are waiting for their forever families. The therapist agreed this is true and also stated that it can still be very hard to leave a foster family you have come to love, and Carlos emphatically agreed.

The therapist told Carlos that they were going to do an activity so that he will always be able to remember these special people and described the Loss Box activity. Carlos chose a shoebox and colored the box the color blue he remembers from his old room with the foster family. He drew pictures of stars and planets with markers because he thought there were pictures like that in this room. He said that he doesn't really like to draw and also doesn't like to play with clay. However, he was willing to try the Model Magic clay and created different shapes to represent the foster parents, their son, their dog Lucy, and his preschool teacher. As he talked about the foster parents, he remembered how nice they were to him and told the therapist that the foster mother would rub his back at night to help him get to sleep. Carlos loved pizza night, and also remembered that the foster parents' son gave him piggy back rides and chocolate chip cookies. Another fond memory was chasing Lucy and rubbing her belly. From preschool, he remembered that he liked when Mrs. Rosen played the guitar. The therapist reflected that there were many things he remembered from that home that made him feel warm and cared about, and complimented him on what a good memory he has.

Parent Session 2: Dealing With Rejection by Child

The purpose of this session is to help parents understand how children with unresolved grief and loss issues often engage in rejecting behaviors. This includes children who have also experienced rejection in previous placements. Parents are helped to deal with their feelings and use coping strategies so that they can respond appropriately and effectively with their children.

Materials for this module include Handout 36: Understanding Child's Rejecting/Testing Behavior.

REVIEW PARENT SESSION 1 HOMEWORK: UNDERSTANDING MY CHILD'S LOSSES AND MY CHILD'S GRIEF REACTIONS HANDOUTS

Discuss what parents have further noted regarding the child's losses and their own adoption-related losses over the week. If parents need help, give examples from what you know about the child's behavior—for example, temper tantrums, fearfulness, separation anxiety. Ask parents to share how they think their child is grieving their previous losses. Praise parental efforts to understand their child's grieving process and also ask about what strategies they think can help their particular child's grieving process. Check in about instances when the parents used de-escalation since the last session, and problem solve any difficulties that may have arisen.

DISCUSSION OF CHILD'S REJECTING BEHAVIORS/ VERBALIZATIONS AND PARENTAL REACTIONS

Tell parents that children with unresolved grief and loss issues may push their parents away as a way of protecting themselves by rejecting their parents before they are rejected themselves. Especially children who have experienced multiple placements may engage in troublesome behaviors to test whether the new parents will reject them as others have in the past. For example, a child who got into trouble for lying in a previous placement may lie to their adoptive parents on purpose, especially if they know it upsets their parents, in an attempt to test whether these parents will be able to tolerate the child's negative behaviors.

In addition to behaviors, children may make rejecting statements. Give parents additional examples:

- "I don't have to clean my room because you're not my real mom/dad."
- "I hate you. I want to go back to Miss Betsy's house."
- "I wish I could have stayed with my real family."
- "I want to go back to Ethiopia!"

Help parents to reinterpret the child's rejecting statements and/or difficult testing behavior in light of the child's past history. For example, you can say, "I can imagine that you want me to know how much it hurt when your foster parents chose not to adopt you." Bear in mind that their child's rejecting behaviors can be very painful and impactful for the adoptive parents. Although the intensity of pushing parent's buttons and trying to upset them by saying rejecting comments happens in all families, they can be particularly hurtful for adoptive parents. Especially with older children who have lived with birth parents, adoptive parents may feel quite rejected when the child expresses their love for birth family with comments like "You're not my real dad," or "I already have a mom."

Explore, accept, and empathize with the parents' feelings and reactions to these behaviors. Help parents to remember that their children's expressions are really indications of intense feelings, as the child usually doesn't mean hurtful statements such as "I wish you were dead" when they are not dysregulated. In accepting parents' feelings, let the parents know it is perfectly understandable to have the impulse to strike back by suggesting the child leave if they are not happy in the home. Remind parents how important it is to keep that impulse in check as it is just what the children are *expecting* to hear, confirming all of their fears.

Remind parents to use the coping strategies for emotion regulation discussed in Module 1. Review deep breathing, muscle relaxation, and use of their calming image and encourage parents to use them when they feel upset by the child's rejecting behavior or words. Emphasize how important this is so that they can respond to their child without rejection and be there to help the child with their conflicting feelings—for example, wanting to be loved but afraid of being vulnerable.

COGNITIVE RESTRUCTURING AND USE OF ALTERNATIVE EXPLANATIONS

Teach parents to reinterpret the child's rejection of them and their testing behavior by using cognitive restructuring and alternative explanations with an adoption-specific lens. Together with the parent, develop appropriate response strategies for their individual child, with emphasis on praise and reward for positive behaviors, ignoring their child's rejecting behaviors, and later commenting on the adoption-specific function of the rejecting behaviors (e.g., "It helped you cope in your birth family," "I can understand why you would want to test if I'd reject you if you misbehaved since that's what happened in the orphanage," "I can understand that you would want to push me away by saying hurtful things to me because it's scary to be close to someone when you've been rejected a bunch of times, but we're your forever family, and will stand by you no matter what," "I can never take the place of your birth mom, and I don't want to, but I can give you lots of caring and love").

DISCUSSION OF TREE OF REMEMBRANCE ACTIVITY IN JOINT SESSION

Inform parents that the activity for the next (joint) session is working on a Tree of Remembrance, where the child names and shares memories of people whom they have lost who were important to them (e.g., birth parents, foster parents, orphanage caregivers, teachers, siblings). Ask the parents to share their feelings about doing this exercise and empathize with their feelings. Discuss the importance of treating the child's losses and memories with care and respect, reminding them again that children often have fond memories of former caregivers who may have hurt them or of cultural elements and language that may not be part of their adoptive home.

HOMEWORK: ADOPTION-SPECIFIC RESPONSE; REVIEW AND PRACTICE OF PRETEACHING

For homework, ask parents to list the child's rejecting behaviors and to write down possible alternative explanations for these rejecting behaviors on the basis of the child's past history. Give them Handout 36: Understanding Child's Rejecting/Testing Behavior, for recording their answers.

Remind parents to continue with the Adoption-Specific Behavior Record. Additionally, ask parents to use preteaching at least two times during the week. Review this concept and role play in the session as needed if parents are not using preteaching at all or incorrectly.

CASE EXAMPLE: THE SPRINGFIELDS

The therapist reviewed with Rachel and Lewis the handouts they filled out on Understanding My Child's Losses (Handout 33) and My Child's Grief Reactions (Handout 34). Rachel shared that she had a better understanding of Maria's aggressive behavior in terms of her grief over the loss of her birth mother and the rejection she experienced in her first foster care placement, although Lewis continued to have some doubts about this connection. Both Rachel and Lewis said they understood Carlos's anxiety in terms of the neglect he experienced and the moves, which impacted him even though he cannot remember them. They stated that they imagined the loss of the second foster family that he cared about deeply contributed to his anxiety.

The therapist then explored with the couple Maria's troubling behaviors, which have escalated since finalization. Rachel brought up how upset she gets when the school calls to tell her that Maria has been in a fight with her peers or has refused to do her schoolwork. She reminded the therapist of how this puts distance in her relationship with Maria. The therapist explained that it is possible that Maria engages in these behaviors to push Rachel away, as she knows that Rachel will get upset with her. With some exasperation, Rachel stated that she can't help but get angry that Maria would knowingly do something to upset her. She admits that once or twice, she wanted to ask if Maria would like to just go back and be with her birth mother. The therapist empathized with Rachel about how hard it is to handle these behaviors and how hurtful it can be, and noted that while we can know cognitively why the child might be rejecting, we still can have painful emotional reactions in response.

The therapist asked Rachel if when she feels rejected and defeated, she's been able to use any of the techniques for emotional regulation that were discussed in an earlier module—such as deep breathing. Lewis laughed and said he tries to suggest that to Rachel, but it only makes her angrier. Rachel agreed that if she can remind herself that Maria says these things because she is sad and struggling, she can better control her feelings of hurt and use these strategies to remain calm or to calm down.

The therapist then suggested that Rachel and Lewis work on making statements to Maria to reinterpret her behavior—to give her an adoption-focused understanding of her behavior. The therapist suggested that after such an incident, the couple try saying to Maria something like,

> I know you are sad and missing your birth mother, and also missing your foster family. Perhaps you feel sad and angry that the foster family did not adopt you. I can understand that you may steal or be aggressive to test if we will reject you because you feel rejected by them. I also think you may feel you have to push us away to not feel disloyal to your birth mother. We care for you and will be here for you. We are not leaving you.

The therapist asked the Springfields if they are experiencing similar behaviors with Carlos, and they said that he sometimes mentions his previous foster family so they know he thinks about them, but they do not experience rejection from him, rather the opposite, in that he is often anxious and clingy and needs reassurance that they are there for him.

The therapist informed the parents that the next session will be a joint one with the children in which they will work together on an activity called the Tree of Remembrance. The children will be asked to name and share memories of people and things they have lost that were important to them. The therapist asked the couple how they think this will be for them. Rachel became tearful and said she thinks it is going to be very hard for Maria to do. The therapist asked if it will be hard for Rachel to hear, and she admitted that she thinks it will be. The therapist validated that it is often hard for parents to hear their children's pain, and it is common for them to wish for their own relationship with the child to take away that pain. Both Rachel and Lewis agreed this is true. However, Rachel noted that on the other hand, she is looking forward to having Maria share anything with her; although there has been some progress on this since the last joint session, it continues to be challenging.

Child Session 2: The Task of Grieving (Continuation of Loss Box Activity)

This session is a continuation of the previous session whose purpose is to assist children in their grieving process. As they continue to work on the Loss Box activity, children continue to identify and explore feelings related to their losses. Sometimes more sessions need to be added to complete the Loss Box activity if there have been many significant losses.

Materials for this module include

- Loss Box and art supplies for decorating (from last session);
- drawing materials such as markers, pens, glitter, etc.; and
- feelings cards or feelings poster.

REVIEW SESSION 1 CHILD HOMEWORK: REVIEW AND PRACTICE OF CALMING IMAGE

Check in with the child about their homework assignment of practicing using their calming image at least two times during the week when they were feeling angry, sad, or worried and recording this on their Coping Strategies Log (Handout 24). Once again, if any difficulties arose with the child being able to do this, problem solve with the child to ensure this happens.

THE LOSS BOX (CONTINUED)

Check in with the child to assess the impact of the last session and the Loss Box activity. Anger and sadness are often the key feelings that children process and express during this exploration. If the child shares that they experienced any emotional or behavior difficulties during the week, explore their feelings further. For example, a child might say, "I felt really sad or angry," or "I got into a lot of trouble." In response, say something like,

> That is perfectly normal. Of course you would have a lot of big feelings as you talk about your pain over all that you have lost. Thanks for telling me. It's really important to get your feelings out. When you work so hard to push them away, they end up hurting more. Talking about your feelings will help you feel better.

Ask the child if they thought about anything else that could go in the box, and help the child to continue with the Loss Box activity and describe and express feelings related to these losses. Note that the next session will be one in which the child and parents meet together and explore the child's feelings about sharing the contents of their Loss Box with the parents. Accept and support any choice the child makes about sharing or not sharing. Let children know that in the joint session, they will be making a Tree of Remembrance to help keep positive memories of people or things they have lost.

HOMEWORK: REVIEW AND PRACTICE OF PROBLEM SOLVING

Review the Kids' Coping Solutions (Handout 21 from Module 1). Together with the child, develop a plan to deal with a problem the child is experiencing, and role play various solutions as needed. For example, a child might say that he is fighting a lot with his older brother. Ask the child to share an example of a fight—for example, he monopolizes the family computer. Ask the child to look over Handout 21: Kids' Coping Solutions to think of what strategies he might use. For example, he might suggest several options to his brother to solve this problem—take turns using a timer, play a game together, alternate days of the week to share, etc. Role play as the brother and have the child approach you with his suggestions for compromise. Congratulate the child for becoming so good at solving problems.

Ask the child to try out the problem-solving strategies with the identified problem and record them on the Coping With My Problem sheet (Handout 22 from Module 1, Session 4). Reinforce with this homework assignment with the parent.

CASE EXAMPLE: THE SPRINGFIELDS

The therapist asked Maria how her week was and she admitted that talking about everything she has lost made her feel sad and angry and that she got into fights with her mother and Carlos. The therapist normalized Maria's experience, saying it is common for kids to feel this way; she may not realize how much she tries to distract herself from her pain and that although it is initially more distressing, it will eventually help her to feel less pain if she can allow herself to remember, share, and express her feelings about her significant losses. She said, "I hope so." The therapist asked Maria if during the week, she thought about anything else that should go in the Loss Box, and she said, "Yeah—I remembered that I lost my beautiful red sweater when I was with my first foster mother. She had given it to me for my birthday, and then took it away a few weeks later when she was angry with me. I said I didn't care at the time because I was so mad at her, but I really loved that sweater." The therapist said, "I imagine that you felt pretty angry to have a gift taken from you like that as punishment." Maria said, "Yeah—she was so mean. I don't miss her!" The therapist said, "No, I'm sure you don't, and it makes sense to feel so angry when someone caring for you doesn't understand you and is unkind to you. I'm glad you can talk about that powerful feeling so it doesn't continue to hurt you. Do you want to put that red sweater in your Loss Box?" Maria responded that she did and made a beautiful drawing of herself wearing the sweater.

After completing the Loss Box activity, the therapist complimented Maria for her courage to explore her losses. The therapist told Maria that she can share her Loss Box with her parents in the upcoming joint session if she's willing, then could take the box home and bring it out anytime she wants to remember the important people, places, and things that she is missing, or she can leave it with the therapist if she is not ready to take it home.

During Carlos's session, he said he had a very good week. When asked about anything to add to the Loss Box, he stated that he cannot think of anything else to add. After looking over all the things he had put into the Loss Box, he seemed to be finished with it. The therapist gave him free time to play, and he enthusiastically threw a soft football around with the therapist.

Joint Session: The Tree of Remembrance

The purpose of this session is to assist the children in sharing with their parents the losses they have been exploring in their child sessions and engage the family in the fourth task of grieving (according to Maria Trozzi's Good Grief Framework)—the task of commemorating—in which the people, places, and things that have been lost are remembered and honored.

Materials for this session include

- a large paper or poster with tree branches on it;
- precut leaves on colored paper (see Handout 37: Sample Tree and Leaves for Tree of Remembrance if not using toolkit);
- markers, pencils, or pens; and
- tape or metal fasteners to fasten leaves onto tree branches.

THE TASK OF COMMEMORATING (CONTINUED)

Drawing on the work that you have done in the previous two child sessions around the Loss Box activity, together with the adoptive parents help children remember and honor the people, places, things, and circumstances that they have lost that they define as significant in their lives—birth family, foster family, orphanage staff, neighbors, friends, teachers, country, culture or language, pets, etc. If children are willing, encourage them to share what is in the Loss Box, but do not push them to do so if they are not comfortable sharing it at this point.

THE TREE OF REMEMBRANCE

Present the family with a pretraced tree with many branches and roots and precut colored leaves (available in toolkit or can be cut from construction paper). See Handout 37: Sample Tree and Leaves for Tree of Remembrance for a sample tree trunk and branches, as well as leaves that you can cut out of construction paper prior to the session if you do not have the toolkit, which includes the leaves. Each branch represents either a family or a transition. Ask the child to write (or you or the parent may do the writing for younger children) on each branch the family name or transition that the branch represents (e.g., birth family, a particular foster family, group home, orphanage, etc.). Then ask the child to write the names of people or things that have been important to them in those contexts on the leaves.

The leaves should represent individual birth family members, friends, foster family members, orphanage caregivers/staff, social workers, teachers, pets, or beloved possessions—anyone or anything that was significant in the child's life. On the other side of the leaf, ask the child (or the parent) to write one memory they have of the person (or pet or object) that was special to them. If the child has trouble coming up with something, ask the child questions like, "How did this person make you feel loved or special?" "What is one thing this person did with you or for you that you will always remember?" If the child brings up bad memories, empathize with the child and ask if that is a memory the child wants to keep. If the child says, "yes," that leaf is included. If the child says "no," suggest that they can discard this leaf and write a positive memory of that person on another leaf if the child has a positive memory of that person they want to keep. For example, a child might say that her foster sister often teased her. If the child states they don't want to keep that memory, you may ask if the child has any positive memories of the foster sister they would like to keep. The child might say, "She used to polish my nails" and indicate a desire to keep that memory. Once the identification of people and the memories about them are written, help the child attach the leaves with clear tape or metal fasteners onto the branches.

This process allows parents to give permission for the child to grieve, and they honor and note connections from the past, acknowledging the child's feelings and fears of disloyalty if appropriate. For example, a parent might say, "I'm so glad that you can share with me how very much you miss your grandmother and the special meals she would cook for you and the songs she would sing you from her home country. And you can always remember her from the leaf you put on your Tree of Remembrance," or "I am glad you can tell me how much you miss your friends in the orphanage and how you helped each other with loneliness."

Helping children to integrate the past with the present as their parents demonstrate interest, understanding, and affirmation during the Tree of Remembrance activity is extremely beneficial in assisting the child to successfully attach to their adoptive parents. Encourage parents to treat the tree with respect and be open to the child adding to it over time either with you or with the parents. Talk about where they might want to hang up the tree in their home. We suggest that parents also make a copy of it in case it becomes damaged.

CASE EXAMPLE: THE SPRINGFIELDS

The therapist told the parents that the children were going to share what they have been working on in the past two sessions as they engage in an important activity to remember and honor the people in particular whom they have lost. Maria did not want to share her Loss Box, so the therapist brought out the Tree of Remembrance and explained what the children were to do.

Maria had separate branches for her birth mother, her aunt, her first foster family, and her second foster family. She made a leaf for her birth mother and shared a memory of how she and her mother used to talk and laugh when her mother would brush and braid her hair; then Maria put the leaf on the tree. For her aunt, she first mentioned a memory of being frightened of the fighting between her and her boyfriend and of hiding in a closet. The therapist asked if this was a memory she wanted to keep, and Maria emphatically said "no." When asked if she had a memory of her aunt that she would like to keep, she said that she made delicious enchiladas and wrote this on the leaf about her aunt. The only memory she wanted to keep from the first foster home was of the guidance counselor at school who gave her hugs, and she made a leaf for this. From the second foster family, she had several memories she wanted to keep. She made separate leaves for her foster mother whom she remembered having fun with while clothes shopping and who talked to her in Spanish, her foster father who played basketball with her in their driveway, her foster brother who played video games with her, and her neighborhood friend with whom she would ride bicycles and braid each other's hair. After she finished, Rachel said how glad she was to know about the sweet and fun times Maria had with her mother, her foster family, and her friend and how lucky Maria was to have a wonderful counselor at school. Lewis agreed and commented on the fact that Maria could beat him at video games so her foster brother must have been instrumental in helping her to get so good at them. Both Rachel and Lewis said they could understand how much these people meant to Maria, how she would always miss them and always want to remember them.

When it was Carlos's turn, Rachel offered to help him with his writing—he only identified memories of the previous foster family, remembering how his foster mother would read to him at night before bed, his foster father would take him to the backyard and play catch with him, and his foster brother would give him piggy back rides. Lewis said that he understood now how Carlos got to be so good at throwing and catching. Both parents thanked the children for sharing these people and memories with them and took the Tree of Remembrance posters, saying they would keep them in a safe place and that the children could look at and add to them anytime they wanted. Maria asked if they would frame her Tree of Remembrance for her, and Lewis quickly assented. The therapist agreed that the children did a great job with a hard task and acknowledged the parents' appreciation for all the significant losses the children have experienced.

Module 4
Attachment and Joining With the Adoptive Family

6

The purpose of the parent sessions of Module 4 is to assist parent(s) in understanding and facilitating the attachment process. Parents learn about different attachment styles and discuss the child's and their own attachment style. Mechanisms to facilitate attachment and "claim" the child are discussed, and new family rituals are developed to help bring the family together and facilitate positive family interaction.

The purpose of the child sessions of Module 4 is to help children talk about their feelings about safety, trust, and security (or lack thereof) in their adoptive family and to participate in activities that help the child feel connected with the adoptive family. Module 4 has two parent sessions and two child sessions and one joint session.

Parent Session 1: Understanding Attachment Styles

This session's goals include reviewing problem areas and progress, as is done in the first session of each module; reviewing the adoption-specific behavior plan and the practice of preteaching; and discussing attachment principles, as well as the child's and the parent's attachment styles.

---

http://dx.doi.org/10.1037/0000096-007
Adoption-Specific Therapy: A Guide to Helping Adopted Children and Their Families Thrive, by J. Waterman, A. K. Langley, J. Miranda, and D. B. Riley

Materials for this session include

- Handout 38: Circle of Security, and
- Handout 39: Attachment Styles.

PROGRESS ON THREE INITIAL PROBLEMS

Begin the session by checking with the parents concerning progress toward the three problems they identified during their first session. Have parents rate current status of these problems, as they do in the first session of each module. Review the relationship between the problem area and the current adoption-specific behavioral plan, and revise the behavioral plan as needed.

REVIEW HOMEWORK: UNDERSTANDING CHILD'S REJECTING/TESTING BEHAVIOR

Next, go over last week's homework, Understanding Child's Rejecting/Testing Behavior (Handout 36). Discuss the rejecting/testing behaviors noted by the parents and empathize with how painful it can be to feel rejected when they are opening themselves up with love and caring for the child. Look at the possible explanations they have for the rejecting/testing behaviors in light of the child's history, and praise the parents for appropriate and accurate reframing of these behaviors, such as understanding that the child's rejection is based on their fears of abandonment and trauma history. If the parents are finding it difficult not to take the rejection personally, help the parents realize that the child is not truly rejecting them and their love, but rather protecting himself or herself from further rejection. Help the parents to reflect what they are noticing back to the child if they are comfortable and if it does not elicit further rejection and upset from the child. For example, if the situation is appropriate, suggest the parent say something like,

> You seem sad and I would like to help you. I know you say you want to be left alone, and I will respect that wish. I wonder if it is possible that getting hurt by your friend reminds you of how many times you have been hurt and you are protecting yourself. I want to be someone who is there for you and for you not to have to worry that I will ever leave you. Let me know if you want to talk later.

For a younger child, perhaps the parent can say, "You are upset and need to calm down. No matter how upset you get or what you do, we will always be your parents and love you."

Relate the child's behavioral problems back to the adoption issues as appropriate. For example, many young children who have been in several placements believe that they will leave their adoptive home as soon as the parents get tired of their troubles, and they may act out to elicit rejection as a way to "get it over with." Children who have experienced physical abuse or trauma may follow patterns that have previously led to them being hurt by adults just so that they can feel a sense of control over the situation and elicit what they predict versus being caught off guard by an adult becoming violent. Although the parent is carrying out the behavioral intervention, they might remind the child that regardless of negative behaviors, the child is theirs forever and is safe from being physically harmed.

PSYCHOEDUCATION ABOUT ATTACHMENT

Remind parents that the focus of Module 4 is on attachment and bonding. Note that strengthening attachment can help families through difficult periods. Suggest that attachment is like the strong foundation of a house that keeps it standing through rough weather and the wear and tear of many years. Ask, "How do you think things are going with the attachment between you and (child's name)?" Allow each parent to talk about their feelings about the attachment, and provide empathy and validation especially if there seem to be issues in the attachment relationship. Note that attachment is a long and interactional process that does not occur immediately with children who have had disrupted attachments (which includes all children adopted past infancy), and empathize with any frustration they may feel about how long it is taking. Ask parents about how the process of attachment has been for them, as well as ways they see their children feeling bonded to them.

CIRCLE OF SECURITY

Next, go over Handout 38: Circle of Security (from Cooper, Hoffman, & Powell, 2017).[1] The idea is that when a parent attends and responds sensitively to the child's needs, the child feels secure and develops attachment to the sensitive caregiver. Discuss with the parents the two parts of the Circle of Security. First, the parent can provide a *secure base* from which the child can venture out and explore the world, providing delight and assistance as the child discovers more and more about their world. Second, the parent can provide a *safe haven* for the child to return to when the child needs comforting or help in dealing with strong feelings. The parents' consistency; ability to be wise and kind; and ability to protect, help, and comfort a child truly builds the security. Ask the parents to reflect on how they may be providing a secure base and a safe haven for the child. Some children have trouble venturing out from the safe base. Other children may venture out readily but tend to have difficulty accepting help or showing vulnerability, particularly if their needs have previously gone unmet. Ask if parents see either of these styles with their child.

Remind parents that the attachment process may take a long time, particularly with traumatized children and those with many previous placements or long orphanage stays. Some parents have trouble understanding that even though the child is now safe with them, the child still feels frightened and untrusting. Help them see how this is something they will build on over time and is critical to their child's healthy

[1]From "Circle of Security in Child Care: Putting Attachment Theory Into Practice in Preschool Classrooms," by G. Cooper, K. Hoffman, and B. Powell, 2017, *ZERO TO THREE, 37*(3), pp. 27–34. Copyright 2016 by Circle of Security International. Reprinted with permission.

development. Empathize with how difficult it can be when they feel very attached to the child, but the child is not yet able to fully reciprocate.

CHILD'S ATTACHMENT STYLE

Next, discuss with parents Handout 39: Attachment Styles (based on work by Ainsworth & Bell, 1970; Ainsworth, Blehar, Waters, & Wall, 1978), noting the characteristics of each of the attachment styles listed. Ask, "Which of these attachment styles do you think fits (child's name) best?" Follow up by asking what behaviors or emotions lead them to see the child as having that particular style. Discuss with parents the adaptive value of different styles for children in difficult situations. For example, the quick, superficial attachment behaviors (preoccupied/anxious attachment style) often shown by children who have had multiple placements or who have lived in orphanages were probably adaptive when there were many different caregivers who might have changed rapidly and without warning. Similarly, the wariness and avoidant behaviors of children rejected repeatedly (avoidant attachment style) would be very adaptive in protecting the child against further hurt and rejection.

PARENTS' ATTACHMENT STYLE AND HISTORY

After identifying their child's style of attachment, ask the parents to reflect on their own attachment styles and histories, using Attachment Styles (Handout 39) if needed. Give them a couple of minutes to think about their own style. Ask them how they think their attachment style developed, based on their own background, and provide empathy and validation if traumatic or difficult information comes up for the parent. Many parents will say they have a secure attachment style. To go more in depth, note that securely attached people generally have a slight leaning toward either an anxious or an avoidant style and ask which one fits them better. Explore how this style would have been adaptive given their history. Next, wonder about how their own attachment style fits with that of the child, or how it does not fit, and help parents look at possible links between parental attachment style and the child's attachment style. For example, what are pros and cons of sharing an attachment style, such as being anxious and fearful of abandonment? How would things be different if the parent had an avoidant style and the child had an anxious/preoccupied style? Or if the parent had an anxious attachment style and the child had an avoidant style? If there are two parents and they seem comfortable with the discussion, also ask for examples about how their styles interact with each other in their own relationship.

HOMEWORK: FAMILY ACTIVITY; CHILD'S ATTACHMENT STYLE; GATHER FAMILY PICTURES

For homework, ask parents to participate in a child-led activity the whole family can do over the next week to build a sense of family togetherness and demonstrate that the parents will honor the child's interests. If parents think the child will have difficulty coming up with a suitable activity, brainstorm possible ideas. Some potential plans might be activities like family game night, going to the beach or taking a hike, having a picnic in the park, seeing a movie, and throwing around a Frisbee. If you suggest such activities, remember to point out to the parents that it should be an activity of the child's choosing and that they should make suggestions for the activity only if the child cannot come up with ideas.

Ask parents to gather further evidence this week about their child's attachment style with parents and others, to reflect on their own attachment style, and to notice how the styles of parent and child may interact. In preparation for the activity for Child Session 2, ask parents to help the child collect family pictures from their photo collection, showing family involvement in various activities; if photos do not exist of the family doing things together, encourage parents to take some photos over the week (e.g., during the planned family activity, cooking together, reading a book, playing soccer) or draw pictures of the family doing things together. Remind the family to continue the Adoption-Specific Behavior Record (Handout 8) and adjust the behavioral plan if needed.

CASE EXAMPLE: THE SPRINGFIELDS

Rachel and Lewis began the session by reviewing progress on the behavioral program for Maria. They both acknowledged that there had been a setback this week when Maria had become very angry with Carlos and tossed him out of her bedroom. As per the behavioral agreement, Maria didn't earn her dollar that day. Rachel and Lewis did not approach Maria immediately, as she had slammed her door closed. However, after giving Maria 30 minutes to calm down, they asked to talk with her. Although at first defensive, Maria admitted that she felt bad about this interaction. They talked about the great progress Maria had made in interacting with Carlos, and the therapist praised their efforts and success. Rachel and Lewis had reminded Maria that they understood that she had to take care of Carlos early in her life and wondered what had triggered her reaction tonight. Maria became tearful and said that Carlos had tried to look at her book of pictures of their birth mother and wouldn't put it down when she demanded he do so. She said that she was afraid he would rip up the book because he said he didn't care about their birth mom and that she was so mad that she needed to kick him out right at that moment. Rachel expressed empathy for what it must have felt like when Carlos wouldn't let go of her book, while Lewis remained unmoved. The therapist suggested that the parents make copies of the pictures in Maria's book, so that even if something happened to her book, the pictures would still exist. They all agreed that they would continue the behavioral program that was working well, and the therapist noted that this was only a small setback.

Rachel and Lewis agreed that the program was also working well for Carlos. He liked earning his "Brave Points" and was becoming more comfortable and able to be alone and independent.

Rachel talked about her response to Maria's rejecting behaviors. Rachel admitted that she has a much better understanding of where Maria is coming from, with both fear of rejection and dual loyalty to her birth mother; however, this understanding has not stopped her from feeling hurt when Maria clearly states she wishes she could still be with her birth mom. Lewis feels that he no longer finds the behavior so rejecting, and they agreed to talk about it as a couple when they see Maria rejecting them so that they can support each other to not take it personally.

As the therapist moved on to discussing the Attachment Styles handout and asked the parents about their impressions of the children's attachment style, both quickly identified that Carlos seemed to have a preoccupied attachment style; he is frightened of abandonment, seeks reassurance and closeness, and exhibits crying and clingy behavior whenever there is a hint of separation. They had more difficulty in thinking about Maria's attachment style, as they saw elements of both an avoidant style and a disorganized style. Rachel noted that sometimes Maria wants to be close but also often avoids interaction. She has trouble trusting and also sees herself as angry and unlovable. The therapist suggested that they keep both styles in mind as they consider further her attachment style over the next week (as well as that of Carlos).

In discussing her own attachment style, Rachel said she definitely thinks she has a preoccupied attachment style. She and her mother were "joined at the hip," and she experienced a great deal of separation anxiety when she was young. Her mother especially saw danger around every corner and was very worried whenever Rachel or her sister took steps toward independence; the mother did not like Rachel to go on playdates without her being present, objected when Rachel wanted to join extracurricular activities in high school, and didn't let her get her driver's license until she was 18. Additionally, her mother suffered from significant depression and there would be times when she would be in bed for days and unavailable emotionally to Rachel, who felt very frightened during those times and even stayed home from school a few days to make sure her mother was OK. She also felt that her mother preferred her sister and remembered doing things to please her mother. Rachel noticed that her own childhood experiences of being so closely bonded with her mother might be making it especially painful for her when Maria pushes her away and doesn't seem to want to be close. On the other hand, she understands Carlos's anxiety and clinginess much better and is able to respond with warmth and reassurance because she and he share the same attachment style.

Lewis reported that he feels he has a secure attachment. He has a good relationship with his mother and his three siblings. His father left the family when he was quite young, and after a period of lack of contact, he reentered the children's lives when they were teens; the father passed away 5 years ago. The therapist acknowledged Lewis's assessment, noting that securely attached people usually lean a bit toward either the preoccupied or the avoidant style, and asked Lewis which one he thought was more like him. Lewis thought about this for a while and studied the Attachment Styles (Handout 39).

He reiterated that he thought he had a secure attachment style but felt that he leaned a bit more toward the avoidant style, noting that he is very independent and likes to rely on himself rather than seek out help. On reflection, he said that although his mother was quite warm and loving, she was very busy as a single working mother of four and was hands-off in her parenting. She encouraged the children's independence and sometimes pushed him away when he needed something she thought he could get himself. Rachel and Lewis laughed about people with an avoidant style having difficulty making commitments, noting that it took Lewis 5 years to propose marriage. The therapist asked Lewis about how he saw his style of interacting with the children, and he said that he understands Maria's style more easily and that helps him feel less rejected by her than Rachel did. On the other hand, he sometimes finds Carlos's dependency and clinginess annoying and frustrating, and he could see how his style is so different from Carlos's. The therapist noted that Carlos's style of seeking closeness with caregivers was previously adaptive because he had so many different placements in his life.

When the therapist suggested they reflect on how their own attachment styles might interact in their relationship, Rachel said that it really made sense now why Lewis would get upset when she asked for a ton of reassurance and wanted to constantly be close to him. Similarly, Lewis said he understood more clearly why Rachel has such a hard time when he wants to go off and have time for himself.

Child Session 1: *The Invisible String* and Child's Web of Connections

The goal of the first child session of Module 4 is to help the child feel more connected to the adoptive family. This is done through two activities. The first is reading *The Invisible String* (Karst, 2000), a book that helps children understand they are connected with their parents and others they love even if they aren't with that person. The second is the Child's Web of Connections. In this exercise, children are asked about who they go to for certain things, such as when they are sad. As the child sees the many connections with their parent, the child may begin to feel more bonded with them—they are doing for the child all of the things parents do for children.

Materials for this session include

- *The Invisible String* by Patrice Karst;
- Handout 40: Family Figures for Child's Web of Connections, cut out on card stock if possible or paper (colors available should represent the different ethnicities of family members);
- markers, glue, scissors, yarn, construction paper, etc., for decorating figures;
- yarn or string for making the connections (or markers can be used); and
- paper large enough to accommodate the family figures.

REVIEW MODULE 3 SESSION 2 CHILD HOMEWORK: USING PROBLEM-SOLVING STRATEGY

Begin the session by going over the homework about problem-solving strategies the child was asked to try out and record on Handout 22: Coping With My Problem from Module 1 Session 4. Ask the child for details about the problem worked on, how the chosen strategy was decided on, and how it worked for the problem. If the child did not do the homework or the strategy was unsuccessful, brainstorm what strategies might be effective. Be sure to praise the child's accomplishments.

READ *THE INVISIBLE STRING*

Read *The Invisible String* (Karst, 2000) to the child, a book in which the parent emphasizes how she remains connected to the children through an invisible string no matter where they are or how far apart they are separated. Encourage discussion by asking, "What did you think about the mom and kids being connected by an invisible string?" If it seems appropriate, follow up with questions such as "Do you feel connected to your parents?" "How does it feel when you are apart?" "Do you feel your parents are connected to you?" "What would help to be more connected?"

CHILD'S WEB OF CONNECTIONS

When children are placed into an adoptive home past infancy, they often struggle to feel that they can trust these new parents to care for and nurture them, especially if there has been trauma in their pasts. This activity helps children realize that their adoptive parents are providing them with some of the essential elements that make up positive parenting and help build mutual attachment. In this concrete way, the child can start to feel connected to the family and become more attached.

Say, "We're going to look at how you and your family are connected, using these figures and this string (or these markers that we are going to use like string) to connect." Present the child and adult figures to the child (cut out for young children or available to cut out for older children) from Handout 40: Family Figures for Child's Web of Connections, and ask the child to pick out ones to represent the adoptive family members. Allow the child to decorate the figures with the art materials available. There should be extra figures available in case the child names someone who is not a family member who fulfills a particular function for them.

When the figures have been decorated, encourage the child to place the child's figure in the center of the page and glue or tape it on. Give the child the yarn or string (or marker), and ask the child to use it to connect the child's figure with the family member who they go to for the following things. Glue or tape on these additional figures. If the child does not spontaneously connect them, encourage the child to make the connection between the child's figure and the appropriate family member's figure with the string, yarn, or marker. If the child wants to add another person, use the extra figures and help the child glue them onto the paper. Occasionally, a child will want to add a pet or object (e.g., blanket, stuffed animal, plant) as who they go to for something; allow the child to draw these on the paper and connect to the child's figure.

Ask the following questions:

- Who do you go to when you want to share something funny that happened?
- Who do you go to when you are scared?
- Who do you go to when you have a tummy ache?
- Who do you go to when you want to share a secret?

- Who do you go to when you need help with your homework?
- Who tucks you into bed at night?
- Who do you go to if you want to play a game?
- Who do you go to if you want a snack?
- Who makes you happy?
- Who do you go to if you are sad?
- Who do you tell when you are feeling proud about something?

Note: Different questions can be substituted if they are more appropriate for a particular child or family.

Discuss the Web of Connections with the child. Ask, "What did you notice about who you go to for what?" Responses may be things like, "I go to my mommy for almost everything," "I think I trust my dog and my sister the most," "I go to my Papa when I'm hurt or need something and I go to my Daddy when I want to have fun." If you notice something that the child has not spoken about, mention what you noticed and ask if the child thinks that is true. Before moving on to the homework discussion, make a statement summarizing what is evident in the child's Web of Connections, such as, "You feel connected to lots of your family members," "You find it hard to trust your parents and seem to be most connected to your sister and brother."

HOMEWORK: FAMILY ACTIVITY PHOTOS; PRACTICE DEEP BREATHING

Tell the child that in the next session, you are going to play a game about family activities. Ask children to bring in photos of them doing things with their family members. These can be photos of the family doing routine family activities, such as eating dinner or cooking together, as well as fun activities, such as playing games or watching a movie together, or pictures from vacations or visits to extended family members. If these aren't available, ask the child to take some pictures of things the family does together or to draw pictures of the family doing things together and bring them to the next session. Make sure to remind parents about the child bringing in pictures of the family doing things together (either photos or drawings).

Next, go over the deep breathing exercise. Ask the child in what situations deep breathing has been used, and praise the child if deep breathing has been used as a coping strategy. If the child has not been doing it, practice about 10 deep breaths with the child, with a reminder that deep breathing comes from the tummy and is slow (in to four counts; out to four counts), and talk about in what situations in the child's life it might come in handy. Ask the child to practice deep breathing at least two times during the week in hard situations and to record this on their Coping Strategies Log (Handout 24).

CASE EXAMPLE: THE SPRINGFIELDS

Carlos responded positively to reading *The Invisible String* (Karst, 2000). He reported that when he is scared, he doesn't feel that his parents will always be there with him. The therapist empathized and noted that he has had experiences where previous parents really weren't there for him and said, "It must be really hard to trust that your new mommy and daddy will really always be there for you." Carlos liked the image of the invisible string and said that it helped him to feel calm thinking that he was always attached to his parents. In doing the Web of Connections exercise, Carlos connected to Rachel for almost everything. He did say that he goes to his dad when he feels proud about something and that he goes to both his dad and to Maria to share something funny that happened. The therapist commented that Carlos seemed like he felt especially safe and connected to his adoptive mom and recognized all the things she did to help him and take care of him. He agreed and said that he also has strings to his dad, and of course, he's connected to Maria because "I've been with her my whole life."

In doing the Web of Connections exercise, Maria wanted figures for her two best friends and one of the friend's mothers as well. About halfway through the exercise, Maria shyly asked whether she could put her birth mother on her paper, because she really feels that there is an invisible string connecting her to her birth mother; the therapist said it was fine to add her. However, when answering the questions, Maria picked current people in her life to whom she goes for various things (friends to share secrets, share something funny that happened, go to when sad; Rachel when not feeling good, wanting a snack, shopping; Lewis for help with homework and tucking into bed; Carlos as well as friends for playing a game). The therapist noted that she had not said anything about her birth mother connections, and Maria said that her birth mother makes her feel happy, but she also noticed that her birth mother had not been around or available to meet her needs like her friends and her adoptive parents do because of her drug problems. Maria emphasized, however, that she still was connected by the invisible string even if her mom couldn't take care of her. The therapist wondered if Maria was feeling disloyal to her birth mom as she noted all the things that her current parents do to take care of her and love her, and Maria agreed with tears in her eyes. Maria said that she feels particularly guilty about her birth mother because she now sometimes has fun with Rachel and Lewis and feels safer and closer with them. The therapist acknowledged Maria's conflicted feelings and reiterated that it is possible and understandable to feel close to both birth and adoptive families.

Both children were encouraged to practice deep breathing over the week when they feel themselves getting anxious. Carlos said he would take some pictures of their family doing activities together to use in the next session, and Maria said she would draw some of the family activities if they didn't have photos.

Parent Session 2: Ways to Encourage Attachment

Goals of this session are to review the child-led family activity that they engaged in and troubleshoot any problems that may have arisen; to further facilitate attachment by checking in on the parents' perceptions of the child's attachment style; and to help parents develop strategies that encourage their children to believe and trust that the parents will be there for them on all levels to facilitate attachment development, taking into account their and the children's attachment styles. Further, the parents work at developing a new family ritual to help the child feel bonded with the family.

Materials for this session include Handout 41: Ways to Encourage Attachment (Fahlberg, 1991).

REVIEW SESSION 1 PARENT HOMEWORK: FAMILY ACTIVITY

Ask parents what child-led family activity they engaged in last week and elicit descriptions of what each family member did and felt about the activity. If the activity did not occur, discuss what barriers got in the way, and brainstorm with parents ways to overcome these obstacles. For example, if one child refused to do the activity, help parents develop plans that are acceptable to all children, including enticements if needed.

CHILD'S ATTACHMENT STYLE

As a follow-up to the last parent session and in response to the homework of continuing observation of the child's attachment style, ask the parents what they noticed this week about their child's attachment style and behaviors. Encourage them to describe a range of behaviors that may be involved in the child's attachment style, such as pushing away from parents when they are anxious and clinging to parents at certain times. For example, the parents might have noticed that their child is very fearful, even when the parent just goes upstairs, and seeks a great deal of reassurance (preoccupied style), or that the child almost always refuses help with any difficult task, insisting on solving the problem alone (avoidant style). With the aid of Handout 39: Attachment Styles, ask them to categorize the behaviors they noticed as indications of secure, preoccupied, avoidant, or disorganized attachment styles. Help parents develop empathy for the child's style by wondering how this style might have been necessary or adaptive in previous living situations and examining the behaviors through the lens of the child's past history. This can assist the parents in being most supportive in moving the child toward feeling secure in the family. Also query the parents about what they noticed about their own attachment style in relationship to the child's since the last session. Praise any insights they may have had.

Next, encourage the parents to talk about what feelings are elicited in them by the child's attachment style. For example, do they feel rejected if the child pushes away from the parents when anxious? Does a parent feel smothered if a child is clingy? Using the adoption lens is particularly useful here. For example, if the parent can understand that the child is frightened of being hurt again when pushing the parent away, they will feel less hurt and angry. Help parents respond in a manner that is likely to make the child feel more trusting toward them. For example, when a child pushes away out of fear, suggest that the parent might say,

> I would like to help you right now, but I can see that you want to handle this yourself. I understand that you couldn't trust some people in your past to be there for you, and I really want to help you. I'm here at any time if there's some way I can help.

Helping parents find specific words to convey their feelings to the child and/or role playing responses to attachment-related situations can aid parents in feeling less helpless and confused. The goal is for the parents to respond with understanding, caring, and empathy; if they can be supportive rather than rejecting, a step toward secure attachment has occurred.

METHODS TO FACILITATE ATTACHMENT

Give parents Handout 41: Ways to Encourage Attachment, adapted from Fahlberg (1991),[2] and go over the three major means for building attachment.

Responding to the arousal/relaxation cycle involves being there consistently to help calm and care for the child at times when they are upset, sick, and vulnerable and most in need of sensitive, nurturing caregiving. Help the parents understand that children are most receptive when emotionally aroused.

Initiating positive interactions involves providing affection and attention physically through hugs and kisses, etc., and verbally through saying "I love you" and other positive loving statements, as well as engaging in a variety of fun activities with the child and helping the child with homework, hobbies, etc. Emphasize accepting the children for who they are rather than who the parents want them to be to develop positive interactions (e.g., a child may not be a star at school but rather is fascinated by art). Many older adopted children do not excel at school and benefit from the parents making clear that they appreciate many things about the child, including traits such as being funny, loving, and hardworking.

Claiming behaviors involves making the child feel part of the family by visiting extended family, developing family rituals, and finding many ways of helping the child become incorporated as a family member. As a claiming behavior, suggest that parents take a family picture that includes all the family members, then enlarge it and hang the framed picture on the wall. Unlike a photo sitting on a table or ledge, hanging it on the wall indicates that this family constellation is permanent. Also help parents to identify characteristics that they and the child share, such as, "You're just like your father in that you both love spicy food," "Both you and your grandmother twirl your hair with your finger when you get nervous."

DEVELOPMENT OF NEW FAMILY RITUAL

In discussing claiming behaviors as ways to stimulate attachment, ask parents to think about a new family ritual, and give time to brainstorm ideas about the new ritual. Parents should consider a ritual that both they and the child will enjoy, such as sharing a special breakfast on Sundays at which everyone picks a special food from their culture or something they have been wanting to try, setting a family game night

---

[2]From *A Child's Journey Through Placement* (p. 62), by V. I. Fahlberg, 1991, Indianapolis, IN: Perspectives Press. Copyright 1991 by Vera Fahlberg. Adapted with permission.

or watching a movie on Friday evenings, going swimming or hiking as a family, cooking together, and having a family dance party. The ritual should occur on a regular ongoing basis so it becomes something the whole family looks forward to. Family rituals are a wonderful way for children to identify with their family. For example, the child can say to others, "Our family likes games and has game night every Sunday," or "Our family likes to hike and goes hiking every Saturday morning." Ask parents to work this week on developing the ritual together with the children so that each family member feels ownership.

Let the parents know that next time they will meet together with the children for a joint session. Ask the parents to think of things over the week that they like about the family and things they would like to change about the family to discuss in the upcoming family session.

HOMEWORK: FAMILY RITUAL; PRACTICE OF DE-ESCALATION

As mentioned previously, parents are asked to choose a family ritual in collaboration with the child and to use the ritual before the next session.

To reinforce the practice of de-escalation, ask the parents to notice whether there are identifiable times of high arousal for the child and how parents respond at these times. Remind them of the importance of reducing their intensity by being quieter and calmer in response to their child's increasing intensity to help de-escalate the situation and help the child reduce their arousal.

CASE EXAMPLE: THE SPRINGFIELDS

When asked what they had noticed about the children's attachment styles over the week, Rachel and Lewis agreed that Carlos had a preoccupied attachment style, noting that he had cried and carried on when they went out for a rare date night on Saturday night. He kept saying that he was worried something would happen and they wouldn't come home—there would be a car accident or terrorist attack or maybe they would get lost and not be able to find their house. Rachel noted that what was interesting was seeing their own attachment styles play out in how they handled Carlos's upset. Lewis said, "You'll be fine, see you later" and walked to the car. In contrast, Rachel felt herself getting very upset and anxious at Carlos's abandonment fears, provided tons of reassurance including agreeing to call Carlos when they got to the restaurant, and wanted to stay home and not go out. It was only because she knew that Lewis would be furious if they cancelled their plans that she finally was able to walk out the door.

The therapist noted that Rachel's own preoccupied style had given her empathy for Carlos but also gotten her so agitated that it was hard for her to provide the calm response that Carlos needed for his sense of security. She agreed and then asked Lewis why he wasn't bothered by Carlos's outburst. He said that he knew that Carlos was safe and didn't want him to be a "scaredy-cat." The therapist noted that feeling more secure himself, he didn't fall into the anxiety with Carlos, and because his style is toward the dismissive end of the spectrum, he focused on Carlos being safe and wanting him to take care of himself, therefore responding to his dependency cues by leaving.

The therapist brainstormed ideas to help Carlos with his separation anxiety when the parents go out, partly to encourage them to continue to take some time together as a couple. These included reassuring Carlos that the parents will be safe and will return; leaving him a favorite bedtime snack; and setting up a favorite movie for him to watch.

Rachel and Lewis were very thoughtful when looking over the Ways to Encourage Attachment (Handout 41). They discussed that Maria had recently been home ill. They were particularly aware that she allowed them to "take care of her" and be with her during times when she felt particularly ill, which was a change from how she was when she first entered their home. They discussed other ways that they could respond to the children to facilitate attachment. Lewis decided that when he reads to Carlos at night, he will sit on Carlos's bed with him rather than beside the bed in a chair. He believes that Carlos will respond warmly to the contact. The therapist praised Lewis for this idea, especially in light of his more dismissive style. Both felt that it is harder to move closer to Maria. Rachel discussed how much fun she had taking Maria to the mall and also noted the fun they had drawing together. She decided to take more of an interest in the fashion outfits that Maria was drawing. Parents were excited about the idea of a family portrait to hang on the wall in the living room and understood how it was a claiming behavior.

Both Rachel and Lewis voiced concerns about finding time for a new family ritual, and they agreed that it would need to be on weekends. Given the spread in age between Carlos and Maria, they thought it might be hard to find something both children would enjoy. The therapist jokingly wondered if it could be something related to food because the whole family likes to eat. Rachel and Lewis decided to have a family meeting to get input from the children about the new family ritual and committed to doing the new activity once before the next session.

Rachel and Lewis agreed to work on de-escalation during the coming week. The therapist returned to their example earlier about Carlos becoming so upset when they were going out to dinner and asked Rachel to think over what she did or might have done to de-escalate. She said over the next week, she would remind herself to remain calm, speak more softly, and move away when either of the kids was escalating in intensity. They both noted that the children respond better when they remain calm, and they agreed to support each other in remaining calm.

Child Session 2: Family Activities Cards and Matching Game

The purpose of this session is to continue to help the child bond with the family, emphasizing all the activities that the child engages in with their adoptive parents. As the child focuses on their family doing typical family activities, the child begins to develop a deeper sense of connection and belongingness with the adoptive family.

Materials for this session include

- Handout 42: Family Activities Cards (as well as blank cards);
- family photos or drawings that the child brings in; and
- paper, markers, pencils, or crayons for the child to make drawings of family activities if they have not brought photos or drawings from home.

REVIEW SESSION 1 CHILD HOMEWORK: FAMILY ACTIVITIES PHOTOS; PRACTICE DEEP BREATHING

Make sure that the child has brought in photos or drawings of doing activities with the family. If for some reason this has not occurred, provide paper and markers or pencils so the child can draw or write down the common family activities.

Review the practice of deep breathing and their Coping Strategies Log (Handout 24). As always, problem solve with the child when things have not gone well. If they have gone well, encourage the child to continue the practice.

FAMILY ACTIVITIES MATCHING GAME

Review the photos or drawings the child brought in of doing things with the family or pictures of things the family does together. Ask the child, "What are the 'every day' and 'special' things that you do in your family?" Ask if the child has pictures of these activities, and express interest and enthusiasm as the child shows them to you. If there are many pictures, say "It looks like your family does lots of things together."

Tell the child that you are going to play a matching game with the pictures. Use Family Activities Cards (Handout 42) to match to the pictures that the child brings in. If other activities are portrayed in the child's photos or drawings, either write down or ask the child to write down the portrayed family activity on a blank card. If there are Family Activities Cards for which the child does not have a picture, ask if this activity happens in their family too. If the child says "yes," ask if the child would like to draw a picture of their family doing the activity and provide paper, blank cards, and markers or crayons. If the child does not want to draw the activities, do not push the child to do so. Throughout the task, comment on the fun things the family is doing and/or ask for details about particular activities; for example, for "Read a book," you might ask what kind of books each family member likes or what the child's favorite book is, or for "Walk the dog," you might wonder what kind of dog it is and ask about the dog's name.

At the end of the activity, count with the child all the Family Activities Cards that the child endorses (whether or not there is a corresponding picture). Comment on how the child's family does lots and lots of activities together and how the parents do a lot of things to take care of the child and show how much they love the child.

Let the child know that next time there will be a family meeting with all family members. Ask the child to think of things over the week that they like about the family and things they would like to change about the family to discuss in the upcoming family session.

HOMEWORK: PRACTICE MUSCLE RELAXATION

Ask the child to practice muscle relaxation at least two times during the week and to record this on their Coping Strategies Log (Handout 24).

CASE EXAMPLE: THE SPRINGFIELDS

The children each brought family photos into their sessions. In these photos, the family was eating dinner together, doing homework, tidying the house, and playing a card game. Carlos had a picture of him and Lewis building with LEGOs, and Maria brought in some photos on her cell phone of her, her mom, and her best friend shopping at the mall, and also some of the fashion drawings that she and her mom had done together.

Carlos engaged in the Family Activities Matching Game and enjoyed matching his photos to the cards. He noticed that there was no card for LEGOs and asked the therapist to make one for him. Carlos said that he really wished the family had a dog, so then they could walk and bathe the dog, but Rachel has allergies to animals. The therapist reflected his desire to have a dog and his sadness that his mom's allergies made it unlikely the family could get one. Carlos said that he liked doing things with his family and felt like they were doing fun activities a lot.

Maria was happy to share her photos with the therapist, but thought the Family Activities Matching Game was childish and refused to play. The therapist improvised and simply asked Maria which of the activities listed on the cards did her family do. Maria answered these questions, reflecting a variety of family activities, but confided that she would much rather be with her friends than her family. The therapist acknowledged that most kids Maria's age cared a great deal about spending time with their friends. The therapist asked Maria to say which of the family activities she actually enjoyed and if there were any others she would like her family to do. When invited to draw these other activities, she enjoyed drawing her friends sleeping over and having breakfast with her family, and she also drew a family trip to Disneyland when she'd been allowed to bring along a friend. The therapist reflected that Maria seems to have found some ways to integrate her family *and* her friends. Maria revealed that when she was with her birth mother, she never wanted to bring friends over because her mother might be drunk or stoned and act weird and also the place was always messy and dirty; she was glad that her adoptive family is pretty normal and welcomed her friends into the home. The therapist noted that these things about her adoptive family seem to make her feel accepted and loved.

The therapist brought up to each child that in the next meeting they would be together as a family. The therapist encouraged both children to think of things they liked about their family and things they would like to change about the family to discuss in the upcoming family session.

Joint Session: Family Rituals/What I Like About Our Family/What I Would Like to Change About Our Family

The purpose of this joint session is to consolidate some of the gains the family has made in attachment during the past few sessions and to help the family focus on things they all like about being a family. An additional goal is to help family members talk about what they would like to change in their family in a positive and constructive manner.

Materials for this session include

- Family Activities Cards (Handout 42 from Child Session 2), plus several blank cards;
- blank paper for each family member and markers for drawing activity; and
- Handout 43: What I Like About Our Family/What I Would Like to Change About Our Family.

SHARING OF FAMILY ACTIVITIES CARDS

Have the Family Activities Cards that the child worked on in the last child session available for the family to look over (with their matching pictures if available). Ask each family member to say the activities they enjoy the most and what they like about doing the activity. Make summary statements that note family closeness and enjoyment such as, "Your family really enjoys doing things together," or "I can see how much you and your mom enjoy the outdoors." Provide the blank Family Activities Cards and ask family members to add at least one or two new family activities they agree that they would like to try. Make sure that every family member is heard in regard to what they would like to do together, including activities that the parents may not easily embrace; for example, if they are very health conscious, they may not want to all go out for donuts on Sunday mornings. Help the family negotiate any disagreements that arise and settle on an activity that they all would like to do. Stress some level of flexibility because it is not just about the child assimilating to what parents are comfortable and familiar doing—also integrate what the child might be comfortable and familiar doing and elements that are culturally relevant to the child.

FAMILY RITUAL FEEDBACK

Next, encourage the family to discuss how the new family ritual is going, making sure to get feedback from each family member. This is an opportunity to solidify the activity as part of the ongoing schedule if it is going well or adjust if not. For example, if two members of the family are athletic and bike riding is a family ritual, a third member who is less athletic may not enjoy it. In this case, perhaps the two members could continue the bike riding, but everyone could enjoy a movie or game night.

WHAT I LIKE ABOUT OUR FAMILY/WHAT I WOULD LIKE TO CHANGE ABOUT OUR FAMILY

For this activity, you will use Handout 43: What I Like About Our Family/What I Would Like to Change About Our Family to write down the family's answers, and give the sheets to them to take home. Ask each family member to say at least one thing that they really like about the family, and write down the responses on the handout. This generally leads to a warm discussion of what members like about being a part of this family. Say encouraging statements, such as "You all like being a part of this family" or "You and your dads really like doing some of the same things." If someone puts in a "but" or begins with any criticism, remind them that the focus is on the positive.

After everyone has talked about what they like about the family, ask each family member to say something they would like to change about their family. Set the stage for this by asking everyone to use "I" statements, saying what it is they would like to see change, rather than "you" statements that blame someone. For example, you might suggest that people say, "I would like each member of our family to follow the rules" rather than "X always ignores the rules." Encourage everyone to be constructive and talk about the future, not the past.

Help the family to discuss these issues and facilitate negotiation and compromise. For example, a child may wish the parents were into sports. If the parents are not athletically inclined, help lead a discussion on how the parents could encourage the child's interest in sports without being athletic. The parent could help organize the Little League team a child plays on, but not coach. Parents could attend all of the games. They could take the child to see a professional game in their favorite sport. Ensure that each family member is allowed a chance to talk, with no interruptions from other family members, and step in to defuse any major conflicts that arise to keep the discussion in a positive vein. At the end, give the handout to the family members to take home.

Note: If significant issues arise out of the discussion about what family members would like to change about the family that are not resolved, an additional family session may be added to process these issues.

DRAWINGS OF FAMILY MEMBERS AS ANIMALS (ADDITIONAL ACTIVITY IF THERE IS TIME)

If there is time left in the session after the previously mentioned activities, engage the family in the following drawing task. Ask each family member to draw the members of their family, including themselves, as the animals they remind them of. Ask them to do this independently, and tell them the drawings will be discussed only after everyone has finished drawing. Give up to 10 minutes time for the drawings and assure everyone that it is not a drawing contest. If a family member strongly objects to doing the drawing, ask the person to write down the animal for each family member.

Facilitate a discussion of the drawings, asking each person to tell what animal they drew and why the family member reminds them of that animal. If birth or foster family members or other previous caregivers are included in the drawings, comment on this, noting that the child can be part of the adopted family without needing to stop caring for or identifying with the birth or foster family or other beloved former caregiver. Ask about and reflect the person's feelings about being drawn as the particular animal. For example, if the father is drawn as a lion because he roars, ask how he feels that both his partner and son see him as a lion, and empathize with his response.

CASE EXAMPLE: THE SPRINGFIELDS

The therapist began the session by asking about how setting up a new family ritual had gone. The parents followed through with having a family meeting to come up with a new ritual. The therapist asked the children to give their impressions of the family meeting. Maria said, "It was boring and hard because Carlos didn't want to do anything I wanted and I didn't want to do anything he wanted because they were all babyish." Carlos objected and said he thought shopping at the mall together (Maria's first choice) would be the worst activity ever. The therapist asked what they decided on, and Lewis said they had decided to go out to brunch every Sunday morning. Rachel noted that she had wanted to make brunch on Sundays and have the family eat at home, but Maria said she specifically wanted Mexican food and that she was not eating bread of any kind, so because that eliminated all the things Carlos liked such as pancakes, pastries, and pan dulce, they had decided to have brunch out so everyone could order what they wanted. The therapist asked if they went out last Sunday, and Maria said they did and it was fun because they ate at a Mexican restaurant overlooking the lake and it was fun to watch the boats.

Next, the therapist asked members of the family to talk about what they like about their family. Carlos went first and said that he liked that his family goes to watch him play soccer at the park. He also likes that his parents help him with his homework and that they watch movies together. Rachel volunteered that she likes how much everyone helps to get dinner ready and the dishes done in the evening. She also likes that the family is starting to hug each other and say "I love you" when they go to bed. Lewis said he likes parenting the kids with Rachel, who is very involved with the kid's school. He also likes taking walks together and enjoys the warmth and honesty he feels is part of their family.

Maria struggled a bit more with this assignment and was reluctant at first to say anything she liked about the family. She finally admitted that she likes having dinner together with her family; it makes her feel better when she has had a bad day with her friends. With slight urging from the therapist based on the last child session, Maria said she likes that her parents welcomed her friends into their home, and she agrees with Carlos that it is fun watching movies with the family.

In saying what family members would like to change, Carlos wished his mom didn't work so she would be home more. He would rather come home with Rachel than attend the after-school program. Rachel responded that she also wished she could pick him up from school and spend afternoons with him, but that she had to work then. She said they could talk further about whether he might like to have a babysitter pick him up rather than stay in the after-school program. The therapist praised Rachel for hearing Carlos out and trying to come up with a solution. Maria went next and said she would like Rachel to give her more space and not ask so many questions about everything. Rachel asked if Maria could be more specific about when she asked too many questions, and Maria responded that Rachel starts out asking her a ton of questions early in the morning like what she wants for breakfast, whether she has after-school activities that day, where her homework is, etc., and it drives her nuts. After some facilitation by the therapist, Rachel agreed that she won't ask Maria any questions until 10 minutes before they leave for school.

When it was Rachel's turn, she said she would like the family more often to remind each other how much they care for one another by saying "I love you" or saying how special the other person is. The therapist suggested each person do that right then in the session, and after each person had done that, they all agreed it felt wonderful and decided to try to give an appreciation to one family member each day. Lewis said he would like to feel closer to Maria and wishes that she would talk with him more often. He perceived that she is much more likely to tell Rachel things than to tell him. Maria said that he is always reading the newspaper or watching sports on TV and besides he doesn't listen that well and just wants to tell her what she should do. The therapist wondered whether Maria would like her dad's undivided attention if she's talking to him. Maria replied that she would, and Lewis suggested that he would listen to her more carefully when they go on walks during child-led play. Maria said that would be good and requested that he just listen and not come up with silly quick solutions if she discusses something that is bothering her.

Module 5
Search for Identity and Transracial Adoption

7

The goal for parent sessions in Module 5 is to understand the complexities of identity development for adopted children in integrating a sense of self that involves birth family, adoptive family, and the child, particularly as the child approaches adolescence. Additionally, this module explores special issues of racial/ethnic identity and multicultural experience for children adopted transracially, either domestically or internationally, and helps transracial and same-sex families discuss and develop coping strategies for dealing with discrimination and microaggressions.

The goal for child sessions in Module 5 is to develop an integrated identity that encompasses the child's heritage and biological roots of the birth family, the heritage of the adopted family, and the child's own uniqueness. Additionally, for children adopted transracially or in same-sex families, coping strategies for dealing with discrimination and microaggressions are discussed.

Module 5 has two parent and two child sessions for all children ages 8 and over and for mature younger children. In addition, if it is a transracial adoption, there are two additional parent and two additional child sessions and one joint session. For other nontraditional families (e.g., same-sex couples, single parents, and grandparents) who may face discrimination and/or microaggressions, there is one additional parent session, one additional child session, and one joint session, as appropriate.

http://dx.doi.org/10.1037/0000096-008
Adoption-Specific Therapy: A Guide to Helping Adopted Children and Their Families Thrive, by J. Waterman, A. K. Langley, J. Miranda, and D. B. Riley

This module may require minor modifications if the child has recently been placed in a family. However, if the child has been with the family for 6 months, the module may be appropriate as stated. The child activities involving the Game of Discovery are most appropriate for children 8 years and older but have successfully been carried out with children as young as 6 years old, depending on their maturity level. Even if the child is too young to participate in the Game of Discovery, it is important to have at least one session in this module with the parents. If the child does not seem mature enough for the Game of Discovery, the young child and child's therapist can have a play session, review concepts, etc. *Even if the child is young and is not in a transracial or same-sex family, the information from Child Session 2 about termination needs to be brought up and discussed.*

Parent Session 1: Understanding Adopted Children's Search for Identity

The goal of Parent Session 1 is to discuss the complexities that adopted children face in developing an integrated sense of self that both honors their birth heritage and incorporates their adoptive family's contributions. Additionally, questions children often ask about their background are incorporated here if not fully discussed in Module 2.

Materials for this session include

- paper and markers or pens,
- Handout 44: Common Children's Questions About Identity, and
- a mirror with a reflective surface on one side and a nonreflective surface on the other side.

REVIEW PROBLEM AREAS AND PROGRESS

Check with the parent(s) about progress toward the three problems they identified during their first session. Have parents rate the current status of these problems, as they do in the first session of each module. Review the relationship between the problem area and the current adoption-specific behavioral plan, and revise the behavioral plan as needed.

REVIEW MODULE 4 SESSION 2 PARENT HOMEWORK: FAMILY RITUAL; PRACTICE OF DE-ESCALATION

Ask for feedback about how implementing the family ritual discussed in the joint session went. If it went well, praise the parents and plan any follow-up or modification needed. If it did not go well, brainstorm with parents about how to overcome any barriers that arose.

Ask the parents under what circumstances they practiced de-escalation since the last session. Empathize with problems that may have arisen, and reiterate that de-escalation means becoming calmer, softer, and less intense as the child's agitation and intensity increases to help the child regulate strong emotions. Inquire whether there were situations with the child where they wished they had used de-escalation and role play how that might have played out.

PSYCHOEDUCATION ABOUT SENSE OF SELF AND IDENTITY DEVELOPMENT IN ADOPTION

Ask parents to think about the child's sense of self, and give them a few minutes to think about it. What would the child list as defining characteristics? Write down the characteristics that the parents mention. Next, query about how their child's sense of self is impacted by the adoption. For example, "How do you think the adoption plays into (child's name) sense of self, how she sees herself?" Note that although the developmental task of identity formation is challenging for all children and adolescents, it is more complex for those who are adopted, and especially complex for those who are adopted transracially. Help parents recognize that not having all pieces of the child's history or integrating difficult information can complicate this key developmental task, and empathize with their feelings about missing or painful information. Note that while children may only occasionally bring up thoughts about their birth family with them, we know that most children think about their birth family very frequently, often daily. Children may worry that these feelings would hurt their adoptive parents and they choose to protect parents from their divided loyalties. Confirm that many thoughts and questions come up for adopted children in adolescence as they work to form a coherent identity, and ask parents how they think this process may play out for their child.

Give parents Handout 44: Common Children's Questions About Identity. Ask parents what questions have arisen, or they think may arise, and discuss how they would answer them. Some of these questions may have been discussed in Module 2, Developmental Understanding of the Adoption Experience; acknowledge and refer back to the Questions For My Parents list (Handout 31) that the child developed if appropriate.

Affirm that children often question and reject their parents during adolescence, and discuss how this may be more sensitive for parents of adopted children. For adoptees, this task of identity development may involve taking on aspects of the birth family that may be painful for the adopted family. For example, the child might want to be called Juan instead of John if the birth family is Latino (either living here or another country) or may choose to use the birth family surname as a middle name. Sometimes an adolescent at this time may try to contact the birth family through social media. Empathize with how "normal" though difficult this would be, and stress the continued need to be supportive and nonrejecting as the child struggles with identity formation.

MIRROR EXERCISE (FOR FAMILIES WHERE THE CHILD DOES NOT KNOW OR REMEMBER THE BIRTH PARENTS)

Use this exercise if the child never knew any birth family members or does not remember anything about the birth parents; this happens frequently with international adoptions and may also occur for children adopted as infants. Use a mirror that is reflective on one side and blank or nonreflective on the other. Give the parents the mirror, and ask them to talk about what resemblances they see to their family members when they look in the mirror. Reflect and validate their responses. Then ask them to turn the mirror over (to the nonreflective surface). Note that this is what adoptees see when they look in a mirror if they have had no or minimal contact with their birth family—there is no sense of where their looks (or personality) come from. Elicit reactions from the parents to seeing the blank side in relation to their child's sense of identity, and pull for empathy about what that would feel like for the child.

HOMEWORK: REVIEW AND PRACTICE OF PRAISE AND ENCOURAGEMENT

Note that the recurrent practice for this session is praise and encouragement. Remind parents to use positive strategies of praise, positive attention, encouragement, and reward. Reinforce the goal of providing eight praises for each criticism or correction.

CASE EXAMPLE: THE SPRINGFIELDS

After checking on their progress with the three primary problems as is done at the beginning of each module, the therapist asked what situations had occurred since the last session that required de-escalation. Lewis brought up a situation with Rachel where he wished Rachel had used de-escalation; she asked Maria to put her dirty clothes downstairs in the laundry basket so Rachel could wash them. Maria grabbed the clothes, threw them over the railing into the living room (which was not where the laundry basket was), and slammed her door so hard the house rattled. This enraged Rachel, who went into Maria's room and screamed at her about how she never helped out family members and was totally selfish. As Maria started to defend herself, Rachel kicked over the wastebasket, left the room, and then *she* slammed the door. After giving Lewis a dirty look for bringing this up, and noting that he wasn't very good at de-escalation either, Rachel acknowledged that she was ashamed of her behavior but felt very provoked by Maria. The therapist asked her and Lewis how they would handle it now if a similar situation occurred. Rachel said she would do nothing at first and give both her and Maria a chance to calm down and then ask her to pick up the clothes and put them in the laundry basket in a gentle manner. She said she would try hard to get calmer and quieter as Maria got louder and more dysregulated. Lewis asked how likely was it that Rachel could actually do this, and they both laughed and acknowledged it would be really hard for Rachel, but she would try.

The therapist then focused on Maria and asked what the parents thought were some of her defining characteristics that made up her sense of self. Rachel said she was artistic, had great fashion sense, had lovely hair, and was physically fit. Lewis added that she probably would think her loyalty to her friends was something that defined her, along with poetry-writing skills, and maybe how quick she was to get angry. The therapist wrote these down and then asked the parents how they thought Maria's sense of self and identity was affected by the adoption. As they looked over the list of characteristics, Lewis seemed really struck by something. When asked what he was reacting to, he noticed they hadn't mentioned her identity as a Latina on their list, even though this was highly important to Maria. The therapist acknowledged the importance of this insight and helped the parents explore ways in which they could continue to recognize the importance of Maria's Latina identity to her sense of self and further encourage this as a positive aspect of who she is.

After the therapist presented Handout 44: Common Children's Questions About Identity to the parents, Rachel noted that many of the questions had come up in Module 2; Maria had been very interested in information about her birth father, about which nothing is known. She remembered that she had promised Maria to contact the social worker to see if it might be possible to find out anything at all about him and felt guilty she had not pursued the information. Lewis said that they thought Maria already knew the answers to the questions on the handout that could be found out, which, of course, left lots of unanswered questions about her birth father. The therapist noted how sad it must be for Maria not to know anything about him.

The therapist was unsure about whether to do the mirror exercise. Of course, Maria knew her mother well, and therefore when looking in the mirror, she would have seen similarities with her mother. However, there would be nothing that Maria could identify with from her birth father. After some internal debate, the therapist decided to go ahead and do the mirror exercise. When they looked in the mirror, both parents spontaneously mentioned characteristics they had gotten from both sides of their family. When they turned the mirror over and thought about what Maria might see, Rachel noted that from the picture of the birth mother that Maria has and treasures, it seemed they shared hair type and face shape. As the therapist started to ask about the other side of Maria's birth family, Lewis interrupted to say sadly, "But she'll never know what she had in common with her birth father." The therapist reflected on his melancholy tone and wondered if he might have felt similarly at Maria's age, given that his father had left the family when he was very young and did not reenter the children's lives until he was 17. Lewis said he needed to think about that. The therapist then asked what physical characteristics Maria might think she got from her birth father, that is, that she did not have in common with her birth mother. Rachel said that according to Maria, she is already taller than her mother was, and her skin tone is considerably darker than what she could see from the picture. The therapist said that this week's session with Maria would explore what she feels she got from her birth family, her adoptive family, and herself uniquely, and reminded the parents that Carlos was too young for the child session.

Child Session 1: Identity Exploration Through Game of Discovery

The goal of Module 5 Session 1 Child is to help children develop an integrated sense of identity that includes contributions from birth family, adoptive family, and their own uniqueness.

Materials for this session include the following:

- Game of Discovery cards (in toolkit—or use attributes listed below to make cards for Game of Discovery). Make sure to include some blank cards.
- If not using the toolkit, make banners or column markers saying *Birth Family, Adoptive Family*, and *Me Myself and I.*

REVIEW MODULE 4 SESSION 2 CHILD HOMEWORK: PRACTICE MUSCLE RELAXATION

Review practice of muscle relaxation as previously discussed, eliciting times during the week when the child used it, and encourage the child to continue using the Coping Strategies Log.

IDENTITY DEVELOPMENT IN ADOPTED CHILDREN

The task of identity formation involves moving toward a stable sense of self and is a major task of adolescence. Developing one's identity involves integrating a variety of perspectives that includes accepting and incorporating the positive personality and cognitive contributions of the family while asserting differences from them. Adopted children often have a more complex road to identity formation because they generally take an extra step and factor in the heritage of both birth and adoptive families. Adopted children must figure how they are like and different from two families, even though they may have limited or no knowledge of their birth family. The search for identity for adopted children may also involve integration of the different racial/ethnic cultures of their birth and adoptive families.

EXPLORING IDENTITY THROUGH THE GAME OF DISCOVERY

The Game of Discovery, developed at the Center for Adoption Support and Education (C.A.S.E.), is an interactive exercise meant for children over 8 years of age; however, we find that mature children 6 years and older can successfully use it. The purpose of the Game of Discovery is to help children understand that their identity is based on characteristics from their birth family, adoptive parents, and self. The cards include physical characteristics such as eye color, height, and skin tone; personality characteristics such as kindness, quick temper, and sense of humor; skill sets such as athletic ability and artistic ability; and cognitive competence such as intelligence. Use cards from the toolkit or make your own cards with the following attributes on them, and feel free to add others that may be appropriate. Make sure to have some blank cards in case the child wants to add attributes that are not written on the cards. Here are some suggested attributes:

- race or ethnicity
- kindness
- birthday
- values
- courage
- skin color
- hair color
- love
- intelligence
- sense of humor
- eye color
- athletic ability
- religion
- height
- self-esteem
- drawing ability
- good grades
- musical ability

Say something like,

> Today we are going to play the Game of Discovery to find out more about how you think about yourself. Each of these cards has a personal characteristic on it that some people identify with (for younger children: Each of these cards has something that describes people). Over here on this felt board, we have three different spots, one for your birth family, one for your adoptive family, and one for you yourself. We will sort the cards into which things you think you get from your birth family, which things you get from your adoptive family, and which things you think are unique and special to you and not related to either family.

If the child does not know much about their birth family, you can ask the child to guess what things they might have gotten from their birth family. If the child does not seem to understand that physical characteristics are likely to come from the birth family, you may note that usually things like hair color, skin color, and how tall a person is come from their birth family. However, if children have the same color skin or hair or eyes as their adoptive family and see that as a commonality, you do not need to correct this. Hand the child the attribute cards one at a time, mixed up with regard to type of attribute, and assist the child with the sorting process by asking questions if needed to help the child decide which spot is best for that attribute (birth family, adoptive family, me myself and I). For younger children, you may need to read the attribute as you hand the card to the child.

After children have finished sorting the cards, including adding any extra ones, ask what they notice as they look over the categories of what they got from their birth family and adoptive family, and what is unique and special to them alone. Summarize the chart and reflect the child's feelings. For example, you might say something about noticing that they seem to get their looks from the birth parents, their interests from their adoptive parents, and their personality from their own self. If the chart is very lopsided, note, for example, "You feel like you got most of the things that define you from your birth family and your own uniqueness, and not much from your adoptive family." Say that you'll be working further on sense of self in the next session, so the child can add other things if desired.

HOMEWORK: PRACTICE CALMING IMAGE

Ask the child to remind you of the calming image they are using, and suggest they practice using this image at least two times during the week when angry, sad, or worried and record this on the Coping Strategies Log (Handout 24).

CASE EXAMPLE: THE SPRINGFIELDS

The therapist introduced the Game of Discovery to Maria, who seemed intrigued with it, and laid out the column markers for Adoptive Family, Birth Family, and Me Myself and I. The first card the therapist presented was *eye color*, and Maria quickly put that on the Birth Family side, saying her eyes and her hair were exactly the same as her birth mother. Next the therapist presented *intelligence*, which she put under the Myself category after pondering whether that came from her birth family or herself. As the game played out, she put *hair color, height, race/ethnicity, artistic ability,* and *skin color* in the Birth Family category and added *scatterbrained.* Under Me Myself and I, she put *kindness, sense of humor, loyalty,* and added *good friend* and *fashion design.* Under Adoptive Family, she put *cooking* and *athletic ability.* When asked to look at her chart and reflect on what she saw, Maria noted that she got a lot more from her birth family than her adoptive family, saying that she still felt more connected to her birth family than her adoptive family, though they were "growing on her." She especially liked the characteristics she saw as belonging to Me Myself and I.

The therapist decided that Carlos was not old enough or mature enough for this activity and instead asked him to draw a picture of his adoptive family and then of his birth family. Carlos reminded the therapist that he did not like to draw, and the therapist encouraged him just to use stick figures if he wanted. He begrudgingly drew the pictures. The adoptive family was drawn playing checkers together, with the checker board drawn carefully and all family members around it, including the stick figure dog (the family had found a hypoallergenic breed that they could afford and are all enjoying having her around despite her puppy destructiveness, especially Carlos who had wanted a dog since he came to live with the Springfields). In contrast, the birth family were just standing there, him, Maria and birth mom. The therapist reflected that Carlos seemed more connected to his adoptive family, and he readily agreed. The therapist and Carlos then played checkers at his request for the few minutes that remained of the session.

Parent Session 2: Game of Discovery/ Positive Similarities With Birth Family

In Module 5 Session 2 Parent, the adoptive parents examine similarities the child has with the birth parents and with themselves, as well as the child's own unique attributes, with an emphasis on noting positive similarities between the birth family and the child.

Materials for this session include

- Game of Discovery cards and banners for Birth Family, Adoptive Family, and Me Myself and I (from Child Session 1); and
- Handout 45: My Child's Identity.

REVIEW SESSION 1 PARENT HOMEWORK: REVIEW AND PRACTICE OF PRAISE AND ENCOURAGEMENT

Review homework about use of positive strategies of praise, positive attention, encouragement, and reward. Check in on goal of providing eight praises for each criticism or correction. If the parents are still finding it hard to use positive strategies, try to understand with them why it is difficult and brainstorm ways to bring more praise and encouragement into the relationship with the child.

THE GAME OF DISCOVERY

Introduce the cards in the Game of Discovery, developed at C.A.S.E. described in the Module 5 Session 1 Child, noting that their child played the Game of Discovery in their last session. The Game of Discovery helps children understand that their identity is based on characteristics from their birth family, their adoptive parents, and themselves uniquely. The cards include physical characteristics such as eye color, height and skin tone, personality characteristics such as kindness and sense of humor, skill sets such as athletic ability and artistic ability, and cognitive competencies such as intelligence. See attributes for Game of Discovery cards in Child Session 1 for a list of suggested attributes, and feel free to add others that may be appropriate. The cards used here are the same as in Child Session 1, so there is no need to make another set. Be sure to have some blank cards available in case the parent wants to add attributes that are not written on the cards.

Ask parents to sort the cards describing the child's attributes into those from birth family and adoptive family, and those that are the child's own unique attributes. They then record these attributes on Handout 45: My Child's Identity. After parents have finished writing down the attributes, ask what they notice as they look over the categories of what they perceive the child got from birth family and adoptive family, and what is personally unique and special. Summarize the chart and reflect the parents' feelings. For example, if you notice that the parents think the child got almost all their attributes from the birth family, wonder what that feels like to the adoptive parents, and then work with them to look for their similarities with the child. Or you might summarize the chart with a statement such as, "It looks like you think (child's name) physical characteristics came from his birth parents, his values and personality style from you, while his interests and hobbies are unique to him."

RECOGNIZING AND HONORING CHILD'S POSITIVE SIMILARITIES WITH BIRTH FAMILY

For children to feel good about themselves, they need to feel that they have positive attributes that are connected to their families. In addition to integrating positive information from both birth and adoptive families, adopted children often have to deal with negative information they may have about their family. Particularly if birth parents have had issues such as a criminal history, drug or alcohol addiction, mental illness, etc., it is really important that the child can identify with something positive about them to develop a positive sense of self. To facilitate adoptive parents being able to help children feel positive about attributes shared with birth parents, you may need to process their own feelings about the birth parents and help them build empathy for the birth parent's struggles and background. If the adoptive parents see the birth parents as completely bad and worthless, it will be hard for them to help the children see positive similarities with birth families. We certainly do not want parents to make statements to the children such as "You stole some candy from your friend; you're a thief just like your birth mother." Instead we want to help parents recognize that stealing food may have been adaptive when the family was homeless and starving and develop a behavioral plan that is responsive to their past history.

Help parents learn to comment on known positive similarities of the child with the birth parents (e.g., "You have beautiful brown eyes like your birth mother," "Your birth dad was an artist, and I bet that's why you are so great at drawing"). If parents have trouble coming up with positive attributes, suggest that they go back through their adoption records or even contact the adoption agency or social worker because of the importance of being able to share something positive about birth parents.

If very little is known about the birth parents, adoptive parents can still comment on what they *think* is a positive similarity. This happens most often when the child has a skill or trait that the adoptive family does not have. For example, if the child is tall and plays basketball and the adoptive parents are short, the parent might comment, "I'm sure glad that you got your height from your birth parents because it really helps you on the court," or "You must have gotten your patience from your birth family because I certainly have a short fuse." Ask parents to role play sharing these known or possible similarities with their child in session.

BEGINNING DISCUSSION OF TERMINATION

Particularly for children who have had disrupted attachments, many moves, etc., it is important to start planning for termination early. At the end of this session, mention approximately how many sessions are left, and elicit feelings of parents about that.

Termination is often a major issue for children being adopted from foster care. Many of the endings of relationships with previous caregivers may have been abrupt, without explanation to the child, or involve traumas such as physical or sexual abuse, domestic violence, or abandonment. Let parents know that it is very important to prepare the child ahead of time for the end of adoption-specific therapy (ADAPT).

Beginning in this session, count down the sessions so that both parents and child know exactly how many are left. Make the following points with parents (and child):

1. This ending is different from some of the ones that have happened before for the child. It is planned; it will be marked by a celebration at the end, and it is the result of positive changes for the child and family.
2. The ending may bring up thoughts or memories of past losses along with strong feelings, so encourage parents to empathize with the feelings such as sadness, anger, and ambivalence that may arise for the child and warn that they may also experience strong feelings.
3. Let parents know that the child will have a say in what happens in the last session, in terms of activities and food. Because many of the traumatic endings

gave the child no choice, note how important it will be to give the child some control in this session.

4. Help parents see that the child's reactions to the end of the intervention make sense when seen through the lens of the child's history.

Termination should frequently be mentioned and processed in the upcoming sessions.

HOMEWORK: SHARING POSITIVE SIMILARITIES; REVIEW AND PRACTICE OF PRETEACHING

Ask parents to share at least one positive similarity to a birth parent and at least one positive similarity to an adoptive parent with the child over the next week.

Make sure that parents are continuing with the Adoption-Specific Behavior Record (Handout 8) and review and update the current plan they are implementing. Additionally, review the concept of preteaching; role play if needed to remind parents or deal with issues that have arisen, and ask parents to make sure to use preteaching at least twice over the week. It is helpful to have them think of a situation or two in the near future in which preteaching would be useful.

CASE EXAMPLE: THE SPRINGFIELDS

In reviewing the use of praise and encouragement at the beginning of the session, Lewis reported that it had been very difficult to be positive with Maria this week because Carlos told them he saw Maria take money from Rachel's purse (as they had earlier suspected). When the parents noted that some money was missing from Rachel's purse and wondered if Maria knew anything about it, Maria vehemently denied taking the money, yelling that the parents don't trust her. When Lewis said that Carlos saw her take the money, she went after Carlos (who looked very scared) and started screaming at him about what a liar he was and how he just wanted to get her in trouble. Although the parents were pretty sure that Maria had taken the money, they weren't positive which child was lying. However, they decided to ground her for a week, causing her to miss her friend's birthday party that included shopping and a movie at the mall. Maria was inconsolable about not being able to go to the party and cried so much for several evenings that the parents were really worried. The therapist empathized about how painful the incident had been for all of them and wondered if the parents were aware of anything in Maria's past that might relate or give them insight into how such an action might have been adaptive in her previous life. Although neither parent could think of anything specifically, Rachel noted that Maria had certainly needed to steal food when with her birth mom so she and Carlos could eat when their mom was shooting up and not available, but she was puzzled because now there is always food around and Maria knows that.

Lewis wondered if maybe she was so upset about not going to the party because she never really had friends before. Maria had mentioned how happy she was to bring friends to her house now because she never had friends over when living with her birth mother because of the state of her mother and the motel room, and both her aunt and the first foster family were very strict and didn't allow her to go to friends' houses or have them come over to their house. The therapist praised their careful reflections. Lewis continued to be enraged that Maria had lied to them repeatedly about taking the money, and the therapist gently reminded him of how children in neglectful and abusive situations often lie because the environment is unpredictable and admitting a wrongdoing could have significant negative consequences, including possible violence. In referencing Handout 20: Behavioral Strategies for Common Difficult Child Behaviors Using Adoption-Specific Lens from Module 1, the therapist and parents went over the importance of looking at both the stealing and the lying as behaviors that were adaptive at an earlier time. They also looked over the strategies for lying and realized they had tried to catch Maria in a lie; they decided they would focus on making sure to praise her when she told the truth. Rachel and Lewis agreed to continue to think about what they could glean about this upsetting incident by using an adoption-specific trauma lens.

The therapist then brought out the Game of Discovery cards, and they continued exploring the children's sense of identity by sorting the cards into attributes from the birth family, adoptive family, and the child uniquely. The parents thought back to what they had talked about regarding Maria last week, and put *hair color, eye color, skin color, ethnicity,* and *height* into the Birth Parent category, and Lewis wanted to add *stealing,* given what had just occurred, so he wrote it on one of the blank cards. Rachel thought Maria's *fashion sense, loyalty to friends, artistic ability,* and *sense of humor* were unique to herself (using a blank card for *fashion sense*). They had more difficulty thinking of things that might come from them as parents, and finally chose *values* and *kindness,* noting that they hope Maria is learning these qualities from being in their family. In reflecting on their answers, Rachel noted sadly that she thinks Maria's attributes are mostly from her birth mother, with many also unique to her, and very little from her adoptive parents at this point in time. The therapist empathized with Rachel's feelings of sadness.

For Carlos, parents chose the same cards as for Maria for the Birth Parent category. Lewis put *athletic ability* as coming from the adoptive parents, since he is coaching Carlos's soccer team and enjoys playing sports with him at the park. Rachel named *generosity* as something Carlos got from her and Lewis; she wanted to add *sense of security* as something he is getting from the adoptive family and wrote that attribute on a blank card. For what is unique to Carlos himself, they chose *shyness, intelligence,* and *kindness.* In reflecting on their answers for Carlos, Rachel felt that they are having a bigger influence on him than on Maria.

When asked about positive similarities with the birth parents, Rachel and Lewis were stumped at first. They had very little information to go on, having never met any of the children's parents, and with Maria's father being unknown. Lewis noted that he thought maybe Maria got her athletic ability from her birth father because she was apparently a star soccer player when in her previous foster home prior to placement in their home. Rachel wondered if her birth mother was a fashionista, because Maria had such a great sense of style. Lewis noted that they knew a lot more about the birth mother's negative qualities than about any positive ones.

The parents decided to contact the previous foster mother as well as the social worker to see if they could find out any information about Carlos's birth father, who had been involved with him up to about the age of 5, to help them determine what positive similarities Carlos might have with his birth father. For the assignment of mentioning something that each child had in common with a birth parent in the next week, Lewis decided that he would note to Maria that her birth father must have been very athletic because she is such a good soccer player, and Rachel was going to talk about Maria's fashion sense maybe coming from her birth mother, especially because Rachel feels that she herself is not stylish at all. They hoped to get some information from the foster mother or social worker to help with talking to Carlos about similarities with birth parents, but noted that maybe Carlos's love of animals was inherited from one of his birth parents, and Rachel remembered that Maria had said that Carlos's beautiful eyes and long eyelashes were just like their birth mother's.

Child Session 2: My Self Chart

In the second child session of Module 5, the child reviews the results from the Game of Discovery and makes an integrated My Self chart, noting contributions of birth family, adoptive family, and what is unique to the child, to further explore the child's sense of identity.

Materials for this session include

- notes or sorted cards from the Game of Discovery or photo of child's completed Game of Discovery board, and
- Handout 46: My Self Chart (to be filled out with the child).

REVIEW SESSION 1 CHILD HOMEWORK: PRACTICE CALMING IMAGE

Review the usage of child's calming image and their Coping Strategies Log (Handout 24). If the child has not used the calming image, go over the details of the image again and ask the child to identify a good situation for using it over the next week.

REVIEW DISCOVERY GAME RESULTS

Remind the child that their sense of identity develops from their heritage and their experience. Say something like, "Last session, we played the Game of Discovery and identified things about you that are like your adoptive parents and some things that are like your birth parents and some things that are just from you yourself. Let's look at them again." Either have the child examine the photo taken of the Game of Discovery board last session or go through the actual Game of

Discovery cards that the child sorted into Adoptive Parents, Birth Parents, and Me Myself and I.

MY SELF CHART

Ask the child to fill out the My Self Chart (Handout 46) based on the results of the Game of Discovery, detailing similarities of the child with adoptive and birth families, as well as what is unique about the child. Note that there may be things the child knows came from the birth parents, such as physical characteristics or specific interests or talents if the child has continued contact with them or if the child remembers what the birth parents looked like. There may also be things that the child thinks or suspects came from the birth parents if they have not had contact with the birth parents or such contact was long ago. For example, the child may think their physical or racial characteristics must have come from their birth parents, or they may think that their baseball skills must be due to athletic prowess in their birth family because their adoptive parents are complete klutzes who couldn't make a hit no matter how easy the pitch.

Try to help the children who know little about their birth parents come up with possible positive similarities with their birth family. You might note that the child has beautiful skin and suggest that maybe one of the birth parents also had lovely skin, or you might note how artistic the child is and comment about how that talent must be from the birth family because when the adoptive parents drew their calming images in Module 1, it was clear that they were not Picasso.

If children come up with negative similarities with their birth or adoptive families (e.g., I am too fat like my birth mom; I stole candy from a store so I guess I'm a thief like my dad), accept and allow the child to put it in their My Self chart. However, note that just because the birth family is a particular way does not mean that the child will necessarily be like that parent in that way. It is particularly important for children whose parents have known difficult histories, such as being in prison, alcohol/drug addiction, domestic violence, child abuse, prostitution, etc., to recognize that they can make different choices for themselves.

DISCUSSION OF TERMINATION

Because of the child's history of past losses and sometimes traumatic endings to relationships, it is important to fully process termination and to allow enough time to do so. Near the end of this session, bring up the number of sessions that are left, and process the child's feelings about this. Note that the child may have a variety of feelings about ending therapy, adding that you and the child will be talking more about termination over the next few weeks. Mention that during the last session, you will do some goodbye activities and then have a party with the parents that will include food and activities the child chooses. Refer to Parent Session 2 in this module for more information on bringing up termination.

HOMEWORK: SHARE MY SELF CHART WITH PARENTS; PRACTICE PROBLEM-SOLVING STRATEGY

Ask the child to share the My Self chart with parents. Elicit what the child feels about sharing the chart, empathize with these feelings, and brainstorm possible solutions for the problems the child may bring up. Let the child know that the parents have done the Game of Discovery in their session so they have also been thinking about the child's identity. If children are concerned their parents will be angry that they feel they share many positive attributes from their birth parents, reflect these feelings and talk about divided loyalties. Note that in earlier sessions of ADAPT, parents were helped to understand the importance of children's ties to their birth family. Ask the child if it would help to invite the parents in at the end of the session so you can help with discussion of the My Self chart or to set up an additional family session to share the My Self chart.

Review problem-solving strategies by going over Kids' Coping Solutions (Handout 21 from Module 1, Session 4). Develop a plan to deal with a current problem the child is experiencing, and role play various solutions as needed. Ask the child to record responses on Handout 22: Coping With My Problem from Module 1 Session 4.

CASE EXAMPLE: THE SPRINGFIELDS

When Maria came into the session, she looked very upset, avoiding eye contact with the therapist and throwing her backpack forcefully onto the ground. The therapist asked what was wrong, and Maria answered sullenly, "Nothing." The therapist started to review the homework about using the calming image and noted that maybe now might be a good time to use it. Maria did not respond. The therapist started to do a bit of guided imagery with Maria's calming image (magnolia trees and flowers with birds flying around, a place she would go to calm down when she and her birth mother had arguments), and Maria burst into tears. She said, "That reminds me of my birth mom—I miss her so much and wish I could be with her." The therapist reflected her feelings of loss, and wondered again what was upsetting Maria so much today. She then told the therapist that her parents grounded her and so she was going to miss her best friend's birthday party at the mall on Saturday. As the therapist began exploring her feelings, Maria sobbed harder and said that she had never had a best friend before and was devastated to miss her party. The therapist reflected that she remembered Maria telling her how pleased she had been about Rachel and Lewis including her friends in family activities, so this must have been really painful for them to prevent contact with her friend at such an important time as her birthday.

The therapist then wondered what led the parents to give her such a painful consequence, and Maria said they thought she stole money from Rachel and then lied to them about it. The therapist was quiet, and after a bit, Maria admitted that she had taken the money. She had wanted to take her best friend and the other girls at the party to her friend's favorite restaurant. Maria knew that paying for seven girls would be expensive and her parents would not have given her the money, but getting special food for her friend was so important to her. The therapist empathized with

Maria's desire and wondered if it might have something to do with all the times she and Carlos had gone hungry; feeding her friend would be both something special in nurturing her and also would solidify the friendship. Through tears, Maria talked about how Rachel and Lewis would never understand her, and she lamented the fact that she had stolen the money, lied and gotten in trouble for nothing, because now not only could she not take all the girls out to eat, but she could not even go to the party! The therapist and Maria discussed whether Maria thought the girl would be friends with her only if she gave her things and whether Maria thought she herself was someone worthy of friendship and love. Because of all the loss and rejection Maria has had, she wondered if she was lovable and a good person.

With this lead-in, the therapist brought out the My Self chart, and suggested that they look back at what she had said last week in the Game of Discovery about where her traits come from. Under "Things I know I got from birth parents," Maria listed *eye color, hair color, skin color* and *race/ethnicity* and *being scatterbrained* (which she was sure she got from her mother). Under "Things I think I got from birth parents," she put *height* and *artistic ability*, thinking she must have gotten these things from her birth parents. She was sad that she knew nothing about her birth father, but she imagined him as pretty tall, good looking, and possibly an artist, like her. She wistfully wondered if she would ever know who her father was. The therapist empathized with how it must feel like there's a missing piece of her puzzle and noted that maybe she got her beautiful smile from him. Under "Things I got from my adoptive parents," Maria listed *cooking* and *athletic ability*; she noted that Rachel is a very good cook and she's learning from her, and she thought playing sports with Lewis was helping her be a better athlete. Things Maria thought were uniquely her were *kindness, sense of humor, loyalty, good friend*, and *fashion design*.

The therapist noted that the parents did the Game of Discovery and made similar charts for her and Carlos, and suggested that Maria share her My Self chart with them. Maria said, "No way, I'm not talking to them." The therapist suggested using the problem-solving steps to develop a plan to work things out with her parents, and they brainstormed ways to resolve the current conflict. After looking at different options, Maria decided that she wanted to tell Rachel what she had wanted the money for and how it related to her not being allowed to have friends in the past, and how important food is to her because of going hungry so many times when she was younger. She also felt she wanted to apologize to both of them for stealing and lying. If this conversation worked out OK, then she felt she might share her My Self chart with them. The therapist praised her problem solving and said the therapist was happy she was willing to share what was bothering her.

Parent Session 3: Racial/Ethnic Identity, Supporting Child's Cultural Heritage

The purpose of Module 5 Session 3 is to help parents explore ways in which they can ensure their child grows up with knowledge and pride in their race, ethnicity, and/or culture, and can support the child's identity associated with their birth family. Parents also reflect on privilege, discrimination, and ways to be aware of and prepare children of color for microaggressions and discrimination they may face.

Materials for this session include

- poster board or large paper for each parent;
- markers, crayons, etc.;
- magazines to use for cutting out symbols for ethnic/racial identity posters (optional);
- Handout 47: Supporting My Child's Racial/Ethnic Identity; and
- Handout 48: Our Joint Transracial Family Identity.

REVIEW SESSION 2 PARENT HOMEWORK: SHARING POSITIVE SIMILARITIES; REVIEW AND PRACTICE OF PRETEACHING

Review homework from the past week with parents about sharing of at least one positive similarity or fantasized similarity to a birth parent and at least one positive similarity to an adoptive parent with the child. Process parental feelings about figuring out possible similarities with birth and adoptive families, as well as about sharing this with the children.

Review the usage of preteaching, and elicit examples of how parents used it in the last week. If they did not use preteaching, explore what got in the way and brainstorm solutions.

DISCUSSION OF TRANSRACIAL FAMILY IDENTIFICATION

Make the following points with the parents: Parents adopting children of a different race (Black, Asian, American Indian/Alaskan Native, White), ethnicity (belonging to a social group that has a common national or cultural tradition, such as Latino), or culture (the customs, arts, social institutions, and achievements of a particular nation, people, or other social group, such as from Peru, Thailand, or Ghana) need to ensure that their children grow up with knowledge and pride in their racial/ethnic/cultural heritage and also are able to integrate the "culture" of the adopted family with that of their birth heritage. It is extremely helpful to the child that the parents make clear that they want to support the child's identity associated with their birth family and heritage/country of birth and that they feel proud of their child's background. For children who are physically identifiable as non-White either through appearance or accented speech, or for children who may be gender nonconforming, parents should let their children know that they are aware that they themselves do not face many of the issues of discrimination that the child faces daily. Help White parents reflect on their own privilege and how different life is for people who have been discriminated against and oppressed. Hopefully, the family will be strong advocates for social justice and equity within their community and support their child's racial, ethnic, and gender identity and their sexual orientation.

Children who are adopted transracially will develop their racial/ethnic identity over time. As young children, they may be focused on skin color. As they grow, they will face the demands of fitting in with youth who are both like them (physically) and different from them (culturally). It can be confusing for children to look like other children they know, but not share a family cultural background. Encourage the parents to have sensitivity to these issues as well as open communication with the child proactively and when issues arise.

When children are part of a transracial family, it can be helpful to think about family identity as well. It is very important to support the child's racial/ethnic identity, and it is equally important that the entire family identify as a multiracial/ethnic/cultural family versus isolating the child as being from a different background. This means seeking out experiences related to the child's heritage as a family, coming together to build a transracial family identity rather than seeking out experiences for the child alone. For example, instead of enrolling the child in weekend Chinese classes, the whole family would learn Chinese together.

Parents must be cognizant of the reactions that others have in viewing their families as different and should be aware of potential negative stereotyping and bias. This happens primarily with racial stereotypes but can also happen with older children who may have non-English accents (such as a native Spanish speaker who is adopted into an English-speaking home). As much as it would be ideal, the world is *not* color-blind and gender neutral. Most children of color report that they experience discrimination in many forms and that these experiences are common. Help parents recognize that the child's experiences with discrimination and racism are likely different from their own experiences. Parents who have experienced the privilege of being White may need support in learning more about the experiences of people of color in the United States and may need help understanding how to support their child. This can be accomplished by talking with other people in their life who may share their child's racial/ethnic background and have similar lived experience. Children experience emotional safety when parents acknowledge these differences and celebrate them, but also empower children with coping skills to respond to racist practices and bias.

Ask the parents the following questions to gain a deeper understanding of their relevant experiences. Ask follow-up questions as appropriate and provide reflections to validate the parent's feelings and communicate your acceptance and understanding of their experiences.

Question 1: What is your own racial/ethnic identity and cultural heritage, and how has that impacted your life? In what way do you incorporate your racial/ethnic identity into your family life?

Question 2: What are your perceptions of racial or ethnic bias in your family and your community?

Question 3: What led you to consider transracial parenting?

Question 4: What role do you think discrimination, racism, and stereotyping may have on your child's development of a positive racial/ethnic identity and positive self-concept?

Question 5: What situations have you or your child experienced that you would consider to be a form of racism or negative stereotyping?

Question 6: How have you or will you prepare your child for dealing with racism and microaggressions?

Question 7: Can you share one or two examples where you advocated for sensitivity to a cultural issue or diversity?

RACIAL/ETHNIC IDENTITY POSTERS

To further explore issues for transracially adopted children, give each parent a piece of poster board or paper and instruct them to use symbols or words that represent their own racial, ethnic, and cultural identity. Provide a list of concepts such as type of food, music, clothing, hairstyle, language, and celebrations as examples to consider.

After each parent completes their own poster, give them another poster board or paper and ask them to work together to create symbols or words for their child's racial, ethnic, and cultural heritage. Discuss with the parents the meaning of the parent and child symbols, objects, or words.

SUPPORTING THE CHILD'S RACIAL AND ETHNIC IDENTITY

Discuss the importance of the family having relationships with people and incorporating traditions from their child's birth heritage/country. Ask parents to fill out the first part of Handout 47: Supporting My Child's Racial/Ethnic Identity, detailing what they currently do to incorporate their child's heritage within their family. Brainstorm ideas with parents for further integrating the child's racial/cultural/ethnic heritage into their family. Ideas might include

- developing family friends of the same race, ethnicity, or country as your child;
- seeking out play dates with children of the same ethnicity or race or from multiracial or transracial families;
- attending cultural events that are related to the child's heritage;
- celebrating family holidays or special events from the child's heritage;
- considering moving to or spending time in neighborhoods representative of your child's culture;
- taking children's race and culture into account when deciding on schools, summer programs, etc., so children do not feel like they stand out as being different;
- going to a hair salon that specializes in haircare and styling for your child's culture, if appropriate;
- learning together about the child's country of origin and the native language of the child's birth family or culture; and
- considering a trip to the child's country of origin if child is old enough.

Ask parents to write down several new ways they might support the child's racial/ethnic heritage in the second part of Handout 47: Supporting My Child's Racial/Ethnic Identity.

DEVELOPING A JOINT TRANSRACIAL FAMILY IDENTITY

Explore the similarities and differences in the race/ethnicity/cultures of parents and child. Discuss the importance of celebrating and honoring the multifaceted cultural heritage of the whole adoptive family, and use the posters they made to assist in this effort. The goal is to help the family achieve an identity that includes their own heritages and the child's heritage in their family life and helps develop an integrated family identity. Write (or have parents write) current traditions as well as the results of brainstorming for possible new integrated traditions on Handout 48: Our Joint Transracial Family Identity, so parents can take these ideas with them.

IDENTIFYING A CONSULTANT

In the last activity, ask the parents if they have someone in their lives they can go to who has personal knowledge of the child's culture to support them when facing issues of racism, discrimination, or general support in raising a child of a different race/ethnicity/culture from the parent, a person or persons they can reach out to when they are not sure how to handle a situation or need advice/support. This person can serve as a "consultant." If parents cannot identify someone who can help play this role in their lives, brainstorm ideas with the parents about whom they know or can access who would be helpful in this role or steps they could take to find an appropriate consultant.

CASE EXAMPLE: THE SPRINGFIELDS

Before presenting the material for this session, the therapist asked how things had played out over the last week with Maria, whom they had grounded after she stole money from her mother's purse and lied about it. Rachel and Lewis reported that they had thought a great deal about how this incident might reflect issues and possible trauma in Maria's past over a glass of wine the evening after the last session. Although they didn't come up with much other than what was discussed in the last session, they reported that after a few more days of sullenness, Maria had apologized for stealing and then lying about it, which Rachel had lavishly praised her for and told Maria how much she appreciated her saying she was sorry. When asked what had been going on for her, Maria gradually shared much of what she had told the therapist in her last session about wanting to take seven girls out to her best friends' favorite restaurant for her birthday and knowing Rachel and Lewis would think it was stupid and extravagant. She noted that she'd never had a best friend before and thought if she could provide a great meal, it would solidify their friendship. Maria became tearful when relating that since she wasn't allowed to go to the party, her stealing and lying had been for nothing, and she had compromised the parents' trust without accomplishing anything. The therapist asked what that had been like for the parents to hear, and Rachel said she was touched and thanked Maria for sharing and helping them understand. She noted that she hoped in the future that Maria would trust them enough to share what she was feeling so they could together work out a solution, for example, maybe having the friend over for dinner or taking her out with the family for a special birthday dinner if it was important to Maria that the gift involved food. Rachel said she slipped in that she knew getting enough food mattered a lot to Maria because she and Carlos often went hungry while their birth mother was using drugs. The therapist said she was really impressed with their response, especially noting that they had tied the issue back to her past history when stealing food was adaptive, as well as with their problem solving. Lewis had been largely silent during this exchange, so the therapist asked how he felt. He said he was glad Maria shared with them, but he was still concerned about her tendency to steal, and the therapist noted this seemed to be an ongoing concern for him. Lewis pondered this, and then said maybe it was because one of his brothers had begun stealing as a teenager and later spent several years in prison for auto theft, and he didn't want this to happen to Maria.

When discussing the parents' own racial/ethnic background, Lewis animatedly discussed how much discrimination he had faced growing up as a young Black male in a racially diverse neighborhood. Especially as a teenager, he reported being followed and harassed by police when in stores and walking with his friends. He and some Korean kids from his school got into several fights as well, and his integrated high school was actually segregated within the school into African American, Korean, and Latino sections. With bitterness, he noted that although he was a better, more cautious driver than Rachel, he had been stopped while driving innumerable times, while Rachel had only gotten stopped once, when she accidentally went through a red light. Lewis feels he has an ambivalent relationship with his race; he is proud to be a Black man descended from a resilient people, but he also finds it annoying and provoking to be racially profiled at times.

Rachel on the other hand, said that she does not have a strong cultural identity. She grew up in the Midwest in a small town where pretty much everyone was White and churchgoing. However, Rachel reflected that at the preschool where she works, almost all the children are Latino, as are most of the other teachers and aides. Sometimes she is slightly envious of their sense of cultural community and feels left out, especially when they speak Spanish and she can only understand a few words.

In doing their own racial/ethnic identity posters, Lewis drew a person with a huge Afro (which he had most of his younger life), sweet potato pie and collard greens (his favorite foods that his grandmother made), some CDs that were his favorites from back in the day (Dr. Dre, Snoop Dogg, and Ice Cube), and a ball and chain, which he said represented slavery. Rachel puzzled over what to put down for herself but after a few minutes drew a stick figure ballet dancer, something she identified as chicken pot pie (a staple of her family meals), a red baseball cap to represent that her family had been rabid St. Louis Cardinals fans, and a church with a large cross on top.

When they did the racial/ethnic identity poster for the children, they drew enchiladas and tacos, which both kids love, and decided to write the word *salsa* with a green hot chile next to it and musical notes on the other to indicate both a food and a music genre, and the word *familia* to represent what they perceived as the importance of family in Latino culture. They also drew the Mexican flag and wrote a few common Spanish words (*adios, buenos dias, te amo*).

The parents felt they were doing a pretty good job of supporting the children's racial/ethnic identity and had thought about these issues quite a bit as an interracial couple prior to having children. They have Mexican food usually two to three times a week, and Rachel and Maria enjoy learning to cook new recipes together from various parts of Mexico; Maria has been teaching the parents to do salsa dancing and Cumbia; and they live in a diverse neighborhood with many Latino families. Lewis noted that Maria is fluent in Spanish whereas the rest of the family only knows random words here and there. In thinking of how to support the children's racial/ethnic identity further, Rachel and Lewis decided to look into taking conversational Spanish classes together at the local community college and to investigate whether they might be able to find a bilingual class or playgroup for Carlos for next year in first grade. They also decided to see if the kids would like to have a party for Mexican Independence Day or Dia de Los Muertos, which some of the neighbors also celebrated.

Child Session 3: Racial/Ethnic Identity

The purpose of Module 5 Session 3 is to help children discuss their racial, ethnic, and/or cultural identity and how this may be similar and/or different from other family members, using books and drawings (younger children) and/or creating a racial/ethnic identity poster (older children).

Materials for this session include

- Handout 49: Books About Diverse Families (for younger children);
- feelings cards for younger children;
- paper, markers, and/or crayons for family drawing for younger children; and
- paper or poster board, scissors, markers, glue, magazines, etc., for racial/ethnic identity poster for older children.

REVIEW SESSION 2 CHILD HOMEWORK: SHARE MY SELF CHART WITH PARENTS; PRACTICE PROBLEM-SOLVING STRATEGY

Review with the child the experience of sharing their My Self chart with their parents. Ask how it felt to share it with their parents, how their parents reacted, and how that felt to them.

Review what problem-solving strategies the child practiced last week in what situation, and record on Handout 22: Coping With My Problem from Module 1 Session 4.

RACIAL/ETHNIC IDENTITY

The goal of this session is to help the child think about and discuss their racial and ethnic identity, including how they self-identify, what characteristics they associate with their group, and how these are different or similar to other family members. Given the different developmental understandings over this time period, activities have been divided into those for younger children (ages 5–8) and older children (ages 9 and older).

RACIAL AND ETHNIC IDENTITY—YOUNGER CHILDREN (AGES 5–8)

Questions young children may have about racial and cultural physical characteristics include the following examples:

- What does it mean, I'm Mexican/I'm Ethiopian?
- Why am I called Black if my skin is brown?
- Why is my skin brown and mommy's is white?
- Why is my nose flat but my sister's nose curls up?

BOOKS

Begin this session by reading the child a book about different types of families from Handout 49: Books About Diverse Families. Say, "We're going to read a book about different kinds of families today." After reading the book, elicit reactions from the children to the book read and relate it to their own family. Note who they identify with in the books and how they characterize themselves versus their family members. Use feelings cards if the child is having difficulty speaking about feelings. It is helpful to give the Books About Diverse Families handout to the parents for use at home.

DRAWING FAMILY PICTURES

Ask the child to draw a picture of their family. Use the books read as jumping off points to discuss racial and ethnic differences as they relate to the child's family. For example, if they read *Rosie's Family: An Adoption Story*, ask the child how people's skin color is the same or different in their family. If they read *The Colors of Us*, ask the child to draw the different colors of the people in their family. If children do not spontaneously draw differences between family members, refer back to the book read and ask the child to make a new drawing that reflects the differences in their family or suggest they modify their original drawing.

RACIAL/ETHNIC IDENTITY POSTER (CHILDREN AGES 9 AND OLDER)

Ask the child to use words or symbols or cut out pictures or words from magazines or from the Internet (if the therapist has Internet access) that tell a story about their culture and heritage, similar to the poster the parents created. Give examples such as food, clothing, music, famous people, people the child looks up to, celebrations, and hair to help them get started. Discuss the poster with the child and reinforce the positive qualities depicted.

CASE EXAMPLE: THE SPRINGFIELDS

In the session with Carlos, the therapist asked how he would describe himself to someone who didn't know him. He said he was a boy, 6 years old, and had a sister and a dog. He did not mention any physical characteristics or racial/ethnic identification. After reading *Rosie's Family: An Adoption Story*, the therapist asked about how Rosie was different from her family members. Carlos said that Rosie was brown and white and smooth while the rest of the family was grey and furry. The therapist asked if people in his family looked different, and Carlos said that he and Maria looked the same, they were brown and had black hair. Mommy was identified as pink and Daddy as dark brown. The therapist then asked Carlos to draw a picture of his family, and he again replied, "I told you I hate to draw!" After some cajoling, he quickly drew almost indistinguishable stick figures, so the therapist said she couldn't tell them apart and asked him to draw them again, using crayons that showed what color each person was. With a big sigh, Carlos drew Rachel as pink, him and Maria as tannish brown, and Lewis as deep chocolate brown. The therapist asked him why he thought he and Maria were the same color, hoping he might say they were both Mexican American or Latino, but he said instead, "Because she's my sister, silly!"

With Maria, the therapist first asked how things had gone at home since she had been grounded last week for stealing and lying, and had been so upset about it. She said everything was OK now. When asked for elaboration, Maria said she had apologized to her parents and that she and Rachel had a good talk and worked out some ideas that didn't involve stealing for getting special food for her best friend. She was pleased at how this worked out, but said she thought maybe Lewis was still mad at her about what happened because he hasn't asked if she wants to take a walk after dinner like he usually does several times a week. The therapist praised her for working to resolve the issue and taking the first step by apologizing.

Next, the therapist introduced the Racial/Ethnic Identity Poster activity, which Maria was excited to do because she loves art projects. The therapist had brought in some magazines and scissors and glue in case Maria wanted to use pictures from them for her poster, but she said she'd prefer to draw pictures. She first drew framed paintings that she said represented paintings by Frida Kahlo and Diego Rivera, saying that they are Mexican artists and she hopes to be a Mexican fashion artist. Then she drew enchiladas, which her aunt and mother had cooked so well, as well as *sopes* and *caldo de pollo*, a TV that she said was playing her favorite telenovela, a Christmas tree with a plate of tamales under it, and a salsa dancer in a sexy outfit. She explained to the therapist why she put each symbol on her poster, noting that she'd love to design dresses for salsa dancers and Ballet Folklorico performers. The therapist commented on how rich and interesting her culture is and complimented how well she had drawn all the symbols.

Parent Session 4: Preparing for and Dealing With Discrimination and Microaggressions

This session is a continuation from the transracial sessions in this module; however, it may also be given for families who are not transracial but are diverse in other ways, and who may face discrimination and microaggressions as well, such as families with lesbian, gay, bisexual, and transgender parents; single parent families; and older parents.

Materials for this session include Handout 50: Positive Responses to Discrimination Situations.

PREPARING CHILDREN FOR DISCRIMINATION AND MICROAGGRESSIONS

Because some of the bias children may experience will be indirect, such as in the media, discuss the possibility of parents arming children to combat dominant media messages about people of color (e.g., all the criminals in the news are African American or Latino; Latino kids join gangs; Native Americans drink too much). Ask parents what messages they think the child may have gotten about their race or ethnicity or other family composition, and suggest they may want to ask the child what they have heard others say about a group they identify with (e.g., Latinos, African Americans, Asians, lesbian moms).

ROLE PLAY ABOUT COPING WITH DISCRIMINATION/MICROAGGRESSION

Encourage parents to think about possible challenging situations that the child may face or may already have faced because of differences in race/ethnicity/culture or family composition. Give parents Handout 50: Positive Responses to Discrimination Situations and discuss the following strategies with them:

- *Psychoeducation*—(a) discussing differences in a nonjudgmental and normalizing manner; and (b) explaining prejudice, e.g., "Some people may be prejudiced—they might not know people who are different from themselves. So they might have wrong ideas about or be scared of people who are different from them."
- *Ignoring*—walking away
- *Seeking adult help*—telling trusted adult such as parent or teacher what happened
- *Sharing feelings*—letting the person know that what they said hurt your feelings
- (For older children) *Journaling or drawing about the incident* at home (with or without parent involvement)
- *Positive self-talk*—For example, "I like myself just the way I am," "It's OK to be different from others; it doesn't make me any less good (smart, caring, special, etc.) than other kids."

Engage parents in a role play about appropriate responses that they can use, and children could be taught to cope with discrimination and microaggressions.

Ask parents if they are aware of a relevant situation that has occurred in the child's life, and use this as the basis for the role play. If no incidents are reported by the parents, the following examples can be adapted. Help parents utilize strategies from Handout 50: Positive Responses to Discrimination Situations if needed.

For Children Ages 5–8:

Example: "Some kid called me chocolate boy. I'm not made of chocolate."

Appropriate sample response: "James, your skin is a beautiful dark brown. And you are right, you are not made of chocolate. There are many colors of skin and they are all beautiful. When a kid says something about the color of your skin, you can say, 'My skin is different from yours, but just as good as yours.'"

Example: "My friend said you can't have two moms."

Appropriate sample response: "There are all kinds of families. Some have two moms, some have a mom and a dad, some have two dads, and some have one parent. In your family, you have two parents who love each other, and they're both moms."

Example: "Selena said, 'She looks like your grandmother, not your mom.'"

Appropriate sample response: "I'm sorry you have to hear that. Although I'm old enough to be your grandmother, I love being your mom. You might tell Selena that your mom is older but she loves you and she's a great mom."

For Children Ages 9 and Older:

Example: "At the sleepover, Samantha said that my hair looks crazy."

Appropriate sample response: "I'm sorry, that must have been really upsetting. Girls who are African American have hair that is different from girls like Samantha who are White—it can be thick and curly. When Samantha says that the next time, you can say 'my hair is different from yours. My hair is just like (insert an African American role model or celebrity in popular culture) who can do all kinds of things with it, wear it natural, in braids, locks, straight, curly or whatever she wants.'"

Example: My friend said "What do you mean, you have two dads? Which one is your real dad?"

Appropriate sample response: "It can be so frustrating that people don't realize that there are all kinds of families. Maybe you can just say, 'They're both my real dads. They both take care of me just like your parents take care of you.'"

Example: "Kids at school keep asking me why I just have a dad and where's my mom."

Appropriate sample response: "I'm sorry that made you feel bad. Can you tell them 'There are all kinds of families, and mine is me and my dad?'"

CASE EXAMPLE: THE SPRINGFIELDS

When the therapist asked Rachel and Lewis what possible instances of discrimination or microaggressions Maria and/or Carlos had experienced, Lewis noted that given the many instances he has experienced of discrimination, he is acutely attuned to what his children may have to deal with. The example he noted with Maria occurred when he and Rachel had their conference with Maria's guidance counselor at the end of the first semester; the counselor had suggested that given Maria's background and the fact that Spanish was her first language, perhaps Maria would do better on a vocational rather than academic track. Lewis had responded that Maria spoke perfect English even if she has a Spanish accent, and that given her background, she was doing amazingly well academically. He told the guidance counselor that Maria had been very upset when the counselor said he thought she'd be better off working toward vocational training instead of a 4-year college.

The therapist asked how Lewis had handled this with Maria. He sheepishly reported that he told Maria that the counselor was an ignorant asshole and to ignore anything he said. In going over the Positive Responses to Discrimination Situations (Handout 50) in relation to this situation, Rachel and Lewis felt that Maria had already sought out adult help by coming to them. They also thought that Maria might want to educate the counselor that her accent had nothing to do with her academic ability, and they could work with her on positive self-talk around the fact that speaking English with an accent does not make her less smart or capable of succeeding in school. They role played these two strategies, with Lewis playing himself and Rachel playing Maria. They felt it was helpful and planned to check in with Maria about whether there had been other situations involving discrimination or microaggressions that she has experienced but not yet shared with parents.

Child Session 4: Handling Discrimination and Microaggressions

The purpose of Module 5 Session 4 is for the child to share situations where someone said something negative about the child's appearance, race, ethnicity, culture, family structure, etc., and to role play ways to respond to these types of situations in the future in a way that feels empowering.

Materials for this session include Handout 50: Positive Responses to Discrimination Situations (from Parent Session 4; give to children 9 years and older).

EXPERIENCES WITH DISCRIMINATION

Ask the child to draw a picture of, write about, or tell about a situation where someone said something that was negative about their looks, racial or ethnic identity, or family structure, or made a stereotypical comment, using child-friendly language. If the child does not have an example, give an example from your own personal or therapeutic experience or use a hypothetical example for younger or older children from those given in Parent Session 4. Discuss the example with the child and use the feeling cards or feeling poster to identify how they felt in those situations. Empathize with their feelings about being discriminated against. For older children, describe what a microaggression is—a comment or action that subtly and often unconsciously or unintentionally expresses a prejudiced attitude toward a member of a sometimes-marginalized group such as people of color, women, or gay people. Discuss the concept and ask if the child has experienced any examples of microaggressions. If the child does not seem to understand the concept or cannot think of examples, give the following examples as appropriate: (a) in a store or museum, the security guard pays particular attention to or follows the African American child but not the White child (even if there is no interaction); (b) the teacher asks a child to take home a newsletter and give to the child's mom and dad (assuming the child has two heterosexual parents) or plans a Mother's Day activity of making cards for the children's mothers (invalidating the child with one or two male parents and no female parent); and (c) the server at the ice cream parlor asks the White parent and child what they want before asking the Latino parent and child.

ROLE PLAY ABOUT COPING WITH DISCRIMINATION/MICROAGGRESSION

Role play the child's own situation or one of the examples from Parent Session 4 to practice responding to discrimination. State the situation, and encourage the child to come up with a response. If they are having difficulty developing an appropriate response, offer the suggested sample responses given previously in the parent session, or give the samples as alternative possible responses.

Provide empathy and reassurance to the child throughout the role play, noting that such situations are not fair and can be very upsetting. Let the child know that they will be discussing situations like this when child and parents meet together in the next session, and that together they will talk about more good ways to handle these situations.

POSITIVE STRATEGIES FOR DEALING WITH DISCRIMINATION

Review the strategies from Handout 50: Positive Responses to Discrimination Situations (discussed in Parent Session 4) with the child, as is age appropriate, and give a copy to children 9 years and older.

CASE EXAMPLE: THE SPRINGFIELDS

The therapist asked Carlos about whether anyone had ever made fun of him about his looks or who he is or said anything about Mexican American people that made him uncomfortable. He said some older kids at school asked him why his skin was so dark when his mother's skin was so light. They also called him a beaner, which he knew was negative but had no idea what they were talking about. The therapist used one of the examples noted previously in helping Carlos respond. The therapist told Carlos, "There are many colors of skin and they are all beautiful. I remember your drawing from last week, where your family had all different colors of skin." The therapist then suggested that "When a kid says something about the color of your skin, maybe you can say, 'My skin is different from yours, but just as good as yours.'" The therapist and Carlos role played this scenario, and Carlos smiled and thought it was a good idea to add that he liked to eat frijoles but that he was a boy and not a beaner.

When discussing possible discrimination situations with Maria, she brought up the incident with the guidance counselor that the parents had also discussed in their session. Maria and the therapist went over the handout on Positive Responses to Discrimination Situations, and Maria felt she wanted to tell the counselor that just because she has an accent and is Mexican does not mean that she's stupid or not able to learn and that maybe the counselor hasn't met a lot of smart Mexican girls before. In asking about other situations, Maria also mentioned that her best friend is White, and she thinks the girl's parents didn't want to let her friend come over to Maria's house because the parents kept coming up with excuses; she wondered if it is because she's Latina and maybe the parents think she lives in an unsafe neighborhood. However, when the families were together at a school event and her friend's mother realized Maria had a White mother, all of a sudden she was fine with her daughter visiting at Maria's house. The therapist asked how Maria felt about this, and Maria responded that she had mixed feelings. She was really glad that the mother would let Maria's best friend spend time at her house, but was angry at the mother and thought she might be racist. The therapist validated Maria's mixed feelings, noting that sometimes discrimination was subtle and could be called a microaggression and said that they would be discussing discrimination further in the joint session next week. The therapist added that she wanted Maria to know that they could always make time and space in session to talk about these situations when they come up so Maria doesn't have to carry them around on her own.

Joint Session: Developing an Integrated Family Identity, Dealing With Discrimination

The purpose of the Module 5 Joint Session is for children and parents to share family drawings and racial/ethnic identity posters and to role play together ways to handle discrimination and microaggressions.

Materials for this session include

- children's family drawings from Session 3 (ages 5–8);
- racial/ethnic Identity posters (made by parents and children ages 9 and older in Session 3);
- large paper or poster board, scissors, markers, glue, magazines, for Joint Transracial Family Identity poster;

- feelings cards; and
- Handout 50: Positive Responses to Discrimination Situations (for families who did not participate in Session 4).

For families who did Session 3 about racial/ethnic identity, proceed with the next two sections. Otherwise skip to the section Role Play About Handling Discrimination.

SHARING OF FAMILY DRAWINGS AND RACIAL/ETHNIC IDENTITY POSTERS

For children ages 5–8, help them share their family pictures and talk about the similarities and differences in their family identified in Child Session 3. Ask parents to share with the child their posters from their own Session 3 about their own and their child's identity.

For children ages 9–14, have both the parent or parents and the child share their Identity posters. Ask parents and child to discuss differences and similarities between themselves and their parents, and reflect the differences and similarities that they bring up. Elicit feelings from family members about these similarities and differences.

JOINT TRANSRACIAL FAMILY IDENTITY POSTER

Give the family a large piece of paper or poster board and ask them to work together to create a poster that reflects their joint transracial family identity, merging aspects of all of their heritages. If they have difficulty coming up with what to put on their poster, suggest they look at their individual ethnic identity posters (for older children and parents) and also encourage them to put any specific family traditions or rituals that they participate in together onto the poster. Help parents talk with the child about race and ethnicity so the child knows that the parent is comfortable discussing these issues, regardless of whether the child's feelings are positive or negative.

ROLE PLAY ABOUT HANDLING DISCRIMINATION

Encourage the child to share the situation involving bias or discrimination that was discussed in Child Session 4 with parents (or bring up the hypothetical example if none was identified in the child's own life). If the child is unable to share the example, you can ask the parents to describe the situations that they worked through in their session. Have a copy of the Positive Responses to Discrimination Situations handout that has already been discussed in both parent and child sessions to guide them in deciding on and trying out different strategies.

Ask the parent to begin the role play with the child, with the child presenting discrimination situations and the parent modeling proactive responses to the situations, using the techniques discussed in the individual parent session or others they have developed. Then ask them to switch roles, so that now the parents present a discrimination or microaggression situation, and the child responds with techniques discussed. Coach the parent as necessary to use reflective listening skills and help affirm the child's feelings associated with negative comments. Provide feeling cards or the feelings poster as a tool for the parents. The skills acquired will empower children to better handle these challenging situations in the future, responding in a manner that reduces the chances for shame or physical response.

CASE EXAMPLE: THE SPRINGFIELDS

The therapist was not sure whether to have the joint session with both Carlos and Maria or to have separate sessions because of the difference in their developmental level. In the end, the therapist decided to include both children in the session, thinking that Maria might help Carlos understand the concepts of race/ethnicity and discrimination. The therapist asked each family member to share their "artwork" related to racial/ethnic identity. Carlos immediately said, "I want to go first!" He showed his family drawing and said that he and Maria have light brown skin, Rachel has pink skin, and Lewis has dark brown skin. The therapist asked the family why they thought people had different skin colors, and Maria said that it was because people were from different backgrounds. She said that she and Carlos have the same skin color because they are both Mexican, and Lewis has darker skin because he's Black. Carlos said "no, he's dark brown!" The parents laughed and Lewis explained that his race is African American and many people refer to people like him as Black even though Carlos is right that his skin isn't black like the Batmobile. Maria thought it was funny also that Carlos said Rachel's skin was pink; Maria noted that although Rachel's skin tone is kind of pink, her race is White. This further confused Carlos. The therapist reflected that this idea of race and ethnicity can sometimes be confusing and suggested that parents and Maria share their racial/ethnic identity posters to help clarify. The family looked over the parents' and Maria's posters about the children's ethnic identity. The therapist asked what things the family noticed were the same or different on the two posters. Carlos excitedly said, "they both have enchiladas and other Mexican food like tacos and tamales," and Maria added that salsa music was included on both posters. Rachel mentioned how beautiful the artwork on Maria's poster was and especially noted the salsa dancer's cool dress. Maria beamed and said that she's thinking she'd like to design salsa and Ballet Folklorico outfits when she's older.

The therapist then asked the parents to share their own racial/ethnic identity posters, and asked the children what they noticed was different about the parents' racial/ethnic identity from theirs. Maria said she noticed that all the posters had food on it, but they were all different types. She asked Rachel what chicken pot pie was and how come she doesn't make it. Rachel replied that it's bad for you and tastes pretty gross but her mom made it once a week when she was a child. Carlos said that all the posters had something to do with music, and Maria said that she spoke Spanish and Lewis spoke rap.

Bringing out a large poster board, the therapist encouraged them to make a Joint Transracial Family Identity poster that brought together aspects of all their ethnic backgrounds and cultures. When the family looked confused, the therapist said that the things on the poster can be things from one person's culture that they would all like to share together as family traditions. Maria thought maybe they could divide the paper into Food, Music, Activities, Sports, and Miscellaneous. The parents thought this was a good idea, but Carlos said he didn't want to draw and didn't even know what Miscellaneous was, and he started to sulk. Rachel suggested that Carlos could be in charge of the markers and crayons, and family members could ask him to find the colors they needed for the poster. Carlos agreed, and the therapist praised Rachel for coming up with a creative solution. Working together on the poster was generally peaceful, though Maria was a bit bossy. They ended up putting a variety of Mexican foods, sweet potato pie, and fried chicken (served in both parents' childhood homes) on the Food section of the poster, deciding to leave off chicken pot pie. In the Miscellaneous section, Rachel brought up Language, noting that only Maria speaks Spanish fluently, and she told the children that she and Lewis were going to take a conversational Spanish class so that they could share the language with Maria and suggested that they also were trying to find a class for next year where Carlos could learn in both Spanish and English. Maria said she thought Rachel would enjoy the telenovelas when she learned some Spanish because they are so dramatic and hoped they could watch them together.

In doing the role play about responding to discrimination, the therapist asked who would like to bring up a situation involving discrimination. When no one responded, the therapist suggested that they might discuss the incident with the guidance counselor because it was discussed in both the parents' and Maria's last sessions. After giving the Positive Responses to Discrimination Situations list to Maria, Lewis took the lead, saying he had been so angry about what the counselor had said, and asked Maria how she felt about it. Maria said she wanted to educate him about not stereotyping Mexican girls, and Lewis said he was proud of her. They then role played the situation, with Lewis playing the role of the guidance counselor, and Maria told him that her abilities had nothing to do with her Spanish accent. Lewis as guidance counselor challenged that, saying her grades weren't that great. Maria responded that her grades were improving and that it had been hard for her to enter a new school for middle school. Both parents praised Maria. Carlos was wiggly and distractible during this section, so the therapist ended the session by praising their work and again looking over their Joint Transracial Family Identity poster together.

Module 6
Adoption and the Outside World

8

Module 6 goals for parent sessions are to help parent(s) and children handle questions and comments they receive about the child's background and adoption that come from other children and adults, including friends and family members as well as strangers, and to help parents make decisions regarding disclosure about child's difficult history to others (e.g., extended family members, pediatricians, teachers).

Module 6 goals for child sessions are to empower children to handle the intrusive, sometimes aversive questions asked and comments made by others about adoption. Sometimes the questions refer to the children's personal adoption stories and other times children are expected to be "experts" on adoption because they were adopted.

Parent Session 1: Dealing With Difficult Adoption-Related Questions, Deciding What Information to Share and With Whom

The goals of this session are to review progress on the child's problem areas, as done at the beginning of each module; review parents' use of preteaching (homework from Module 5, Session 2); discuss difficult adoption-related

http://dx.doi.org/10.1037/0000096-009
Adoption-Specific Therapy: A Guide to Helping Adopted Children and Their Families Thrive, by J. Waterman, A. K. Langley, J. Miranda, and D. B. Riley

questions that parents and child have been asked; help parents decide about whom to share difficult child information with; and introduce the W.I.S.E. UP! Program that children will be learning to help them handle difficult questions.

Materials for this session include

- Handout 51: Difficult Adoption-Related Questions, and
- *W.I.S.E. UP! Powerbook* (in toolkit, or it can be purchased at http://www.adoptionsupport.org).

REVIEW PROBLEM AREAS AND PROGRESS

Check in with the parents to assess the progress on the problem area(s) the parents identified on the behavioral measure at the beginning of treatment, having them rate how significant the problem is now. Review the relationship between the problem area and the current adoption-specific behavioral plan, and revise the behavioral plan as needed.

REVIEW MODULE 5 SESSION 2 PARENT HOMEWORK

Ask about how the parents are doing with preteaching and request a recent example of when they used this strategy. If this has not occurred on a regular basis or has not gone well, brainstorm ways to improve.

DIFFICULT ADOPTION-RELATED QUESTIONS

Encourage parents to reflect on and discuss the challenge they and their children face regarding how to respond when either they or their child are asked questions or receive comments about being an adoptive family or regarding the child's adoption story.

On the two-sided Handout 51: Difficult Adoption-Related Questions, ask parents to write down on one side the types of questions that they are aware their child has received about being adopted and/or being in a nontraditional family or looking different from other family members, and on the other side, the types of questions they themselves have received from other parents, relatives, friends, acquaintances, and strangers. Additionally, ask the parents to also write down, on the relevant sides of the handout, any questions and comments they worry will be asked of their child and of themselves that they are not sure how to answer.

Using the handout, review the comments made and comments they worry they will receive. Parents of transracially adopted children will likely share that the common questions and comments made to themselves and their adopted children center on the difficulty that others have around viewing them as a legitimate family—for example, "She must be adopted—she is a different race than you," "She can't be your mom—your skin is darker than hers," "How can you be sisters when she's White and you're Black?" "Did your babysitter pick you up today?" Similarly, there are often special challenges that children with a single parent, relative caregivers, older parents, and/or same-sex parents face around family formation—for example, "Why don't you have a dad/mom?" "Which one is your real mom/dad?" "You can't have two moms/dads," "Why is your dad so old?" "Why do you live with your grandma and not your real mom?"

If the parents do not offer really intrusive questions such as "Where is her real mother?" or "Were his parents drug addicts?" which can feel especially troubling, you should ask if either they or their child have encountered these kinds of questions. Encourage the parents to share their feelings about these questions and empathize with their feelings. Explore what they know about their child's experiences with these kinds of questions, emphasizing how these questions can make their children feel—embarrassed, angry, confused, sad, lonely, and/or different from other children. Highlight the fact that these questions/comments can be especially troubling and wounding to children because they mirror the questions/thoughts/feelings that children may have inside themselves. For example, it can be extremely upsetting to a child who is already pondering, "Why didn't my birth mother keep/want me?" to hear someone ask, "Why were you adopted?"

Discussion in this session will include educating parents about why adults unfamiliar with adoption ask intrusive questions. Adults usually do not know that a child's adoption story is private and therefore that asking questions about a child's adoption story is intrusive. Adults unfamiliar with adoptive families may hold myths and misunderstandings about adoptive families. Allow space for parents to talk about their frustration when other adults ask intrusive, inappropriate questions/comments and validate those feelings (i.e., anger, confusion, vulnerability). Explain to parents that refuting myths and educating others about adoption, as well as about the privacy of their child's story, is something parents can do to support their children. For example, when someone says, "Oh, those kids are so lucky," parents can say, "Oh, *we* are the lucky ones!" Or if asked "Do you know anything about his background?" parents can respond, "I'm sorry but that is my child's private story."

Nonadopted children ask questions for a variety of reasons including curiosity about something they know little about, as well as their own possible feelings of confusion, sadness, and fear around the fact that adoption means the loss of one's biological parents. With this understanding, parents can intervene to protect their child's privacy while appropriately increasing the nonadopted child's positive understanding of adoption. So, for example, if asked "Why was he adopted?" the parent can answer: "Adoption happens for many reasons—sometimes parents are unable to raise or take care of their children. Adoption is a great way to build a family and we are a great, loving family!"

DECISIONS ABOUT SHARING INFORMATION

Help parents understand that they should not feel obligated to share information about their child's adoption story with others, emphasizing again the need to educate others that their child's story is private, and as children grow, they will be in charge of information sharing. Expect that parents will have a variety of opinions and questions about sharing information with family and close friends, teachers, etc., and explore these feelings, respecting the comfort levels of disclosure of various parents. Some parents may feel very strongly about educating others about adoption, whereas others may wish to disclose nothing at all. Some parents may have already shared much information with close family and friends and feel regret and concern. Reassure parents that they can go back to their family members/friends and ask them to respect the confidentiality of the information that was shared.

Regarding school personnel, tell parents that teachers are often much more understanding and supportive of meeting a student's needs when they have some knowledge of the child's past. Given appropriate concerns regarding the confidentiality of the information, parents do not need to share the details of their child's story, but it can be very useful to let school personnel know, for example, if a child has experienced trauma, multiple moves, breaks in attachment, institutional care (orphanage), neglect, abuse, etc. These experiences may compromise the child's cognitive, emotional, behavioral, and social development, which can impact their academic performance and behavior at school.

One way to maintain the child's privacy while dealing with the functional issues that may arise in the school setting is to address the behavior or need without revealing the details of the child's history. For example,

> He has a very hard time with transitions so at home we give him a 5-minute and then a 2-minute warning before we transition from one thing to another, and we offer him appropriate choices to help him feel a sense of control. I wonder if there would be a way to use some of these strategies at school to make transitions easier for him.

And another example is the following:

> She is very sensitive to loud noises, so at home we try to moderate our voices to be sensitive to this, and we stand closer to her when there are loud noises to offer comfort. I am wondering if there are ways to use similar strategies at school to provide warning before fire alarms or adult proximity when noises do escalate.

This enables the teacher to address the child's needs without having to reveal the details of why the child has a hard time with transitions or with loud noises.

Parents do need to be warned that some teachers may have a negative view of adoption or foster care and may not respond with empathy or appropriate intervention. In almost all cases, there is no need to tell school personnel about prenatal substance exposure. It is not necessary when describing the child's symptoms and may label the child negatively for the rest of their school career. Despite these caveats, remind parents that there are many dedicated teachers who want to find strategies to assist the children.

Note that ultimately it will be the child's decision about whom they wish to share sensitive information with. Refer the parents to the Sample Scripts for

Discussing Difficult History With Children (Handout 28) from Module 2, Parent Session 2, to assist their children with how to share information if they make that choice.

THE W.I.S.E. UP! PROGRAM

Inform parents that the W.I.S.E. UP! Program centers on teaching children a simple, but effective tool that gives them the power to decide how they want to respond to intrusive questions and comments about adoption and/or their family. Show the parents the *W.I.S.E. UP! Powerbook* and tell them that it will be used with their child to teach them about the four choices they have to respond to questions and comments about adoption. These are

W—Walk away or choose not to pay attention.
I—It's private; I can choose not to share information.
S—Share some information about my adoption story.
E—Educate others about adoption in general, by telling them correct information and helping them understand it.

Let the parents know that their child will be learning this tool in their session and that it will be discussed in more detail in the next parent session.

HOMEWORK: COMPLETE DIFFICULT ADOPTION-RELATED QUESTIONS HANDOUT

Give parents Handout 51: Difficult Adoption-Related Questions, and ask them to add any other questions/comments of concern to them that their children might face in the future and bring the handout to the next session.

PRACTICE OF PRAISE AND ENCOURAGEMENT

Remind parents of the importance of continuing to develop a positive relationship with the child, and check in with how they are doing in giving five to eight praise or encouragement statements for each criticism. Brainstorm any problems parents may be having and ask them to count the number of praise and encouragement statements as well as criticisms for 1 or 2 days over the next week.

CASE EXAMPLE: THE SPRINGFIELDS

The therapist told Rachel and Lewis that this new module was about exploring the challenge that adoptive parents and children face around questions and comments made to them by others about adoption. The therapist asked them to talk about what their experience has been and if they were aware of adoption-related questions/comments made to Maria and Carlos. Rachel shared that she is often uncomfortable in public when people are staring at the family—which is even worse when both parents are present—and someone in a grocery store line once asked her if Maria and Carlos were her kids. Lewis shared that Maria asked him to wait for her in the car when he picked her up from school, and when he asked her why, she told him that it was because she was tired of kids asking if he was her "real dad." Maria had also told him that they have asked her if she wanted to find "her real dad." Neither Rachel nor Lewis were aware of any questions posed to Carlos but admitted they had never asked him about this.

The therapist empathized with how troubling these questions/comments can be for everybody. The therapist explained that these questions/comments from outsiders reflect the very thoughts, questions, and feelings that children have about their adoption. The therapist gave the couple the Difficult Adoption-Related Questions (Handout 51) and asked them to record any questions/comments that they have received and ones they know their children have received, as well as ones they fear may be coming. After they finished completing the handout, Rachel and Lewis noted they had received the following comments: "Oh, you're such saints to adopt those children." "Did their parents do drugs?" "Might you still try to have your own child?" The couple worried that Carlos will be especially upset by questions about his birth parents because he barely remembers them. The parents also shared anxiety over the constant pointing out of the racial differences and discussed the fact that adoption-related questions/comments can easily cross the line into racist comments and that the parents will have to prepare the children for this. The therapist reminded them of the strategies discussed in Module 5 about handling discrimination and microaggressions, and Rachel said they used them when Maria reported that kids at school said Lewis couldn't be her real dad because he was Black.

The therapist discussed with Rachel and Lewis the reasons why adults ask intrusive questions or inappropriate questions and emphasized that adoptive parents can take on the role of "adoption educators" when confronted with inappropriate questions/comments. As opposed to getting angry, which teaches people that "adoptive parents are overly sensitive and if the children are present teaches them to respond to questions with distress," the therapist encouraged the couple to correct myths that come their way and, most important, to teach others that the questions they are asking are inappropriate—because the answers are part of their child's story and that this information is private and belongs to the child and is up to the child to share if and when they choose. Rachel exclaimed that she had shared a lot of the children's history with her mother and best friend. The therapist assured Rachel that this is not uncommon and that she can reinforce with her loved ones the importance of keeping this information private. Lewis said he is a much more private person than Rachel in general and that he has discussed the children's background with no one.

The therapist then explained that in their own session, the children were each exploring with their therapist the questions and comments they have been dealing with, including their feelings. The therapist explained that the children are learning a simple but powerful tool to help them with this challenge. The therapist showed them *W.I.S.E. UP! Powerbook* (Center for Adoption Support and Education [C.A.S.E.])

and explained how the tool works. The therapist noted that more will be discussed about W.I.S.E. UP! in the next session. The therapist gave them blank copies of the Difficult Adoption-Related Questions handout and asked them to complete these forms with any additional questions/comments that they may become aware of and to bring the handout with them to the next session.

The therapist again reminded the parents that there are only a few more sessions in adoption-specific therapy (ADAPT) and wondered how they were feeling about ending. Rachel said she is very nervous to try things on their own but expressed deep gratitude for all the help the therapist has given their family, noting that they are much closer and more open about everything, including adoption. Lewis acknowledged the progress with enthusiasm but also said it will be somewhat of a relief not to have to leave work early each week.

Child Session 1: W.I.S.E. UP! Program for Responding to Difficult Questions

The purpose of this session is to explore with the child their experience of being asked questions or having comments made to them about adoption, and to introduce the W.I.S.E. UP! tool for handling this challenge.

Materials for this session include

- premade 3 × 5 cards with questions from the Difficult Questions list in the next section (available in toolkit or you can write them on the cards),
- blank 3 × 5 cards, and
- *W.I.S.E. UP! Powerbook* and pocket guide.

REVIEW MODULE 6 SESSION 1 CHILD HOMEWORK: PRACTICE DEEP BREATHING

Review with the child their use of deep breathing, noting what is on the Coping Strategies Log (Handout 24).

DIFFICULT QUESTIONS ABOUT ADOPTION

In this session, you will be asking children to identify questions they have been asked or comments they have heard about their adoption experience and/or their adoptive family at school; in the neighborhood; and from teachers and other school personnel, relatives, friends/peers, and strangers.

Tell children that you know from working with many adopted children that they often get asked a lot of questions about adoption and/or their adoptive families. Ask them if that has happened to them and to write those questions down on 3 × 5 cards; for younger children, offer to assist them with writing. If the child has a hard time identifying questions, show the child the premade cards from the toolkit or on which you have written the questions from the difficult questions list presented next. Ask the child how being asked these questions feels and empathize with how intrusive (personal) these questions are. Ask how the child has responded to these questions or comments in the past.

- Why were you adopted?
- Where are your *real* mom and dad?
- Why aren't you with your real (birth) parents?
- Why didn't your real parents want you?
- Why don't you look like your mother, her skin is light and yours is dark?
- Do you want to find your *real* mother?
- Do you have a father?
- Why do you have two dads (moms)?
- What was it like in foster care?
- Do you have any brothers or sisters?
- Is that your real sister/brother?
- Where did you live before?
- Did your real mother do drugs?
- Your eyes are strange.
- Why is your nose flat?
- I wouldn't want to be adopted.
- That can't be your mother, she's White and you're Black/Asian/Hispanic.
- That's your grandmother, not your mother, right?

TEACHING THE W.I.S.E. UP! PROGRAM

Introduce the child to the *W.I.S.E. UP! Powerbook* and read pages 1–4 with the child, then review the feeling chart in the book. Introduce the "Wise Owl" and the special program he has created to help children handle questions/comments about adoption. Teach the child the W.I.S.E. UP! tool. Children learn they have four choices in how to respond to intrusive questions/comments:

W—Walk away or ignore what is being asked/said.
I—It's private; communicate I will not respond.
S—Share some information about my adoption story.
E—Educate others about adoption in general, by telling them correct information and helping them understand it (but not information about my personal story).

Ask the child about reactions to these options for intrusive questions and comments, and which ones would feel most comfortable to use in different situations or with different people. Children may choose to respond very differently to a question from a close friend in a private space versus someone they do not know well in a public setting. Remind children that how they respond will also depend on how they are feeling at that particular moment. Also tell children that if they are being teased or bullied, they should use the *W*—walk away—with "attitude," saying, "Whatever . . ."

or something similar that communicates that they are not bothered by what is being said. This can help prevent the bullying from continuing. Children should also never have to cope with being teased or bullied alone. Encourage them to always share this with their parent and/or teacher if it happens in school.

HOMEWORK: PRACTICE OF MUSCLE RELAXATION

Ask the child to practice using muscle relaxation at least two times during the week when angry, sad, or worried and to record this on the Coping Strategies Log (Handout 24). Reinforce this homework assignment with the parent. Remind the child that there are only a couple of more sessions of ADAPT. Process feelings the child may have and share your own feelings about termination if appropriate. In addition, ask the child to think about activities and foods that they would like for the termination party.

CASE EXAMPLE: THE SPRINGFIELDS

The therapist met first with Maria and told her that from working with many adopted children and teens, she has learned that most kids get asked a lot of questions about being adopted. She asked Maria if she has ever been asked questions about being adopted. Maria made a face and said, "Of course—all the time! It's so annoying." When asked to share specifically what she's been asked, Maria said, "Oh dumb things like, 'What happened to your real parents?' 'Why is your dad Black?' 'Were you taken away?' 'Did your mom use drugs?'" The therapist empathized with how intrusive and upsetting these questions are and asked Maria to write them down on 3 × 5 cards and add any others she recalled being asked—including troubling comments that she has heard. Maria frowned and said the class bully told her that she should be deported! The therapist asked how she responded and she told the therapist that she told him to shut up.

The therapist asked how Maria responded to the other questions she's been asked. She said she usually gets angry and has gotten in trouble in school for fighting over these incidents and others. The therapist reiterated that she understands Maria's anger completely but that she'd like to teach her a program that has a simple tool that may help her cope better and not let these other kids upset her and then get herself into trouble. The therapist showed Maria the *W.I.S.E. UP! Powerbook* and explained that the "Wise Owl" may seem silly to her as the book is geared to younger kids, but the program/tool is used by adopted teens and even adults—as well as by adoptive parents. The therapist reviewed each of the tools with Maria. Maria said that it probably would be much better for her to either walk away or tell people that it's none of their business. The therapist suggested that doing the homework activity of muscle relaxation or using the calming image may help Maria to remain calm and effectively use the W.I.S.E. UP! tool. The therapist told Maria that they will practice this program again in the next session.

The therapist met with Carlos and asked him whether he gets asked questions about adoption. Carlos shared that he gets asked questions similar to the ones that

Maria shared—about looking different, and where his real parents are, and if he wants to go back to live with them. He said these questions make him feel sad and confused because he doesn't even remember his birth family. He said that he wishes the other kids would leave him alone and he wishes he didn't look different from his parents. When asked how he responds, he usually says what his parents have told him—that his birth parents couldn't take care of him. Carlos added that then he gets asked even more questions, which he usually answers by saying that he just doesn't know. The therapist empathized with Carlos about how miserable these experiences are for him and told him that she is going to teach him a program that has helped thousands of other kids to handle this situation.

The therapist showed Carlos the *W.I.S.E. UP! Powerbook* and taught him what the letters stand for—that they describe the choices he can make whenever someone asks him a question or makes an unkind comment about adoption. Carlos loved the Wise Owl and asked if he could have some markers to color him. The therapist told Carlos that they will talk more about W.I.S.E. UP! in the next session and practice acting out some scenarios to learn how to use the tool. Carlos said he can't wait. The therapist reminded Carlos to practice muscle relaxation two times during the week and record it on the log.

Parent Session 2: Helping Child Use the W.I.S.E. UP! Program

The purpose of this session is to teach and practice the W.I.S.E. UP! tool. The parents' understanding and use of the tool is in preparation for the joint session with their children where they will be practicing the tool together.

Materials for this session include

- *W.I.S.E. UP! Powerbook,*
- Handout 51: Difficult Adoption-Related Questions (filled out in last parent session), and
- 3 × 5 index cards.

REVIEW SESSION 1 PARENT HOMEWORK: COMPLETE DIFFICULT ADOPTION-RELATED QUESTIONS HANDOUT AND PRACTICE OF PRAISE AND ENCOURAGEMENT

Review with parents Handout 51: Difficult Adoption-Related Questions that was completed at home. Discuss any additional questions that the parents added to the handout during the week focusing on their feelings, concerns, and questions about these additional questions/comments.

Review with the parents how using praise and encouragement is working at home, discuss the request from the last session to count the number of praise and encouragement statements as well as criticisms for 1 or 2 days last week, and brainstorm about any problems that have arisen.

USING THE W.I.S.E. UP! PROGRAM TO RESPOND TO DIFFICULT QUESTIONS

In the last session, you briefly described the W.I.S.E. UP! Program developed at C.A.S.E. In this session, you will provide more detailed information about how the program is used as a mechanism for helping children cope with questions or comments about their background, their family, or their adoption. Teach the parents that the letters *W, I, S,* and *E* represent the four choices that their children (and they themselves) have in deciding how they wish to respond to adoption-related questions/ comments from others. Refer to the *W.I.S.E. UP! Powerbook* (or the last child session) to review what the letters represent. Engage the parents in a role play exercise using the W.I.S.E. UP! letter choices.

Tell the parents that you will ask them the questions they noted on the Difficult Adoption-Related Questions handout, and you would like them to choose how to respond using the W.I.S.E. UP! tool. We suggest you use at least two questions from each area of the handout for this role play (i.e., questions parents have been asked, questions parents fear they will be asked, questions their children have been asked, questions parents fear their children will be asked). Ask the parents to use all four choices at some point as they practice responding. Point out that many times a response may reflect two (or more) of the choices. For example, Question: "Where is your real mother?" Answer: "She's at work now and she's picking me up after school." Choices used: the *I* (It's private: I know you are asking about my birth mother, and I am choosing not to talk about her) and the *E* (Educating others: If you use the word *real,* to me that is my adoptive mom).

If the parents appear to be struggling with choosing how to respond, remind them that this is exactly what this program was designed to address—that feeling of being caught off guard and unprepared. The parents are likely struggling because they feel they owe some kind of answer (*S*: Share), and they don't want to really answer the question. Explain that is the perfect time to choose the letters *W* or *I*, and not the *S* (or *E*). Let the parents know that the children often understand this suggestion more easily than their parents and feel incredibly empowered to escape this struggle! The children are happy to "walk away" or say some version of "It's private."

Remind the parents that learning W.I.S.E. UP! will encourage discussion of their children's feelings about this challenge. Let the parents know that W.I.S.E. UP! teaches the children that their decisions about responses will depend on many factors: who is asking the question/making the comment (is this a close, trusted friend or adult, or a stranger?); how they feel about the question/comment (does it make them feel sad and/or embarrassed—maybe they have not yet even thought about these pieces of their story); or what mood the child is in at that particular time (are they in a good mood or feeling tired?).

It is also imperative that you encourage the parents to support their children in understanding that whenever the child chooses the *S* option to respond to a question, they can decide what they feel ready to share without feeling obligated to continue "Sharing" should follow-up questions continue. The children have the power to stop at any time and choose another option (*W, I, E*). For example, if asked "Why are you adopted?" the child may respond "My birth parents weren't ready to raise a child." If asked the follow-up question, "Do you think you'll ever go to live with them?" the child may choose to deflect the question and respond using the I, saying, "I'm hungry, let's go get some lunch."

Discuss with parents that sometimes children might wish to choose the *S* and share but don't quite know what to say. Reviewing some of the questions on the handout, discuss some comfortable answers that the children can use to respond. For example, "Why were you adopted?" Answer: "Because my birth parents were not ready to be parents/not able to raise children/couldn't take care of children." "Why don't you look like your parents?" Answer: "Because I was adopted." "Where are your real parents?" Answer: "My birth parents live in (another state, an hour away, in Guatemala)" or "I don't know where my birth parents are." It is also OK to add "My adoptive parents are my real parents because they love and take care of me."

Remind the parents that as W.I.S.E. UP! encourages parent–child discussion of the challenge of responding to outsider's questions/comments about adoption, these questions often mirror what children are thinking about inside. As a result, this discussion may open the door to further dialogue about adoption. Although this is a desirable consequence, parents need to prepare themselves for further conversation about adoption, as they did in earlier modules.

PLANNING FOR JOINT SESSION

Tell the parents that their child will be sharing what they have learned about W.I.S.E. UP! in the joint session. Prepare the parents that the children will be sharing the questions and comments that they have received and their feelings about these questions. Note that parents and children will be doing role plays together to practice the W.I.S.E. UP! tool. Ask the parent to select two to three questions that their child has been asked or they fear their child will be asked from Handout 51: Difficult Adoption-Related Questions, and write them on the 3 × 5 cards to be used for the role plays. Using the handout, ask the parents to also select several of the questions that they have been asked that they would be comfortable sharing with the child in the joint session and have them write those questions on the 3 × 5 cards—for example, "Why did you adopt?" and "What do you know about her birth family?" For the role plays, it is safest at this time to help parents choose developmentally appropriate questions that their children can handle. It is best to steer them away from questions that their children may not yet be ready to process. For example, for a 6-year-old—even if a parent fears their child will be asked "Were you a mistake?"—it is best not to overwhelm the child unless that is a question the parents know their child has been asked.

HOMEWORK: REVIEW AND PRACTICE OF CHILD-LED PLAY

Ask the parents to continue with the Adoption-Specific Behavior Record (Handout 8). Additionally, ask the parents about how things are going with having a regular time for child-led play, and brainstorm ideas if they are not regularly involved in one-on-one child-led play. Ask parents to make sure to engage in this activity at least three times next week.

CASE EXAMPLE: THE SPRINGFIELDS

The therapist reviewed the handout on Difficult Adoption-Related Questions and discussed the new ones added that referred to racist comments Rachel and Lewis worry the children will hear, including why their parents would adopt Latino children. The therapist empathized with the parents' desire to protect their children, especially from racism, but noted the sad reality that parents need to prepare their children for this possibility and equip them with strategies to cope.

The therapist reminded the Springfields about the W.I.S.E. UP! tool introduced last session. After reviewing the tool, the therapist asked them to use the *W*, *I*, *S*, and *E* as responses to the questions/comments on their Difficult Adoption-Related Questions handout. The therapist asked Rachel and Lewis to take turns responding. They realized with the therapist's help that sometimes the responses represent more than one of the four choices. During this exercise, Rachel seemed to be struggling with how to respond, and the therapist reminded her that she seemed to be searching for a "Share" answer and that she didn't have to come up with one—she could choose the *W* and the *I*. Realizing this, Rachel was able to respond much more quickly to the questions. However, the therapist and parents discussed some of the common, comfortable answers that either they or their children could give if they did want to choose the *S* and Share. Question: "Why don't you look like your parents?" Answer: "Because I was adopted." Question: "Why?" Answer: "My birth parents could not take care of me/children."

The therapist highlighted again the fact that these outsider questions are often especially troubling to children because they mirror the questions that children have inside about their adoption. The therapist explained that talking about W.I.S.E. UP! may therefore likely lead to the children wanting to talk with Rachel and Lewis again about their adoption story, as they did in earlier modules, and that they should be prepared for this dialogue.

The therapist then talked with Rachel and Lewis about making decisions regarding sharing their children's adoption stories. Rachel said that because the school knows that they are a transracial family, she has explained to the teachers that the children were adopted from foster care and have been through a lot. She said that up to this point, she has been pleased with the school's support.

The therapist told the Springfields that in the joint session, the children will be sharing the questions that they have been asked and that they will be practicing together role plays using the W.I.S.E. UP! tool. The therapist asked the Springfields to select two of the questions they wrote down on their handout that they would be comfortable sharing with the children to use in the role plays and to write them on 3 × 5 cards. They selected, "Why did you adopt older children from foster care?" and "Where is their real mom?"

The therapist asked the couple to continue with the Adoption-Specific Behavior Record (Handout 8). Additionally, the therapist asked them to focus on child-led play during the week.

Child Session 2: Practicing With W.I.S.E. UP!

The purpose of this session is to strengthen children's understanding, comfort and ability to use the W.I.S.E. UP! tool. Children will prepare to practice using W.I.S.E. UP! with their parents in the joint session.

Materials for this session include

- 3 × 5 cards from last session,
- *W.I.S.E. UP! Powerbook* and pocket guide, and
- feeling cards.

REVIEW SESSION 1 CHILD HOMEWORK—PRACTICE MUSCLE RELAXATION

Review with child their practice of muscle relaxation and their Coping Strategies Log (Handout 24). Brainstorm solutions for any problems that may have arisen.

REVIEW W.I.S.E. UP!

Review the concepts from the W.I.S.E. UP! Program that were discussed in the last session. Give the child the W.I.S.E. UP! pocket guide and review the four letter choices. You may need to review some typical *E*—Educate responses: "Children are adopted because their birth parents are not ready/able to be parents," "There are 5 million adopted children in this country," "Children are adopted from countries all over the world."

DIFFICULT QUESTIONS EXERCISE

Using the questions written on 3 × 5 cards in the last session, role play a scenario in which you ask the child the difficult questions and have the child respond by choosing one of the four W.I.S.E. UP! letter responses. Make sure that each letter choice is demonstrated and also show how a response can represent more than one letter, for example, "Where are your real parents?" Answer, "My parents are at work." This demonstrates the *I*—It's private and the *E*—Educating that adopted children think of their adoptive parents as real parents. Comment on the child's positive efforts in learning this program.

Using the feeling cards, ask the child how it felt to have each question asked of them and validate their feelings. Practice at least four or five questions until the child understands and seems comfortable using the W.I.S.E. UP! tool.

Talk with the children about "comfortable" *S* (Share) responses they can use if and when they would like to share something about their adoption. For example, "Why were you adopted?" Answer: "Because my birth parents couldn't take care of me, they weren't ready to be parents." Reinforce with the children that whenever they choose the *S*—Share in response to a question, they are not obligated to continue choosing the *S* in subsequent, follow-up questions. For example, if the next question is "Do you know where they (your birthparents) are?" the answer might be, "I don't want to talk about my birth parents anymore. Let's go to lunch."

PLANNING FOR JOINT SESSION WITH PARENTS: PRACTICING W.I.S.E. UP! AND PROBLEM-SOLVING STRATEGIES

Tell the child that they will be practicing the W.I.S.E. UP! scenarios together with the parents in the joint session, as parents have been learning the program in their own sessions. Ask the child to select several of the 3 × 5 cards role played with you to role play with the parents in the joint session, and ask the child to tell the parents about the W.I.S.E. UP! Tool in the joint session.

HOMEWORK: PRACTICE W.I.S.E. UP! AND PRACTICING CALMING IMAGE

Ask the children to try using the using the W.I.S.E. UP! tool if the opportunity presents itself during the coming week and record on Handout 22: Coping With My Problem, from Module 1, Session 4. Also encourage children to practice their calming image at least two times over the week, using it if they get asked difficult questions to help them focus on answers from W.I.S.E. UP! If the child does not remember their calming image, remind the child and see if that image is still a helpful one. If not, assist the child in choosing a new calming image, and guide the child through practice in using it, noting smells, sounds, textures, etc., in the image.

CASE EXAMPLE: THE SPRINGFIELDS

The therapist gave Maria the W.I.S.E. UP! pocket guide and reviewed the W.I.S.E. UP! tool with her by asking if she remembered what the letter choices are. Maria remembered them well, except for being able to give examples of *E*—Educate. The therapist reviewed the general statements she could make about adoption to give an *E* response. (See Session 1.) The therapist then suggested they role play the questions that Maria had written on the 3 × 5 cards in the previous session so that Maria could practice giving responses to reflect each letter choice. The therapist reminded Maria that a response can be a combination of letter choices.

Using Maria's card, the therapist asked Maria, "Why were you adopted?" Maria responded by walking away—using the *W*. The next card read, "Don't you miss your real parents?" Maria responded by saying, "Why would I miss them? They're at work," using a combination of the *I* for It's Private, as Maria knew the question was about her birth parents, and the *E* to educate that she thinks of her adoptive parents as the "real parents." The therapist asked Maria to now demonstrate the *S*—Share and read the card, "Are you really sister and brother?" Maria responded, "Yes, Carlos is my biological brother. We have the same birth mother."

The therapist then asked Maria to talk about how she felt about each question. Maria stated that they all annoy her and she doubted she'd ever choose the *S*—Share.

The therapist empathized with how uncomfortable and upsetting these questions are and asked if she would feel the same way if someone close to her, such as her best friend, asked her these questions. Maria thought about it and said if her one friend Maya asked, it would be OK, but she still wasn't sure what to say. The therapist then offered some *S* responses that might feel comfortable to her—for example, to the question, "Why were you adopted?" Maria could respond, "Because my birth parents couldn't take care of me." Maria looked doubtful and said that most likely a friend would then want to know the reason why her birth parents couldn't take care of her, and she did not want to talk about her mother's problems. The therapist reassured Maria that anytime she chooses to share something, she can stop sharing any time—even after the first question, no matter who it is. So to a follow-up question, "Why couldn't they take care of you?" Maria could always say, "I don't want to talk about my birth parents anymore."

Given that there were only two more sessions to ADAPT after this one, the therapist said that she had another question that she hoped would get an *S* response. The therapist reminded Maria that ADAPT was ending soon and wondered how she was feeling about it. Maria got a little teary and said that she was really going to miss the therapist. The therapist said she would also miss Maria and reiterated what an honor it had been to watch her grow and process her feelings about adoption and her birth family. Maria confided that she was worried it would be harder for her not to lie if she didn't have the therapist to talk with. They discussed who else she could share things with and also some ways to share her honest feelings with her parents. Maria thought it would be easier to be honest if she had done something wrong with Rachel rather than Lewis, and they role played a situation in which Maria had not told her parents that she was going to a friend's house after school.

The therapist told Maria that in their sessions, her parents were learning the W.I.S.E. UP! Program as well, and that in the next joint session, Carlos, Maria, and their parents will demonstrate what they have been learning by practicing the W.I.S.E. UP! scenarios together. The therapist told Maria she will be asking Carlos and her to explain W.I.S.E. UP! to their parents and that they would then engage in role plays similar to the ones they have been practicing in their sessions. The therapist asked Maria to select a few of the cards with the questions to use for these role plays.

For homework, the therapist suggested that Maria use the W.I.S.E. UP! tool if the opportunity came up at school during the coming week and to record it on Handout 22: Coping With My Problem from Module 1, Session 4.

The therapist next met with Carlos and gave him the pocket guide and reviewed the W.I.S.E. UP! tool. Carlos recalled the *W*—walk away and the *I*—"It's private" but had trouble with the *S* and the *E*. The therapist gave some examples of comfortable *S* and *E* responses. The therapist then asked Carlos if he likes to role play and he enthusiastically said yes. The therapist explained that she was going to use the cards on which he wrote the questions he gets asked about adoption, and he would practice an answer using each letter of W.I.S.E. The therapist reminded Carlos that an answer may be combination of two of the letters. The first card read, "Why don't you look like your mother?" Carlos hesitated for a moment, then turned around and stomped off in an exaggerated manner smiling all the while. The therapist "asked" if he used the *W*, and he said he said yes and the therapist said, "Terrific." She took a card that said, "Why were you adopted?" and Carlos frowned and said, "I don't want to talk about it." Again, the therapist praised Carlos. The therapist said, "OK, here comes the harder ones—see if you can do the *S*—'How does it feel to be adopted?'" Carlos exclaimed, "I feel happy!" The therapist said, "That's a good *S* answer. It's also an *E* answer in educating other children to know that children love their adoptive families. Now let's try other *E* responses. Remember some of the things you can say to Educate others about adoption without sharing your adoption story?" Carlos said, "Yes!" The therapist read the card with the statement, "I'd hate to be adopted." Carlos said, "Well, there are 5 million adopted children in this country!"

The therapist asked Carlos how he felt about each of the questions and the comment. Carlos said that he doesn't really care, but if he does, he'll just "walk away." The therapist then reminded Carlos that if and when he chooses to share something from his adoption story or his feelings about adoption, he does not have to keep sharing if he doesn't want to—that he can switch to any of the other choices any time he wants. The therapist gave Carlos the example of his "I'm happy" response. A follow-up question could be, "But don't you miss your birth parents?" The therapist told Carlos he could answer with the *S*—share if he wanted to, but what if he didn't want to? Carlos stated, "I could just walk away or say, 'Let's go play.'" The therapist said, "Wonderful, you've got this!" and gave him a high five.

The therapist told Carlos that the next session would be a joint one with Maria and his parents and discussed with him the same information about the session noted previously with Maria. The therapist asked Carlos to pick at least two or three of the cards that they just role played in this session to use for the role plays with his parents in the joint session and asked him if he thought this would be hard to do or fun, or both, and Carlos said, "Oh this will be fun!"

The therapist asked Carlos to look for opportunities to use W.I.S.E. UP! during the week and record it on Handout 22: Coping With My Problem and get his parents' help if needed. Reminding Carlos that there were only two more sessions of ADAPT after this one, the therapist asked how he felt about it. He said, "*I*—It's private" and started running around the room. The therapist said maybe he was sad about ending, that they had both learned a lot and had lots of fun in ADAPT, and that he would be missed. Carlos came and sat right next to the therapist and didn't want to leave. The therapist commented that he has had a lot of people leave him, so endings are hard, and reminded him about the party on the last day. He perked up immediately and said, "I want chocolate cupcakes!"

Joint Session: Practicing W.I.S.E. UP!

The purpose of this session is for parents and children to practice and discuss the W.I.S.E. UP! tool to encourage continued use and comfort using the tool. It is also to reinforce continued family communication around the challenge of responding to questions about adoption as well as other adoption-related conversations.

Materials for this session include

- 3 × 5 cards with questions on them from Parent Session 2 and Child Session 2,
- *W.I.S.E. UP! Powerbook* and pocket guide, and
- feelings cards.

REVIEW W.I.S.E. UP!

Ask the child to teach the parents what W.I.S.E. UP! is and what it is used for (a tool created to help children and parents respond to questions/comments about adoption). Then ask the child to explain what each of the four letter choices represents. Praise the child for teaching the parents about the choices and encourage the parents to share their reactions as well.

ROLE PLAY DIFFICULT QUESTIONS

Using the 3 × 5 cards from both Child and Parent Sessions 2, have the parents and child take turns practicing asking and responding to the questions on the cards using the four letter choices. Do at least four or five scenarios (or more) to ensure that each letter response has been demonstrated. Remind parents and children that a response can represent more than one letter and have them demonstrate this if this hasn't already been shown in the role plays. Praise the family for understanding and using the W.I.S.E. UP! tool.

Using the feelings cards, ask the child to share with the parent what feelings these questions elicited, and validate the child's feelings. Using the 3 × 5 cards the parents made in Session 2 in preparation for the joint session, ask the parents to share with the child some of the questions that they have been asked and how those questions made them feel, and validate the parents' feelings as well.

If the parents and/or the child appear to be struggling with choosing how to respond, remind them that this is exactly what this program was designed to address—that feeling of being caught off guard/unprepared. Remind everyone that struggling to answer may indicate that they feel they owe some kind of answer (Share) and they really don't want to answer the question. Remind them that this is the perfect time to choose the letters *W* or *I* or *E* and not the *S*. "How come you have two moms and you don't look like either of them?" "I was adopted." "Do you wish you had a dad?" "It's late, let's go get some lunch." However, if the parent or child would like to use the *S* and share something, review some of the comfortable Share responses discussed in previous parent and child sessions.

DISCUSSION OF SPECIAL CIRCUMSTANCES REGARDING USE OF W.I.S.E. UP!

Review with parents and children that their decisions about how to respond will depend on many factors: who is asking the question/making the comment, how they feel about the question/comment, and what kind of mood they are in at that particular time.

Ask the children how they want to handle questions when they are together with their parents. For example, do they want their parents to choose, or do they want to decide for themselves how to respond?

Give the family the *W.I.S.E. UP! Powerbook* and encourage parents and children to review the book at home together and continue practice using the W.I.S.E. UP! tool. Encourage the child to use the W.I.S.E. UP! tool with others and facilitate the parents in encouraging their child to always feel free to talk with them when they experience questions/comments from others so they can troubleshoot and plan together as well as provide support. Remind the parents to periodically inquire if their child is being asked questions and seek avenues to team together as a family to problem solve and apply the W.I.S.E. UP! skills.

Remind the family that next session there will be a party to celebrate the end of the ADAPT intervention. Note that parents and children will meet separately with their therapist for about half the time, then the family will come together for a joint party including food and activities chosen by the children. Make any final arrangements needed for this.

CASE EXAMPLE: THE SPRINGFIELDS

The therapist began by asking the children to decide who wanted to explain the W.I.S.E. UP! Program to their parents. Carlos enthusiastically asked if he could, and Maria agreed. Carlos said, "It is a tool to help children answer questions about adoption." Rachel praised Carlos and said she and his dad learned that they can use it too . . . that anyone can use it and it's so helpful! The therapist then suggested that Maria explain what each of the four letter choices represents. Maria rolled her eyes a little in typical teenage fashion as she correctly explained the four letters. When Maria explained the *I*, Carlos interrupted and gave some examples of *I* responses: "Let's go play," "It's none of your beeswax," and laughed.

The therapist was concerned that the family have fun, while acknowledging the seriousness of the feelings behind the questions that everyone gets assaulted with. The therapist said,

> You're both doing a great job. We also know how hard these questions can be, and how hard it is to figure out what to say and do when they happen. So let's now take a look at those difficult questions/comments that all four of you have shared that you dread getting asked, and let's practice responding using W.I.S.E. UP!

Rachel and Lewis were given the children's cards, and they took turns asking the children the questions. The therapist emphasized that a response can represent more than one letter. For example, Lewis asked Maria, "Where are your real parents?" and Maria responded, "They are at work, silly. Oh, you mean my birth parents—they live about an hour away." This demonstrated the *E* and the *S*. Rachel asked Carlos, "Don't you want to find your parents?" and Carlos said, "I know exactly where they are. My dad's in the garage, and my mom's out shopping. If you mean my birth parents, it's none of your beeswax!" and he laughed.

The therapist encouraged the parents to ask how these questions make the children feel. Maria said they are really annoying, and Carlos said they are just "stupid." The therapist invited the parents to share the questions they get asked and how these questions make them feel. Rachel gave Maria a card to read that asked, "Why did you adopt? Couldn't you have children of your own?" Rachel hesitated and seemed unsure of how to respond. The therapist used this as an opportunity to state that Rachel is likely struggling because she thinks she owes some kind of *S* response, and if she doesn't want to do that, she can make a different choice! Rachel then responded, "Adoption is a wonderful way to build a family and these children are my own!" Asking Maria what letter(s) her mother chose, she answered correctly, the *I* and the *E*. The therapist asked Rachel to share how this question made her feel, and she shared that it has made her feel angry that people think of adoption as not being as good as biological families. She stated that now she sees she can use it as an opportunity to "educate others!" Lewis then gave Carlos his card, and Carlos asked Lewis, "Do you know anything about their birth family?" Lewis simply responded, "Yes." Everyone laughed as they stated that this is a combination of the *S* and the *I*! The therapist used this an opportunity to reassure the children that their parents have learned that their adoption stories are private to them and that only they can choose to share details with others.

The therapist reviewed comfortable *S* responses the family members can use if and when they do want to choose the *S* response and share something from their story. They discussed how their responses will likely vary depending on who is asking the question, when the question is being asked, and how they feel about the question/comment. The therapist also discussed the children's preferences about who should decide how to respond when a question/comment is made when the children are together with a parent. Maria stated that she wants to decide, and Carlos followed suit, but then whispered something in Rachel's ear. Carlos didn't mind his mother sharing what he said, so Rachel said that Carlos had said that sometimes he may want his mom or dad to handle it. Everyone laughed. The therapist highlighted that humor is a great coping skill.

The therapist gave the family the *W.I.S.E. UP! Powerbook* and encouraged them to use it to practice, practice, and practice. The therapist emphasized that the children should not have to deal with this challenge on their own and said the children should always inform their parents and enlist their parents' comfort and support with any future experiences regarding being asked questions or receiving comments about adoption. The therapist also advised the Springfields to periodically check in with Maria and Carlos to learn if this is happening and how the W.I.S.E. UP! tool is working for them.

The session ended with preparations for the termination party next session. Carlos told the therapist, "Remember, I want chocolate cupcakes!" Rachel and Maria decided that they would like to bake something to bring, and the family also decided that they would bring sparkling water to drink. Maria wanted to play her favorite songs during the party, and Carlos wanted them to all play a game together. The therapist said that the party would celebrate the many gains that all family members had made, but it would also be sad to say goodbye. All family members acknowledged these mixed feelings, except Carlos.

9 Module 7
Trauma Treatment

This module is to be inserted into the curriculum if the child has a trauma history that is interfering with current functioning and seems higher priority than continuing with the adoption-specific therapy (ADAPT) modules in order. It may be inserted at the beginning of any other module after Module 1, which should always be completed first. The first parent and child sessions can be administered by any ADAPT therapist. We assume that most therapists working with this population have been trained in trauma treatment and can proceed with the rest of the module if it appears that there has been significant trauma and current posttraumatic symptoms. However, if the therapist has not been trained in or does not feel comfortable treating trauma and posttraumatic stress disorder, the child and family should be referred to a trauma treatment expert.

The purpose for parent sessions of the trauma treatment module is to help parent(s) understand that later placed children adopted from foster care or orphanages are more likely to have experienced traumatic events and will need time, nurturance, and specialized therapy to heal. Parents will also need support in accepting children's disclosures of trauma, providing a safe and trusting environment for them to talk about what happened to them, and seeking their own support so they can best be there for their child. These traumatic events

http://dx.doi.org/10.1037/0000096-010
Adoption-Specific Therapy: A Guide to Helping Adopted Children and Their Families Thrive, by J. Waterman, A. K. Langley, J. Miranda, and D. B. Riley

often include physical and/or sexual abuse, neglect, deprivation, domestic violence, and witnessing or experiencing community or school violence.

The purpose for child sessions of this module is to aid the child's recovery from symptoms of child traumatic stress by providing an opportunity for the child to process their memory of the traumatic event(s) with a competent trusted therapist and potentially with the adoptive parent(s) in a safe environment. The therapist must be able to join the child/adolescent and accept the journey of revisiting the traumatic events, acknowledging the injustices, and reframing maladaptive beliefs children may hold about the event and/or their role in it. If a child is currently experiencing posttraumatic stress symptoms that are distressing and interfering in any way, it may be recommended that the child engage in the trauma narrative process with their therapist in combination with other anxiety management, coping, and adoption-specific skills from previous modules.

Parent Session 1: Trauma Education, Child's Trauma History

The goals of the first parent session of the Trauma Treatment module are to help parents understand the impact of the child's trauma, provide psychoeducation about posttraumatic symptoms, help parents develop empathy for what the child has gone through, process parents' own reactions to the child's trauma, and focus on the child's resiliency in the face of adversity.

Materials for this session include

- Handout 52: Common Reactions to Trauma and Stress, and
- Handout 53: My Child's Trauma History.

TRAUMA EDUCATION

Acknowledge to the parents that many children in the foster care system or institutional care entered care because of abuse and neglect, and note the importance of parents understanding the impact that their children's history of trauma may have had on their development and on their current functioning and experience in the world. Also support them in the fact that while we know that children adopted from foster care may have experienced a variety of traumatic events including sexual abuse, physical abuse, neglect, deprivation, witnessing domestic violence, community or school violence, and/or living in a drug-abusing environment, it can be both painful and frustrating for parents who may see the aftermath of abuse or other trauma. Highlight that it is especially difficult when parents may notice a reaction or a behavior but not have all of the information about the child's traumatic events or history to understand it better within that context. For example, a parent may notice age-inappropriate sexual activity or hypervigilance but not be able to trace its origin or understand its connection with the child's trauma history.

Provide the parents with a copy of Handout 52: Common Reactions to Trauma and Stress and review these common reactions to normalize some of the child's behaviors given their background and context and to encourage parents to look at such behaviors through the lens of the child's particular story. As you review the information with the parents, make a note of the posttraumatic symptoms that they or you have noticed the child experiencing. Ask them to reflect on whether the child is currently exhibiting any of the symptoms on the handout, drawing the connection between the symptoms/behaviors and the child's history of trauma. For example, it can be quite revealing to understand that a child's difficulty concentrating or sleeping or overreaction to loud noises or close proximity may make a lot of sense given that they have witnessed domestic violence between their parents, experienced physical abuse themselves, or watched a parent fight with the police and be taken away in a police car and then was led away by an unfamiliar social worker and separated from their family. It makes a lot of sense that a child may have terrible nightmares, may be afraid of nighttime, and may avoid boys and men and even bathrooms if sexually abused by an older cousin or foster sibling in the bathroom after dark. Sometimes information and details about past events may not be known, and children can have more generalized avoidance behaviors following trauma, such as not wanting to be alone or sleep alone or go to school, that are hard to tie to the specifics of an event but are certainly common posttraumatic responses. Enabling parents to build empathy around the context for these reactions and behaviors allows them to view their child through a trauma lens and the context of what they have been through rather than just finding it difficult or annoying that their child has difficulty separating from them or refuses to go certain places.

CHILD'S TRAUMATIC EVENTS

Give the parents Handout 53: My Child's Trauma History. Use the process of creating a list of the traumatic events they know the child has experienced to build empathy and to highlight the child's resilience. On the handout, parents also note where they acquired the information about their child's traumatic experiences (i.e., written records, a social worker, the child told them) and whether the child has disclosed the trauma to them. Although it may be emotionally difficult to create this list, it is important to get a sense of what the child has been through and to see it all in one place. Allow the space for imagining what this must have been like for the child and for parents to build empathy for their child's life history and understanding of its potential impact on their current functioning. Likewise, reflect on the tremendous resilience of their child and how inspiring it is to reflect on the child's strengths and all that has been overcome.

Help the parents to deal with their own, sometimes powerful, reactions to what the child has experienced. Parents may have difficulty coping with their anger or sadness about what the child has already been through in their young lives, such as murder of a parent, sexual penetration prior to adolescence, cigarette burns, being homeless, and scavenging in dumpsters. It is not uncommon for parents to feel horror, sadness, anger, and guilt that they could not prevent what happened to the child. It is important to encourage the parents to also create a plan for how they can receive support for themselves from trusted adults to help them manage these feelings. It is also important to assess whether the parents themselves have prior trauma exposure and evaluate how the child's exploration of trauma could trigger their own trauma.

Child Session 1: Trauma Education, Trauma History, Reactions, and Coping Strategies

The goal of Child Session 1 is to provide psychoeducation to the child to normalize reactions to traumatic experiences and to help children understand that these symptoms make sense given what they have been through. In addition, children are given the opportunity to share what their traumatic experiences have been and draw a link between current symptoms and their traumatic events. They also can share how they have been coping and how they may apply any new coping strategies they have learned in ADAPT to help manage traumatic stress symptoms.

Materials for this session include the following:

- Handout 54: Prevalence Graphics
- *A Terrible Thing Happened* by Margaret Holmes (2000; for children under age 10)
- Handout 55: Common Reactions Checklist for Kids (for children under age 10)
- Handout 52: Common Reactions to Trauma and Stress (from Parent Session 1, for children ages 10 and over)
- Tokens for reactions to traumatic events activity (at least five tokens each; green for "reexperiencing," yellow for "avoiding," orange for "on edge," and blue for "negative thoughts and feelings"). Tokens can be round or square and cut from construction paper or copied onto colored paper. If possible, write the category on them (e.g., reexperiencing, avoiding). Premade tokens are also available in the optional toolkit.
- Handout 56: What Happened to Me
- Handout 57: Coping Strategies for Posttraumatic Stress Reactions

TRAUMA EDUCATION—PREVALENCE

Provide the child with age-appropriate information about both the prevalence of trauma exposure (they are not the only ones) and common reactions to stressful or traumatic events, with the intention of normalizing such reactions given what they have been through. Using Handout 54: Prevalence Graphics, say something like the following:

> Did you know that you aren't the only child who has gone through something stressful or scary or who has seen stressful or scary things happen to someone else? About one fourth (25%) to one half (50%) of young people have had this type of experience that we sometimes call *trauma* or *traumatic*—something that is very stressful or scary or that feels really bad (show first prevalence graphic). And about 10% of kids, or 10 in every 100, have a really hard time feeling better afterward (show second prevalence graphic).

Help the child put these numbers into a context that makes sense for him or her and relate them to the child's experience. For example, you may say,

> So if you have about 400 kids in your school, that means there are probably about 100 or even 200 kids in your school who have been through some tough stuff and about 40 kids who are having a really hard time because of it. You may not know that very many of these other kids have been through these things because most kids have a hard time talking about what they've been through and maybe that's also been hard for you.

TRAUMA EDUCATION—COMMON REACTIONS PICTURE BOOK (FOR CHILDREN UP TO AGE 10)

Introduce the picture book *A Terrible Thing Happened* by Margaret Holmes (2000). Read the picture book aloud to the child, showing them pictures as you read. When you finish reading the book, ask the child to help you reflect on some of the symptoms that Sherman the raccoon talked about having after he saw a terrible thing. Note that some kids have been through or witnessed many things that were very scary, stressful, or terrible. Try to get some information on which of these symptoms the child may also be experiencing. Say something like,

> Did you know that all human beings react to going through something really stressful, terrible, or scary? Just like Sherman Smith the raccoon, it is very normal for us to have some pretty common feelings and problems when we have been through something like this. It is part of being human (and a raccoon in Sherman's case) and normal. We are going to talk about some things that a lot of people start to feel after a stressful thing has happened, and even though everyone doesn't have all of these reactions, most people have at least a few and sometimes a lot of them. Sherman described some of the feelings and problems that came up for him after he saw something terrible. Can you remember some of those things?

Pause to allow the child to respond or review the following yourself as they come up in the book:

- tried not to think about what he saw,
- did not feel as hungry,
- had stomachaches and headaches,
- felt sad,
- felt scared or nervous,
- had trouble sleeping,
- had bad dreams, or
- felt angry all the time and got in trouble.

As you and the child review these symptoms, and the child shares whether they are having similar reactions, it is very important to try to further elucidate the symptom to help the child understand why it may be happening. Specifically, always try to (a) normalize the symptom, (b) provide hope for how treatment can help, and (c) make a connection between these symptoms and what the child has experienced.

For example, if the child is having nightmares, flashbacks, or intrusive thoughts, you can note that this is normal and a way for their mind and body to try to process or make sense of the really overwhelming things they have been through. Let children know that working with you on telling their story of their experience will help them to understand and deal with what they have been through. Reassure the child that the nightmares or intrusive thoughts then won't happen as often, and when they do, they won't feel as upsetting. Say something like the following to normalize children's experience: "It really makes sense that you have been feeling _____, given that you experienced something(s) that was/were so stressful/scary."

Review Handout 55: Common Reactions Checklist for Kids to cover additional symptoms that Sherman did not mention in the book that are also quite common. Next, have children check off anything from this discussion that they would like to share with their parents about any of these feelings or problems (symptoms) that they have been personally struggling with. For younger children who may not read easily, say something like,

> I am going to read through the list of common reactions kids have when stressful things happen. Some of these things we just talked about because Sherman was having them, but there are other, very common feelings and problems that kids can have after something stressful happens. As I read through the list, I would like you put a check next to the things that you have been feeling yourself so you can share this with your parents. (Langley & Jaycox, 2015, p. 19)

Read through each item on the list, helping the child follow along and prompting them to check or not check each one according to what their experience has been.

TRAUMA EDUCATION—COMMON REACTIONS (FOR AGES 10 AND OLDER)

Using Handout 52: Common Reactions to Trauma and Stress, from Parent Session 1, review the various types of reactions that are common for children and adults after very stressful or traumatic experiences, noting that these reactions are normal responses to trauma. For each item, the child indicates whether they have had or are having that experience or symptom. For each symptom endorsed, give the child a round color-coded token (cut from construction paper—or from the optional toolkit) for each item the child has endorsed and described. A different color token is given for each of the symptom clusters (e.g., green for "reexperiencing the trauma," yellow for "avoiding the trauma," orange for "feeling more on edge," and blue for "negative thoughts and feelings"). Afterward, help the child count the number of tokens of each color to reflect on the child's style of reacting to their traumatic experiences.

CHILD'S TRAUMATIC EVENTS

Engage the child in creating a list of his or her traumatic experiences. Discuss different types of traumatic events and provide children with space and permission to talk about any of these that have happened to them. It is helpful to have a sense for their history so that you can help guide them if they aren't sure what types of things would be listed. It can also be helpful to have a list of potential traumatic events for children to read through, such as a child measure or checklist of trauma exposure, ensuring that events common to children in child welfare are present, such as removal from parent or caregiver, witnessing violence between parents or grown-ups; being hurt physically, sexually, or emotionally by a parent or grown-up; and loss of a family member or loved one (from death, deportation, or incarceration). But also include other types of traumatic events such as accidents, natural disasters, school shootings, and community violence to be sure to get a broader sense of the child's experience. Assist the child in writing down the list of events on Handout 56: What Happened to Me. For younger children it is important to clarify that events happened in real life and were not something seen on television or as part of a video game. This can be queried sensitively by saying something like, "Did that happen in real life with real people or did you see that on TV or in a video game?"

Ask children if they would be comfortable with the therapist sharing their list with the parents, and if so, let children know that you can share it with them in the next session to help them better understand their child's experience, as parents are also learning about common reactions to having been through terrible things. It may be the case that the child is open to sharing some of the things on the list, but not all, so be sure to respect the child's wishes and only share the experiences assented to in the next parent session. If a child does not wish to have their list shared, again, it is important to be respectful and also to explore this as it can give context to how the child is feeling in the family dynamic. Commonly, it can at least be agreed on that the child's separation from known loved ones can be included, given that the child and parents are all aware of this because it may be the reason the child has needed an adoptive family.

COPING STRATEGIES

Review with children any coping strategies currently used to manage the posttraumatic symptoms and note their existing strengths and resilience. Review coping strategies that they learned in Module 1 of ADAPT (i.e., deep breathing, muscle relaxation, calming image) to see which strategies might be most useful to them in dealing with the current symptoms. Help the child make a list or check off items on Handout 57: Coping Strategies for Posttraumatic Stress Reactions.

Parent Session 2: Processing Child's Trauma History

The goals of this session are to provide parents with an opportunity to continue to process their own reactions to the child's traumatic events and history, to hear about the child's list of traumatic events, to review coping strategies for the child and the parent during this time, and to better understand the trauma narrative process.

Materials for this session include

- Handout 56: What Happened to Me (from Child Session 1), and
- Handout 57: Coping Strategies for Posttraumatic Stress Reactions (from Child Session 1).

PROCESSING CHILD'S LIST OF TRAUMATIC EVENTS AND PARENTS' FEELINGS

Begin the session by sharing with parents the list of traumatic experiences the child came up with on Handout 56: What Happened to Me in Child Session 1, as long as the child has agreed to this. As noted in the child session, it may be the case that the child is comfortable with some of their experiences being shared with the parents, but not all of them. If this is the case, it is important to ensure that the child's wishes are respected. Compare the child's list with the list that parents generated in Parent Session 1. Provide empathy and guidance for the parents in dealing with their own feelings about the child's trauma history and help them reflect also on how this may (or may not) influence their feelings about their child. It is important to support parents around whatever feelings come up for them by providing understanding and empathy and connecting how this information and understanding may be used for parents to better understand and support their child.

COPING STRATEGIES FOR CHILD AND PARENT

Given that reviewing a child's traumatic history can be very emotional for the child and the parents, be sure to spend adequate time discussing the heightened need for coping strategies to best support the child as well as to provide self-care for the parents. Discuss coping strategies to help the child, using Handout 57: Coping Strategies for Posttraumatic Stress Reactions from Child Session 1. Assist the parents in considering their own sources of social support and mechanisms for self-care. Encourage them to make a plan to avail themselves of these resources during this time and when they can foresee difficult times in general. It is important that they understand that they need appropriate adults to reach out to for support, distraction, and self-care during times of heightened emotion or stress. Help them consider the steps they will take to reach out to their support system (whom and when) and things they can do to bolster their own self-care (make an appointment for a massage, schedule time to exercise, plan a date night, etc.).

TRAUMA NARRATIVE AND PARENT ROLE

Explain to the parents that the child will spend the next two or more sessions telling the story of the traumatic event, verbally, and by creating a My Story book. Let them know that children will also practice sharing the story with the parent in a role play with the therapist before the joint session. Inform parents that in an upcoming session, you will role play with them responding to the child's trauma disclosure and sharing of the My Story book, and fill them in on any information the child has provided that will assist them in further supporting the child in preparation for the joint session that will subsequently take place.

Child Session 2: Trauma Narrative

This and future trauma sessions are given only if the child has significant trauma history and symptoms and if the therapist has training and experience with child trauma treatment. The purpose of this session is to provide the opportunity for children to process the memory of their traumatic event (or events) through creating a trauma narrative.

Materials for this session include

- My Story book with about six pages—put together with a cover the child can decorate;
- Handout 11: Feelings Thermometer (from Module 1 Child Session 2); and
- crayons, markers, pencils, lined and unlined paper.

PROVIDE RATIONALE FOR SHARING OF TRAUMA STORY

Provide the child with an explanation for why processing or working through their trauma story helps to reduce the frequency and intensity of their symptoms. The idea is that although what they have been through was terrible and frightening, the memory of the events cannot harm them now and children can recover and lead full and healthy lives. Thinking and talking about their experience in a supportive environment with you enables the child to process their memories so that when they are reminded of their traumatic experiences, they do not feel as upset or scared by the memory. It is a way they can take charge of their symptoms.

Using an analogy can be a good way to start off the discussion. You may say something like,

> Have you ever had a splinter? If you get a splinter, say in your hand, and you just ignore it and try not to think about it, will it go away? No, it doesn't go away. Instead it keeps bugging you and getting red and swollen and hurting and getting worse so it seems like you will never be rid of that splinter. When we go through something really stressful or scary, it is kind of like that splinter. We try to ignore it, avoid thinking or talking about it, but what we saw or experienced still affects us and keeps bugging us. To get rid of a splinter we sometimes have to dig at it a little bit and then pull it out. Now the digging and pulling may hurt temporarily, but then the splinter is out and the body can heal itself. Before we know it, we aren't thinking about the splinter so much anymore as it is healing over.
>
> Today I am going to ask you to tell your story, and by talking about it and drawing it and sharing your memories of what happened, just like taking the splinter out, you will be able to start healing and not be so bothered by what happened. Even though you went through some really hard and scary (use wording applicable to the child) things, we know that you can recover and

> lead a full and healthy life. The more you are able to work through your story, the easier it gets each time and the less you will find yourself thinking or worrying about it.

VERBAL TELLING (AND RETELLING) OF TRAUMA STORY

Some children who are adopted may have experienced chronic abuse or neglect or exposure to domestic violence, and others may list multiple traumatic events that they have experienced (i.e., one parent deported or incarcerated, removal from other parent, physical abuse by relative caregiver or foster family, witnessing of a fight between parents, and a shooting or robbery in the community). You can approach the trauma narrative in a couple of different ways, either of which can offer the space to bear witness to the child's sharing of their memories and experience. One option is to explore with the child the event that stands out the most or is currently the most bothersome or distressing. For example, what are they having intrusive thoughts or flashbacks about when they are trying to take a test at school or trying to get to sleep at night? So for the previous examples, for a child who experienced ongoing domestic violence in the home, there may be a fight between parents that is still particularly distressing (maybe the time the child thought dad was going to kill mom, or a time when dad was taken away by police, or a fight in which the neighbors got involved and the child felt a mix of shame and relief). Children with multiple traumatic experiences may be struggling with flashbacks and intrusive thoughts or avoidance around one particular event (e.g., when they witnessed a loved one being held at gunpoint or when they were pulled away from mom and taken to the police station to await social services). They can then start the trauma narrative process about that particular event. Other times children may prefer to talk about the ongoing domestic violence more in general in their story as they recount more than one event or episode (e.g., may title their story "My birth parents fought a lot" or "My birth dad hit me and my mom"). In other words, allow children with multiple or chronic trauma to choose whether to focus on a specific event or a more general distressing pattern that includes multiple events.

If the child will be focusing on a single traumatic event, ask the child to tell you the story of what happened just before, during, and just after the traumatic event (usually this is all within one day). If the child will be talking about something more general, such as "fights at home," "my mom used to hurt me," or "my terrible things," then they can start where it makes sense for them. Let children know in advance that you will be jotting down parts of their story as they share to help them later in the creation of their My Story written narrative. As they are telling their story, try not to interrupt them, other than being an empathic and encouraging presence, writing down the parts of the stories they convey. The following is a sample dialogue that may be used to get the story started if the child is focusing on a single event:

> I would like you to tell me about your story of what happened or what you saw. I am first going to ask you what was going on just before it happened, then ask you to tell me about the event, and then what happened just afterward. As you tell me your story, I am going to be writing down the parts of the story, so you

> will see me jotting things down on this page (show them the paper). When you finish, we are going to go through each part of the story together to make sure we got it all down. We will also use this outline later when you write or draw out your story. Why don't you go ahead and start by telling me what was happening just before your stressful event (note child's particular stressor) happened.

After children have told their story from beginning to end, thank them for their courage and use empathy to acknowledge the terrible thing they have experienced and how proud you are that they were able to tell you what it was like for them. Then, repeat back to them what you heard. The following is a sample dialogue for ending the first telling of the story:

> You did a great job telling me your story. I am really proud of you for having the courage to do that. Let's take a couple of our deep breaths and think about your calming image. Good. Now, you can correct me if I got things wrong, but I'd like to read back to you the parts of the story I heard you say just now. I would like to ask for your Feelings Thermometer (Handout 11 from Module 1) rating for thinking or talking about each part of the story right now. OK? The Feelings Thermometer is right here, so you can just point to a number or you can use your hands to tell me or you can say a number out loud—whatever works best for you.

Read back the parts of the story from just before to just afterward, pausing to ask for a Feelings Thermometer rating for each part. Ask, "What is it like to think or talk about that part of the story right now?" for each part of the story. When you have ratings for all parts of the story, ensure the child is satisfied that everything relevant is included. You may say something like, "Does it sound like we got all the parts to your story in there?" If "no," add in the extra parts.

Ask the child to tell you the story again from the beginning, this time stopping to ask for Feelings Thermometer ratings at the two parts of the story that garnered the highest ratings during the previous telling of the story. These ratings are to give you a sense of the child's feelings and when habituation (anxiety reduction) begins to occur. The following is a sample dialogue that may be used to progress to the retelling of the story:

> OK, now that we have gotten your story written down, I'd like you to tell it to me again from the beginning. I am going to ask you to tell me your story several times. Remember, I am not asking you to tell your story over and over again because I didn't hear you; it is because we know that the more you are able to tell it, the easier it should get and the less you will worry about it. Like the splinter, right? It feels so hard to dig it out at first, but then it can heal so much easier and gets better with time. I will be checking in with you a few times as you tell your story by asking for Feelings Thermometer ratings. Again, you can tell me the number you are feeling on your Feelings Thermometer at the moment I ask for it, or you can point to a number on the thermometer here, or hold up the number of fingers to show your Feelings Thermometer rating at that moment. So let's start at the beginning again with what was happening just before (the stressful event).

If any new parts were added, say "and this time, please include the extra parts we just talked about."

For the final step in this exercise, ask the child to repeat the story one or two more times. You should start to notice that the child's anxiety and Feelings Thermometer ratings are beginning to go down during each retelling of the story. Note that not all children will demonstrate anxiety in the first place, and not all will demonstrate anxiety reduction. All different kinds of patterns of distress are possible, but the long-term goals of repetition and accompanying anxiety reduction remain the same.

If distress/anxiety starts high and reduces, then you are on the right track. Continue with additional practice (writing) to consolidate gains.

If distress/anxiety starts high and stays high, use the remaining time in the session to continue with the verbal storytelling to try to reduce it. If it is still high at the end of the session, reassure the child that more practice (verbal and written) will lead to beginning to feel better. Schedule an extra child session if possible.

If distress/anxiety starts low and stays low, that's fine. Stick with the process because disclosure has been found to be helpful for people even if they do not have significant levels of anxiety.

If distress/anxiety starts low and gets worse, use the remaining time in the session to continue with the verbal storytelling to try to reduce it. If it is still high at the end of the session, reassure the child that more practice (verbal and written) will lead to beginning to feel better. Schedule an extra session time if possible.

PLANNING AND STARTING MY STORY PAGES

Next, with the child's input on what they would prefer to do, select a format for My Story. This can be created with simple binding of six or so pages of paper including a cover page. Some options are

- drawing pictures on the pages and having the clinician write the narration and create "thought and feeling bubbles" based on quotes from the child about their picture (younger children),
- creating a My Story book with a mixture of drawings and words or captions describing each page, or
- writing their story without pictures on lined paper (older children) or on a computer.

Begin to outline the written trauma narrative. If the child has chosen to do a small My Story book, use a four-to-six-page paper booklet to assist the child in planning out what they want to draw or write on each page and making a note of it from start to finish. After you have a plan for how they will use the pages of their book to describe their story, allow the child to begin their title page (if they would like a title) and the first page, assisting them with writing in narrative or thought or feeling bubbles as needed. To elicit more details and/or engagement in the storytelling process, respectfully probe for details regarding thoughts and feelings during the various portions of the trauma story. These can be added to the text, captions, etc.

If the child would like to only write out the story, allow them to do so on lined paper or type on a computer. Once the child has completed the title page and first page of the My Story book or has written out their story on paper, ask them to read it aloud and check in regarding Feelings Thermometer ratings. Let them know that you will continue working on the story and drawings in subsequent session(s).

RELAXATION OR GROUNDING ACTIVITY

Leave time in the session for a relaxation exercise or other short activity to help the child feel grounded in the present and ready to transition out of the session. This may take the form of time to talk about what they are doing that evening or the coming weekend or something they are looking forward to. Because of the important therapeutic work that the child is doing, it can be helpful to develop a plan to check in with the child later that day or in the coming days and to help them make a plan for how they can access social support if they become upset. Refer back to the splinter analogy—"it may hurt a bit temporarily because it is like we just dug out and pulled your splinter." It may be helpful to also engage the parents in planning positive family activities during this time to bolster support for the child.

Child Session 3 (and as Many Extra Sessions as Needed): Continue Completion of Child's Trauma Story Book

This session will follow the Child Session 3 or other child sessions needed to complete the processing of the trauma memories.

Materials for this session include

- art supplies and pencils, and
- child's partially completed or planned My Story book.

COMPLETE THE MY STORY BOOK

Reflect on the progress made in the previous session with the telling of the story and completing the trauma narrative book. You may say something like, "You did such a nice job last time we met. Today you will have a chance to continue your My Story book or to write out your story." For children who are doing the My Story book, say: "Last time we made a plan for how you were going to use the pages of your book. Now, you can spend some time finishing (or continuing to work on) those pages."

Allow the child to continue working on the drawings and written narrative for their My Story book. Assist the child with writing down the narrative or thought or feeling bubbles as needed. To elicit more details and/or engagement in the storytelling process, respectfully probe for details regarding thoughts and feelings during the various portions of the trauma story. These can be added to the text, captions, etc. If the child is writing out their story, allow them to do so on lined paper. Once the child has completed the My Story book or has written out their story on paper, ask them to read it aloud or have you do so, and check in regarding Feelings Thermometer ratings. Provide labeled praise and encouragement for their bravery in writing and sharing their story.

As the child completes or reads back the written narrative or the My Story book, pay careful attention to any maladaptive cognitions and help the child to observe and challenge these thoughts, providing realistic information (i.e., most 8-year-olds do not have the power to stop something like that from happening) and using other coping strategies they have learned in ADAPT (i.e., deep breathing, muscle relaxation, calming image). Make note of any maladaptive or negative thoughts that may be impacting the child so you can share them during the next parent session and strategize around the best way to help the child reframe them when they come up or interfere.

Here are some special considerations to note:

1. *If the child's memory differs from the record.* It is not uncommon that a child's memory of their experience differs from what may be noted in the child's record or the accounting of an adult. Memories are encoded individually and are dependent on developmental level, previous experience, perspective on the situation, emotional state, etc. It is important to allow the child to tell their story without correcting it—what it was like for them and their understanding of their experience. When children are not given information about an event or allowed to process it and ask questions, they will often fill in the missing information on their own. For example, an older sibling may remove a child from the room if the parents begin to physically fight, but the child still hears everything and puts together images and visceral feelings of what is occurring in the other room based on what they are hearing, and because this fight will likely never be discussed or processed, that becomes embedded as part of the child's memory. Once the child has had the opportunity to share the story, if there is more information or detail available, you may let the child know that you have some further information about that event and wonder if the child would like to know it. Children then may be able to integrate this new information into their story and understanding of the experience.
2. *What language to use for the storytelling.* Oftentimes it can be most effective to have the child process the traumatic memory in the language in which it was encoded. For example, if you are working with a child from a Spanish-speaking country who witnessed or experienced a traumatic event in their home country when they were Spanish-speaking at age 4, then it may be easiest for the child to access and process their trauma memory in Spanish, even if they now speak predominantly English as an 8-year-old.
3. *What about traumatic events that occur in preverbal infancy or toddlerhood?* When a traumatic event occurs when children are very young, they may not have a verbal memory to share about their experience. Oftentimes, very young children still seem to have a visceral memory of their experience, and adop-

tive parents may notice that certain sensations or situations trigger distress in the child that they cannot connect to a specific event. For example, any time a child hears a knocking sound or someone knocking on the door, the child becomes immediately distraught and jumps into the parents' arms or wraps arms around the parents' leg.

4. *Traumatic loss.* When children experience a traumatic loss, it is important to extend the My Story process to allow them to integrate a full memory of the person they lost. For example, if a child's mother was shot and killed, or a child finds his father hanging from a rope, every time the child thinks *mom* or *dad,* the traumatic image may pop into the child's mind. When a child has experienced the traumatic death of a loved one, each time someone mentions that person or even just mentions the words *mom* or *dad,* the child is likely to be triggered, which can clearly impact functioning in all domains. To assist children in being able to have a full memory of their parent or other important person and not just think of the traumatic image, it can be helpful to add to the story or create a different My Story about their favorite memories of their loved one and spend some time remembering and reflecting on those positive memories as well. For example, a 9-year-old girl witnessed her father being shot and killed when she was 6, and every time the teachers at school would say the word *dad,* she would touch her chest to the very place her father's gunshot wound was and had a lot of difficulty being redirected. You can imagine for a school-age child how many times each day this word comes up. After she completed the trauma narrative of her father's shooting, the therapist directed her to then start to remember and draw some of her favorite memories of her father and their times together. In being able to both process the traumatic memory and also reflect on her full memory of her 6 years of experience with her dad, not just the moment of his being shot, she was able to bring a fuller picture and memory of dad to mind when she heard this word or his name. If the child has completed Module 3 on Loss and Grief, you can also refer to the memories discussed in the joint session in the Tree of Remembrance activity.

PREPARE FOR THE JOINT SESSION (WHEN CHILD HAS COMPLETED STORY)

Once the child has completed the creation of their story, prepare the child for sharing their trauma story with their parents. This may include role playing sharing their My Story book as well as asking them if there is anything in particular that they may need to hear or see from their parents in the joint session to feel supported through the process. Say something like,

> Now that you have worked so hard on your story, I would like to help you share your story with your parent(s). This will give you another chance to think about it and make it easier to talk and think about. It will also help you be better able to talk to your parent(s) about what you have been through later on in the future when you might be thinking about it or worrying about

something related to it. Next week we will meet together with your parent(s). I will meet with them first to talk about all of the progress you have made and how proud I am of your hard work. I will share your story with them so they can see what you have been working on. Then we will meet together and you can go through your story with them and I will be there to support you.

ROLE PLAY THE CHILD SHARING STORY WITH PARENTS

Help children role play sharing the story with their parents so that they will have practice doing so and be more comfortable. Sometimes it can be helpful to start with you being the child and the child being the parent so you can get a sense for how they think their parents are likely to respond. Then you can move into the child practicing sharing the story as you role play being the parents in the room: "Right now, let's practice telling your story using your My Story book with your parents. I will pretend that I am your parent and you are sharing your story. Let's give it a try." Complete role play and process what it felt like to the child.

Ask the child if there is anything that his or her parents could do or say that would make the child feel supported by them and make note of this to bring up in the next parent session. For example, children may request to sit next to a certain parent (or the therapist), or they may want someone to give them a hug afterward or to make (or not make) eye contact or they may want to hear something in particular such as "I am sorry that happened to you" or "I am glad you are telling me about this."

Parent Session 3: Sharing Child's Trauma Story With Parents and Processing Reactions

This session is to occur after Child Session 3 or as many sessions as the child needs to complete their narrative, once the child's trauma story is complete and they have had the opportunity to role play the sharing of their story with their parents.

The goal of this session is to review the child's progress in this module with the parents and to facilitate the sharing of the child's story with them. In addition, the parent is provided with guidance around the best ways to support the child as they share their narrative.

Materials for this session include

- Handout 58: Tips for Listening to Your Child, and
- child's completed My Story book.

REVIEW CHILD'S PROGRESS WITH PARENT

Provide a brief review for the parent of progress their child has made in this module and the child's ability to use any coping strategies they have learned in ADAPT. Let the parents know that you would like to review their child's story with them so that they have a chance to see/hear and process it with you before their child presents it to them in the joint session. Normalize that hearing or seeing the narrative can be difficult, but that it is important for their child to be able to process the memory of their traumatic event(s) and feel comfortable sharing about it with their parents. This can open the lines of communication so that their child can come to them in the future when thinking or worrying about the event(s).

READ THROUGH CHILD'S TRAUMA STORY WITH PARENT

Using the child's My Story book, share the child's story with the parent, providing empathy and support as they hear it. Review any negative or maladaptive thoughts, such as self-blame or guilt, that the child has related to the traumatic event, and discuss how you have tried to help the child address this, if applicable. Note and process parental feelings that arise during the sharing of the story, providing normalization and empathy.

PREPARE PARENTS TO SUPPORT CHILDREN AS THEY SHARE AND ROLE PLAY

Prepare parents for the best way to support children when they share the story with them in the joint session by telling parents what the child has requested to help them with telling the story. Given your work with the child, let the parents know what they may expect from their child's response and anything their child expressed during previous child sessions related to how their parents may be able to best provide support.

Review Handout 58: Tips for Listening to Your Child with parents and give them a copy to take home. Briefly role play reading the child's story as if you are the child, allowing the parents to practice responding to the child in the manner you have just discussed. You may say something like, "I am going to go through your child's story again with you, but this time I would like us to pretend that I am your child, so that you can practice responding to me (playing your child) in the ways we just discussed."

Provide feedback to the parents as necessary, asking the parents to maintain eye contact, nod, encourage, and say something positive at the end. Answer any of the parents' questions. Also, discuss with the parents if there is somebody that they may be able to talk to within their social support network after the session in case they need to further process any feelings that come up. Normalize that just like the child needs support in processing their stressful events, the parents may also need a support person in their lives that they can go to as they are processing their child's disclosures. This is a good time to encourage some positive family time and activities that they can do together and look forward to as they are working through this intense process.

Following the role play with the parents, assess if the parents have had sufficient time to process the story and be able to respond appropriately during the child's sharing of the story. If you do not feel they will be able to hear the child tell the story and remain supportive, you will need to continue helping the parents work through and process the information and understand the importance of their conveying support to the child. Sometimes you may suggest that an additional parent session or more may be needed for this work, and you can also let parents know they can call you or request an extra session if they are feeling overwhelmed with the child's trauma disclosures.

> Remember that parents may be hearing some of this information from their child's perspective for the first time. They may need guidance and support in getting over some of the shock and some time to deal with it. This does not mean that the joint session should be avoided. It means that some time may be needed to work through their responses and appropriately prepare the parent for the session, engaging them in understanding the critical role that the child's sharing of the story can play in their recovery. It is best to convey to the parent that the joint session will only take place when the parent is ready to hear the child share their story and be supportive. You may have to repeat the role play again to ensure that they are able to respond appropriately. (Langley & Jaycox, 2015, pp. 82–83)

Joint Session: Child Shares Trauma Story With Parents

The purpose of the joint session is to facilitate the child sharing their My Story book with their parents.

Materials for this session include the child's completed trauma My Story book.

SHARING OF TRAUMA STORY

Have the child share their trauma narrative with their parents by reading through their My Story book, showing pictures and captions, etc. Encourage parents to use supportive language and stance practiced in parent sessions, and model this process for them if needed. The following is a sample dialogue you may use to help introduce the reading of the trauma narrative:

> Today you have the chance to share your story with your parent(s). I know you might have talked about it before, maybe even a lot, but we're going to do the whole story here today. This will help you (the child) feel better when you talk about what happened, and it will help you (the parent) be able to hear it and talk about the event(s) more often at home. It's important to share stories like this, just the way you share stories of fun things that happened to you, or stories from when (the child) was younger, or things about your (adult) life when you were younger.

Allow the child to read the story to the parents. Here is a sample of what you may want to say to help get the child started: "Just like we talked about, this is the time for you to share your story (hand child the My Story book). I will be here if you need any help."

Acknowledge both child and parent for taking the important step of sharing the story and prompt parents to provide any supportive statements discussed in the earlier session by reminding them to look at the Tips for Listening to Your Child (Handout 58) as needed. Help the child and parent process any issues that may arise for them in the retelling or immediately afterward. Encourage children to try to set aside time to talk with their parent again about their story if they are thinking or worrying about it, but let them know this is not a story for bedtime. Have child and parent identify where and when this can happen.

If you have worked with the child on restructuring any maladaptive thoughts about the stressful event, help the child to share this so parents are aware of how the child is currently working on thinking about elements of the event in a more adaptive manner.

Acknowledge that processing stressful events can lead to an increase in feelings about what happened for a short time, even though it will help lessen those feelings over time (refer back to splinter analogy, saying "This is kind of like when you have to dig in and get the splinter out so that it can then heal"). If the session is early in the day, you may want to tell the child that you will be checking in later that day or evening to make sure that the child is doing well. Remind parents of their plan to check in with an adult support person as needed.

If at any time during the joint session, the parent responds in an unsupportive manner and cannot be redirected, or behaves in a way that is countertherapeutic for the child (e.g., being so overwhelmed by their own feelings that the focus on the child is lost, parents blame each other), end the session at this point by doing a quick relaxing or regulating activity (e.g., calming image or deep breathing), and try to end on a positive note of progress. Let the child know that you will meet with him or her alone during the next session and figure out another plan for continuing to share the story at a later time. Resume meeting with the child and the parent separately.

TRANSITION ACTIVITY

End the session by guiding the child and parents through one of the following regulating activities, with the goal of ending on a positive and optimistic note:

- Ask the child to help lead a relaxation exercise.
- Ask the child to share some of the skills they have been using to deal with big or scary feelings (i.e., calming image).
- Ask parent and child what some of their favorite things to do together are and then help them plan a time to do one or two of those activities in the coming days.
- Talk to the parent and child about any upcoming family activities that they are looking forward to.
- Discuss what are some favorite family foods and have them plan a meal out this week.
- Ask the child about something happening in school or their social life that day or the next that they are looking forward to.

Use the selected activity as an opportunity to reinforce the child and parents and acknowledge the hard work they have put in during the module. Make an effort to guide the end of the session so that the child and family leave on a hopeful note.

The Termination Session 10

The purpose of the termination session is to help parent(s) and children discuss their feelings about adoption-specific therapy (ADAPT), focusing on positive gains. In the session (as in the preceding couple of sessions), therapists and children process not only this goodbye, but also past goodbyes that often have been abrupt and traumatic for the children.

Parents and children meet separately with their therapists for about half of the last session, then come together for the celebration part. Refer back to Module 5 Parent Session 2 about discussion of termination in planning for this last session to make sure that the important material is presented.

Parent Termination Session

The goals of the parent termination session are to discuss therapeutic gains parents feel they and the child have made over the course of ADAPT, to talk about their feelings about the various parts of the intervention and about ending the treatment, and to make final behavioral plans and discuss generalization of gains made.

http://dx.doi.org/10.1037/0000096-011
Adoption-Specific Therapy: A Guide to Helping Adopted Children and Their Families Thrive, by J. Waterman, A. K. Langley, J. Miranda, and D. B. Riley

DISCUSSION OF GAINS OF CHILD AND PARENTS

After acknowledging that it is the last session of ADAPT, ask the parents what they feel the child has gained and what positive changes they have noticed as a result of the intervention, as well as what the parents feel they have gained from their own participation. Ask questions to clarify and probe for more detail if the parents give vague answers. Be sure to reflect any feelings that come up for the parents. Ask them for final ratings on the three problems that they identified at the beginning of treatment. After the parents have given their perspective, share your own sense of the gains made by both child and parents, being as specific as you can. Emphasize what skills they have learned that can be used in the future, and discuss with them what situations may arise in which it would be appropriate to use these skills. For example, you might note that their son gained competence in using deep breathing and the calming image to deal with situations in which he gets very angry and is likely to hit or kick someone, and then ask the parents if there are upcoming situations where these skills may be particularly useful (e.g., regional soccer tournament, sleepover for brother's birthday).

EVALUATION OF THE INTERVENTION/SHARING FEELINGS

Ask parents what parts of the ADAPT intervention they found most useful and why, as well as which elements they felt were less or not at all useful. For example, you might query about which particular modules seemed to be most helpful or meaningful for the child, and also which ones parents felt were most useful to them. If you felt there were particularly meaningful moments, mention them to the parents, along with whatever feelings you had about them. For example, in the joint session in Module 2 when child and parents share their adoption stories, there are often loving, tender moments that may elicit tears from everyone, including the therapist. To commemorate such a moment, you might say something like,

> I'll remember that special moment when (child's name) crawled up in your lap after you were able to talk with her about her birth mom's drinking and how scary it must have been for her to have been left alone. It brings tears to my eyes to think of it now.

Elicit from parents their thoughts and feelings about the ending of the ADAPT intervention. Accept and empathize with whatever feelings parents bring up. Common feelings include happiness about the progress made, fear that they or the child will slip back into old dysfunctional patterns without the therapist, gratitude at how hard the family worked at improving their family, and sadness at ending after having shared this experience with the therapist and the child. If appropriate, share your own feelings about the ending of therapy. Often therapists have mixed feelings, being happy with the progress made, but sad about no longer meeting with the parents or the child. If your feelings are positive, it is a gift to the family to share these with them.

FINAL BEHAVIORAL PLANS AND GENERALIZATION

Check in on the current behavioral plan and ask parents to anticipate other behaviors or situations that the parents want to work on in the near future. Ask the parents to develop a behavioral adoption-specific strategy to deal with this current or anticipated behavior, with the therapist providing only minimal guidance to help boost parents' confidence that they can do it alone now that they have the skills. Mention that the skills they have learned will generalize to other new situations that will arise, and go over the recurring positive parenting skills of praise and encouragement, child-led play, preteaching, and de-escalation that they have been practicing throughout the ADAPT intervention. If further intervention is needed, make treatment recommendations and discuss options with the parents.

CASE EXAMPLE: THE SPRINGFIELDS

Rachel and Lewis came into the session holding hands and said they had been talking last night about their last session today, and had told each other how sad they were that ADAPT was ending. The therapist asked them to talk more about their feelings. Lewis said that they loved the fact that they got together every week and came to ADAPT as a family and had a family ritual of going out to eat after each session. Except for Maria's occasional sulking and sighing that she wished she was home so she could text her friends (they have a no texting at the table rule), they had come to value this special family time. The therapist wondered if they couldn't continue the tradition of going out to dinner every Wednesday night, and the parents thought that was a good idea.

In talking about gains made, Rachel said she realized that their family closeness had changed as a result of ADAPT in what she saw as helpful ways. Specifically, the parents have felt much closer to Maria; she discloses more to them, is lying less, seeks out affection, and frequently says she's so pleased that she can talk about her birth mom and the parents understand and accept how important she still is to Maria. When asked why they thought this closeness had developed, Rachel thought it was partly because of the conversations about adoption and her birth mother they had in therapy and partly because of the child-led play that they worked so hard on with Maria. Lewis said it seemed like now she felt that they would love her even if she made mistakes and wasn't perfect. With Carlos, Rachel said she felt less close and that was a good thing. The distress over separation in the morning has disappeared, and he seems more willing to try to do things on his own and is so pleased when he succeeds.

When asked what they felt was most and least helpful to them as parents about ADAPT, Lewis said that he thought the emphasis on positivity, which involved positive interactions like play and his trips walking to the convenience store with Maria, really trying to use praise and encouragement every day, and on de-escalation were really useful, especially because he thinks he's kind of a critical person. Rachel said she's still struggling with de-escalation, and what she found really helpful was the discussion about attachment styles and noticing how the family's various styles meshed and clashed. Other things she really liked were writing the adoption story, having the scripts to talk about sharing difficult information, and using the lens of the child's past history when trying to understand the meaning of a particular behavior for the child.

In talking about feelings about ending, Rachel became tearful, asking the therapist to remember that she has a preoccupied attachment style. She is worried about being able to succeed on their own and also knows that Maria has grown very attached to the therapist. The therapist replied that she has been honored to be part of their journey and noted that for the last month or so, the parents have done an amazing job of using the positive parenting strategies like praise and encouragement, preteaching, and child-led play, as well as using the adoption-specific lens in their interactions with the children. Lewis said that he definitely felt more confident as a parent and was having more fun as well.

Child Termination Session

The purpose of the child termination session is to discuss what children feel they have learned in ADAPT as well as what they liked best in the sessions, to share positive feelings between therapist and child and discuss feelings about ending the treatment, and to give children a certificate for successfully completing ADAPT.

Materials for this session include

- Handout 59: What I Like About You (adapted for termination session);
- card stock or construction paper;
- markers, glue, or other art materials for card making;
- photographs of child and therapist (possibly including photos of child and therapist together); and
- Handout 60: ADAPT Certificates.

DISCUSSION OF GAINS MADE

Ask children what they liked best about the ADAPT intervention and what they think they've learned from participating. Guide the discussion at a level appropriate to the child's development. Younger children may focus on specific activities, for instance, the family activities cards or reading *The Invisible String* or *Murphy's Three Homes*, whereas older children may be able to talk about concepts and skills. For example, a preteen boy may say he really liked feeling more comfortable talking about his birth family with his adoptive parents now that he realizes they understand how important his birth mom is to him, or he may note that problem solving about how to deal with peer pressure has already helped him to respond in a way that didn't make him seem nerdy when he turned down his friend's invitation to try marijuana. Praise and reinforce children's responses about gains made with enthusiasm. Make sure to remind all children that they learned skills for coping with upset feelings, including deep breathing, muscle relaxation, and using the calming image. Note that the child also has learned and practiced problem-solving strategies to deal with conflicts that may come up.

WHAT I LIKE ABOUT YOU

Use Handout 59: What I Like About You, previously used in the joint session of Module 1 with regard to family members, to allow the child and you to say positive things you like about each other. Say what you like about each other out loud, and then write down what was said on the What I Like About You handout. Aim to have at least three things each likes about the other. Ask children if they want to write down what they said about you, or whether they prefer that you write it. Give the child the sheet with what you like about them to take home and keep. Thank the child for the nice things said about you and note that you plan to keep it as a reminder of your time together.

GOODBYE CARDS

Have construction paper or card stock, markers, scissors, glue, glitter, and other art materials for you and the child to use to make goodbye cards for each other. If there are photos available, you can put a picture of yourself in the card, and the child may want to give you a photo as well. Sometimes children want to have a picture with you and/or a family picture that includes you. If the child wants to put such a picture in the card for you, let the child know that this can be brought up during the party and a picture taken then.

Use the opportunity of making the card to write how much you have enjoyed working with the child and how special the child is in a way that recognizes the child's uniqueness. Make it as personal and specific as you can, knowing the child may keep it for a long time.

GIFT?

Although it is not necessary to give the child a small gift, it is OK to do so if you feel that would be helpful, especially if it is something that has symbolic meaning in the child's life or the ADAPT intervention. For example, one child really loved *Murphy's Three Homes* and asked the therapist to reread it in several sessions, so the therapist bought him a copy. Other examples might be a special kind of ball that the child has used during sessions, a small stuffed animal that is the same as the one that the child made in the Clay Animal activity, art material, etc. For children with many losses, this small gift can serve as a kind of transitional object.

CERTIFICATES

At the end of the session, give the child a certificate (preferably with a gold seal or other embellishment) signifying successful completion of the ADAPT intervention. Sample ADAPT Certificates are included (Handout 60), but feel free to use your creativity to make a certificate that is appropriate for the particular child and developmental stage.

CASE EXAMPLE: THE SPRINGFIELDS

Carlos was more active and distractible than usual as he came into the session. He wondered when would he get to eat the cupcakes and was disappointed when the therapist said they were going to do some goodbye activities first. The therapist asked what things in ADAPT that he liked best. He thought for a moment and said he liked reading books like *Murphy's Three Homes* and *Rosie's Story*. When asked what he liked about those books, he replied that they were about dogs and he loves dogs. The therapist remembered that Carlos had chosen a dog for the animal he would like to be in the very first session they had. When asking about what he thought he had learned through ADAPT, he said he learned not to be so afraid that his mom would leave him and not come back. He still worries sometimes but uses deep breathing and muscle relaxation to calm him down. He said he also really likes the Lifebook he made. The therapist praised Carlos for all the progress that he has made. When asked if there were parts of ADAPT he didn't like, he emphatically said, "Yes! There were too many times you wanted me to draw something even though you know I hate to draw." The therapist thanked Carlos for sharing his feelings. After participating well in the What I Like About You activity, Carlos balked at drawing anything on the goodbye card. He asked if his mom could send the therapist a picture of him rather than him drawing, and the therapist said that would be very nice. Carlos wrote "To (therapist's name)" and signed it "Your friend Carlos." At the end of the session the therapist gave him a small stuffed dog that looked a lot like Murphy from *Murphy's Three Homes*; his face lit up and he said, "I'm going to name him Murphy and I'll think of you when I hug him."

For her session, Maria came in and burst into tears. She said that she had shared more than she had with anyone with the therapist and was going to miss the therapist very much. The therapist got teary as well as she comforted Maria and told her how much respect and caring the therapist has developed for Maria, noting she had to grow up fast when she essentially had to parent Carlos and then had so many changes of caregivers. The therapist wondered if the end of therapy was particularly painful for Maria because she has had so many other losses. Maria said that she feels like ADAPT helped her really connect with Rachel in particular, partly because she tried so very hard to find a way to reach her. The therapist said that it seemed like being able to talk about her birth mother and her previous experiences and have Rachel and Lewis begin to understand how much her birth mother meant to her allowed her to open her heart a little and gradually. Maria thanked the therapist for helping her and her parents work out the issue when she took money from her mother's purse and lied about it. She says she still sometimes lies, but is pretty sure she won't need to steal again. The therapist said Maria's feedback was really appreciated. When asked what she liked and didn't like about ADAPT, Maria noted that she loved doing the collage for the identity module and also thought the Tree of Remembrance was so meaningful for her. Her calming image has also been very helpful. She thought the family ritual part was dumb because she prefers to be with her friends.

In making the goodbye cards, Maria took her time and made a beautiful drawing of her and the therapist on the front and wrote lovely appreciative things on the inside, signing it "Love always, Maria." The therapist felt a bit inadequate as her card was not nearly as nice as Maria's. At the end of the session, the therapist gave Maria a book about how to make sketches for fashion design, and Maria was pleased and touched.

Joint Termination Session and Party

After parents and child have 30–40 minutes of meeting separately with the therapist, they come together for the celebratory party.

Materials for this session include

- food;
- games to play, especially if child has requested a specific family game; and
- art materials in case the family wants to do a family drawing or activity.

BRING FOOD

You and the family will have planned in the last session who would bring what kind of food. Usually you would bring some food that the child requested, and sometimes the parents also want to bring food to celebrate. Make sure to check with the parents that whatever the child has requested is OK with them for the child to have. The therapist usually brings some food of the child's choice or the family may choose to bring the food. Have a lighthearted atmosphere and have fun with the family.

NOTE POSITIVE CHANGES

As you interact with the family, note positive changes you have noticed. For example, you might say how relaxed and affectionate they are with each other. Ask if there are other positive changes that family members have noticed, and encourage them to share. However, do not push for this type of interaction if the family seems to just want to relax and enjoy.

ENGAGE IN FUN ACTIVITIES

In the last session, the child and you talked about possible fun activities to do during the party. If the child asked to play specific games, be sure to have them available, as well as art materials to draw with to make a family drawing or other art project. Allow the child to determine what activities if any the family engages in. End the session by again sharing feelings about the family, child, intervention, etc., that seem appropriate.

CASE EXAMPLE: THE SPRINGFIELDS

The family got together for the party. The therapist had baked chocolate cupcakes at Carlos's request and also brought some fruit. Maria and Rachel had baked a cake, decorated it with flowers and a big heart, inside of which was written "Thank you with love from Rachel, Lewis, Maria, and Carlos." They took pictures of all of them with the cake and enjoyed eating it. Carlos had calmed down but after a cupcake and a piece of cake, he was running around a lot. Maria played music from her phone and she and Rachel danced a bit, with Carlos clapping. He wanted everyone to play Jenga, so they sat down and had fun with it. The therapist really found it fun to engage with the family, and they all found it hard to leave at the end. The therapist gave the children their certificates to take home.

Conclusion

You have now completed adoption-specific therapy and the ADAPT curriculum. Hopefully, the parents have been able to examine problematic child behaviors through the lens of the children's past history, develop parenting strategies that take this understanding into account, recognize the child's strengths and resiliency, feel more comfortable with children's feelings about their birth family and other previous caregivers, and discuss adoption and related identity issues openly and comfortably with the children. Similarly, hopefully, the children have developed and used their coping strategies, talked about their developmental understanding of their adoption experience and made a Lifebook, processed their previous losses, and thought about the identity issues common in all adopted children and especially those adopted transracially. In the same vein, we hope family closeness and openness have increased. And hopefully, you have found the ADAPT curriculum to be easy to use, covering all the major issues that children adopted past infancy, either from foster care or internationally, and their families face as they grow together and develop closer family bonds.

If you feel that further psychological intervention is needed after completing ADAPT, you and the family can discuss whether it makes more sense for you to continue with them or whether other specialized treatment may be indicated. In our experience, the most common further interventions are usually more in-depth trauma treatment if there was severe trauma that was not completely resolved through Module 7, Trauma Treatment, or sometimes in-home therapeutic behavioral services if severe behavior problems have not completely subsided.

To end *Adoption-Specific Therapy: A Guide to Helping Adopted Children and Their Families Thrive*, here are some quotes from qualitative interviews with family members after completion of ADAPT.

"Every time we went to a session we learned something from it. And I liked how it was broken down into different ways of explaining, different modules. That was very helpful."

"ADAPT showed me how to deal with issues. I feel more comfortable now. Overall, the adoption and his behavior—I totally understand it."

"It prompted us to have conversations we wouldn't have otherwise necessarily had."

"I loved the way ADAPT just got to the point. I wish all therapy was like that. I've been a foster parent for many years and in therapy they just go around in a little circle, and it's, like, why don't you go to the main thing, rather than just going on and on. With ADAPT it was useful."

"I think what sticks out to me is the positive reinforcing, doing more of that rather than the negative. ADAPT taught us how to every time he did something well to really reflect on that instead of what he did wrong. That's what really sticks out to me."

"It helped to be closer to our daughter and it helped us all express feelings better to each other and be more honest with each other and not be afraid to hurt feelings."

"I think she is kind of torn between her two families and ADAPT took a lot of stress away and it was OK to talk about it."

"Well I think it was helpful for both of us to help understand the issues that he was going through and help me come up with a better strategy . . . the issues that would come up, you know related to the whole foster care situation."

"To understand where some of those feelings are coming from . . . for her particularly around loss and things that we don't always think about."

"One thing ADAPT helped us with, was how to accept the fact that one day he may ask to see his birth parents or know who they are, because we were reluctant to do that. We have to accept that he may want to do that one of these days."

"She's gotten really pretty good at being able to talk more openly about her feelings. For instance, when she first came, she really didn't say much."

"Talking about my past, my adoption and current family. It helps you to relieve feelings and stuff like that like if I am bothered by something."

"His whole attitude towards us, he learned how to calm himself down, how to express himself a little better, he learned that he's not alone. That there's a lot of kids out there."

References

Achenbach, T. M., & Edelbrock, C. S. (1983). *Manual for the Child Behavior Checklist and revised Child Behavior Profile*. Burlington: University of Vermont, Department of Psychiatry.

Adoption and Safe Families Act of 1997, Pub. L. 105-89, 111 Stat. 2115 (1997).

Ainsworth, M. D. S., & Bell, S. M. (1970). Attachment, exploration, and separation: Illustrated by the behavior of one-year-olds in a strange situation. *Child Development, 41*, 49–67.

Ainsworth, M. D. S., Blehar, M. C., Waters, E., & Wall, S. (1978). *Patterns of attachment: Psychological study of the strange situation*. Hillsdale, NJ: Erlbaum.

Bada, H. S., Das, A., Bauer, C. R., Shankaran, S., Lester, B., LaGasse, L., . . . Higgins, R. (2007). Impact of prenatal cocaine exposure on child behavior problems through school age. *Pediatrics, 119*(2), e348–e359. http://dx.doi.org/10.1542/peds.2006-1404

Bandura, A. (1977). *Social learning theory*. Englewood Cliffs, NJ: Prentice-Hall.

Barth, R. P., & Brooks, D. (2001). Outcomes for drug-exposed children eight years post-adoption. In R. Barth, D. Brodzinsky, & M. Freundlich (Eds.), *Adoption and prenatal drug exposure: The research, policy, and practice challenges* (pp. 23–58). Washington, DC: Child Welfare League of America.

Barth, R. P., & Miller, J. M. (2000). Building effective post-adoption services: What is the empirical foundation? *Family Relations, 49*, 447–455. http://dx.doi.org/10.1111/j.1741-3729.2000.00447.x

Berry, M., & Barth, R. P. (1989). Behavior problems of children adopted when older. *Children and Youth Services Review, 11*, 221–238. http://dx.doi.org/10.1016/0190-7409(89)90022-4

Berry, M., & Berry, K. (2016). *The adoptive parent toolbox: Insights and stories for the journey*. Morrisville, NC: Lulu Publishing Services.

Besharov, D. J. (1989, August 6). Crack babies: The worst threat is mom herself. *The Washington Post*, p. B1.

Bimmel, N., van IJzendoorn, M. H., Bakermans-Kranenburg, M. J., Juffer, F., & De Geus, E. J. (2008). Problem behavior and heart rate reactivity in adopted adolescents: Longitudinal and concurrent relations. *Journal of Research on Adolescence, 18*, 201–214. http://dx.doi.org/10.1111/j.1532-7795.2008.00557.x

Boss, P. (1999). *Ambiguous loss: Learning to live with unresolved grief*. Cambridge, MA: Harvard University Press.

Brand, A. E., & Brinich, P. M. (1999). Behavior problems and mental health contacts in adopted, foster, and nonadopted children. *Journal of Child Psychology and Psychiatry, 40*, 1221–1229. http://dx.doi.org/10.1111/1469-7610.00538

Brody, J. E. (1988, September 6). Cocaine: Litany of fetal risks grows. *The New York Times*. Retrieved from http://www.nytimes.com/1988/09/06/science/cocaine-litany-of-fetal-risks-grows.html?pagewanted=all

Brodzinsky, D. M. (1993). Long-term outcomes in adoption. *The Future of Children, 3*, 153–166. http://dx.doi.org/10.2307/1602410

Brodzinsky, D. M., Schechter, D. E., Braff, A. M., & Singer, L. M. (1984). Psychological and academic adjustment in adopted children. *Journal of Consulting and Clinical Psychology, 52*, 582–590. http://dx.doi.org/10.1037/0022-006X.52.4.582

Caughman, S., & Motley, I. (2009). *You can adopt: An adoptive families guide*. New York, NY: Ballantine Books.

Cederblad, M., Höök, B., Irhammar, M., & Mercke, A. M. (1999). Mental health in international adoptees as teenagers and young adults: An epidemiological study. *Journal of Child Psychology and Psychiatry, 40*, 1239–1248. http://dx.doi.org/10.1111/1469-7610.00540

Chamberlain, P. (2003). The Oregon multidimensional treatment foster care model: Features, outcomes, and progress in dissemination. *Cognitive and Behavioral Practice, 10*, 303–312. http://dx.doi.org/10.1016/S1077-7229(03)80048-2

Chamberlain, P., Leve, L. D., & Degarmo, D. S. (2007). Multidimensional treatment foster care for girls in the juvenile justice system: 2-year follow-up of a randomized clinical trial. *Journal of Consulting and Clinical Psychology, 75*, 187–193. http://dx.doi.org/10.1037/0022-006X.75.1.187

Chamberlain, P., Price, J., Leve, L. D., Laurent, H., Landsverk, J. A., & Reid, J. B. (2008). Prevention of behavior problems for children in foster care: Outcomes and mediation effects. *Prevention Science, 9*, 17–27. http://dx.doi.org/10.1007/s11121-007-0080-7

Chamberlain, P., & Reid, J. B. (1998). Comparison of two community alternatives to incarceration for chronic juvenile offenders. *Journal of Consulting and Clinical Psychology, 66*, 624–633. http://dx.doi.org/10.1037/0022-006X.66.4.624

Chasnoff, I. J., Burns, W. J., Schnoll, S. H., & Burns, K. A. (1985). Cocaine use in pregnancy. *The New England Journal of Medicine, 313*, 666–669. http://dx.doi.org/10.1056/NEJM198509123131105

Child Welfare Information Gateway. (2017). *Foster care statistics 2015*. Washington, DC: U.S. Department of Health and Human Services, Children's Bureau.

Children's Bureau. (2011). *How many children were adopted in 2007 and 2008?* Retrieved from https://www.childwelfare.gov/pubPDFs/adopted0708.pdf

Chorpita, B. F., Daleiden, E. L., & Collins, K. S. (2014). Managing and adapting practice: A system for applying evidence in clinical care with youth and families. *Clinical Social Work Journal, 42,* 134–142. http://dx.doi.org/10.1007/s10615-013-0460-3

Cohen, J. A., Mannarino, A. P., Berliner, L., & Deblinger, E. (2000). Trauma-focused cognitive behavioral therapy for children and adolescents: An empirical update. *Journal of Interpersonal Violence, 15,* 1202–1223. http://dx.doi.org/10.1177/088626000015011007

Cohen, J. A., Mannarino, A. P., & Deblinger, E. (2006). *Treating trauma and traumatic grief in children and adolescents.* New York, NY: Guilford Press.

Cooper, G., Hoffman, K., & Powell, B. (2017). Circle of security in child care: Putting attachment theory into practice in preschool classrooms. *ZERO TO THREE, 37*(3), 27–34.

Dave Thomas Foundation for Adoption & Evan B. Donaldson Adoption Institute. (2002). *National Adoption Attitudes Survey: Research report.* Retrieved from https://davethomasfoundation.org/wp-content/uploads/2012/10/2002-Adoption-Exec-Summ.pdf

Dickson, L. R., Heffron, W. M., & Parker, C. (1990). Children from disrupted and adoptive homes on an inpatient unit. *American Journal of Orthopsychiatry, 60,* 594–602. http://dx.doi.org/10.1037/h0079211

Dozier, M. (2003). Attachment-based treatment for vulnerable children. *Attachment & Human Development, 5,* 253–257. http://dx.doi.org/10.1080/14616730310001596151

Dozier, M., Lindhiem, O., & Ackerman, J. P. (2005). Attachment and Biobehavioral Catch-Up: An intervention targeting empirically identified needs of foster infants. In L. Berlin, Y. Ziv, L. Amaya-Jackson, & M. T. Greenberg (Eds.), *Enhancing early attachments: Theory, research, intervention, and policy* (pp. 178–194). New York, NY: Guilford Press.

Dozier, M., Peloso, E., Lewis, E., Laurenceau, J. P., & Levine, S. (2008). Effects of an attachment-based intervention on the cortisol production of infants and toddlers in foster care. *Development and Psychopathology, 20,* 845–859.

Eddy, J. M., Bridges Whaley, R., & Chamberlain, P. (2004). The prevention of violent behavior by chronic and serious male juvenile offenders: A 2-year follow-up of a randomized clinical trial. *Journal of Emotional and Behavioral Disorders, 12,* 2–8. http://dx.doi.org/10.1177/10634266040120010101

Edelstein, S. B., Gonzalez, A., Langley, A. K., Waterman, J., Paasivirta, M., & Paczkowski, E. (2017). Preparing and partnering with families to support the adoption of children from foster care. *Adoption Quarterly, 20,* 119–133. http://dx.doi.org/10.1080/10926755.2016.1170087

Eldridge, S. (1999). *Twenty things adopted kids wish their adoptive parents knew.* New York, NY: Dell Publishing.

Elmund, A., Lindblad, F., Vinnerljung, B., & Hjern, A. (2007). Intercountry adoptees in out-of-home care: A national cohort study. *Acta Paediatrica, 96,* 437–442.

Eyberg, S. (1988). Parent–child interaction therapy: Integration of traditional and behavioral concerns. *Child & Family Behavior Therapy, 10,* 33–46. http://dx.doi.org/10.1300/J019v10n01_04

Fahlberg, V. I. (1991). *A child's journey through placement.* Indianapolis, IN: Perspectives Press.

Fahlberg, V. I. (2012). *A child's journey through placement.* London, England: Jessica Kingsley.

Fanaroff, A. A., Stoll, B. J., Wright, L. L., Carlo, W. A., Ehrenkranz, R. A., Stark, A. R., . . . NICHD Neonatal Research Network. (2007). Trends in neonatal morbidity and mortality for very low birthweight infants. *American Journal of Obstetrics and Gynecology, 196*(2), 147.e1–147.e8. http://dx.doi.org/10.1016/j.ajog.2006.09.014

Fergusson, D. M., Lynskey, M., & Horwood, L. J. (1995). The adolescent outcomes of adoption: A 16-year longitudinal study. *Journal of Child Psychology and Psychiatry, 36,* 597–615. http://dx.doi.org/10.1111/j.1469-7610.1995.tb02316.x

Fisher, P. A., Burraston, B., & Pears, K. (2005). The Early Intervention Foster Care Program: Permanent placement outcomes from a randomized trial. *Child Maltreatment, 10,* 61–71. http://dx.doi.org/10.1177/1077559504271561

Fisher, P. A., Gunnar, M. R., Chamberlain, P., & Reid, J. B. (2000). Preventive intervention for maltreated preschool children: Impact on children's behavior, neuroendocrine activity, and foster parent functioning. *Journal of the American Academy of Child & Adolescent Psychiatry, 39,* 1356–1364. http://dx.doi.org/10.1097/00004583-200011000-00009

Fisher, P. A., & Kim, H. K. (2007). Intervention effects on foster preschoolers' attachment-related behaviors from a randomized trial. *Prevention Science, 8,* 161–170. http://dx.doi.org/10.1007/s11121-007-0066-5

Gilman, J. L. (2009). *Murphy's three homes: A story for children in foster care.* Washington, DC: Magination Press.

Gleitman, I., & Savaya, R. (2011). Adjustment of adolescent adoptees: The role of age of adoption and exposure to pre-adoption stressors. *Children and Youth Services Review, 33,* 758–766. http://dx.doi.org/10.1016/j.childyouth.2010.11.020

Gray, D. (2002). *Attaching in adoption: Practical tools for today's parents.* Indianapolis, IN: Perspectives Press.

Greeson, J. K., Briggs, E. C., Kisiel, C. L., Layne, C. M., Ake, G. S., III, Ko, S. J., . . . Fairbank, J. A. (2011). Complex trauma and mental health in children and adolescents placed in foster care: Findings from the National Child Traumatic Stress Network. *Child Welfare, 90*(6), 91–108.

Griffin, K. W., Botvin, G. J., Nichols, T. R., & Doyle, M. M. (2003). Effectiveness of a universal drug abuse prevention approach for youth at high risk for substance use initiation. *Preventive Medicine, 36,* 1–7. http://dx.doi.org/10.1006/pmed.2002.1133

Grotevant, H. D., McRoy, R. G., Elde, C. L., & Fravel, D. L. (1994). Adoptive family system dynamics: Variations by level of openness in the adoption. *Family Process, 33,* 125–146. http://dx.doi.org/10.1111/j.1545-5300.1994.00125.x

Gunnar, M. R., Bruce, J., & Grotevant, H. D. (2000). International adoption of institutionally reared children: Research and policy. *Development and Psychopathology, 12,* 677–693. http://dx.doi.org/10.1017/S0954579400004077

Harold, G., Hampden-Thompson, G., Rodic, M., & Sellers, R. (2017). *An evaluation of the AdOpt parenting programme*. London, England: Department for Education (DfE).

Hazen, A. L., Hough, R. L., Landsverk, J. A., & Wood, P. A. (2004). Use of mental health services by youths in public sectors of care. *Mental Health Services Research, 6,* 213–226. http://dx.doi.org/10.1023/B:MHSR.0000044747.54525.36

Hirschi, T. (2002). *Causes of delinquency*. Piscataway, NJ: Transaction.

Hjern, A., Lindblad, F., & Vinnerljung, B. (2002). Suicide, psychiatric illness, and social maladjustment in intercountry adoptees in Sweden: A cohort study. *The Lancet, 360*(9331), 443–448. http://dx.doi.org/10.1016/S0140-6736(02)09674-5

Holmes, M. (2000). *A terrible thing happened*. Washington, DC: Magination Press.

Irner, T. B., Teasdale, T. W., Nielsen, T., Vedal, S., & Olofsson, M. (2012). Substance use during pregnancy and postnatal outcomes. *Journal of Addictive Diseases, 31,* 19–28. http://dx.doi.org/10.1080/10550887.2011.642765

Jaffari-Bimmel, N., Juffer, F., van IJzendoorn, M. H., Bakermans-Kranenburg, M. J., & Mooijaart, A. (2006). Social development from infancy to adolescence: Longitudinal and concurrent factors in an adoption sample. *Developmental Psychology, 42,* 1143–1153. http://dx.doi.org/10.1037/0012-1649.42.6.1143

Jones, J., & Placek, P. (2017, February 15). *Adoption: By the numbers*. Alexandria, VA: National Council for Adoption. Retrieved from http://www.adoptioncouncil.org/publications/2017/02/adoption-by-the-numbers

Juffer, F., Hoksbergen, R. A., Riksen-Walraven, J. M., & Kohnstamm, G. A. (1997). Early intervention in adoptive families: Supporting maternal sensitive responsiveness, infant–mother attachment, and infant competence. *Journal of Child Psychology and Psychiatry, 38,* 1039–1050. http://dx.doi.org/10.1111/j.1469-7610.1997.tb01620.x

Juffer, F., & van IJzendoorn, M. H. (2005). Behavior problems and mental health referrals of international adoptees: A meta-analysis. *JAMA, 293*(20), 2501–2515. http://dx.doi.org/10.1001/jama.293.20.2501

Kaminski, J. W., Valle, L. A., Filene, J. H., & Boyle, C. L. (2008). A meta-analytic review of components associated with parent training program effectiveness. *Journal of Abnormal Child Psychology, 36,* 567–589. http://dx.doi.org/10.1007/s10802-007-9201-9

Karst, P. (2000). *The invisible string*. Camarillo, CA: DeVorss and Company.

Kerman, B., Freundlich, M., & Maluccio, A. N. (Eds.). (2009). *Achieving permanence for older children and youth in foster care*. New York, NY: Columbia University Press. http://dx.doi.org/10.7312/kerm14688

Keyes, M. A., Sharma, A., Elkins, I. J., Iacono, W. G., & McGue, M. (2008). The mental health of US adolescents adopted in infancy. *Archives of Pediatrics & Adolescent Medicine, 162,* 419–425. http://dx.doi.org/10.1001/archpedi.162.5.419

Kohler, J. T., Grotevant, H. D., & McRoy, R. G. (2002). Adopted adolescents' preoccupation with adoption: The impact on adoptive family relationships. *Journal of Marriage and Family, 64,* 93–104. http://dx.doi.org/10.1111/j.1741-3737.2002.00093.x

Langley, A. K., & Jaycox, L. H. (2015). *Bounce Back: Elementary school intervention for childhood trauma*. Unpublished manual, University of California Los Angeles. Available at https://bouncebackprogram.org/

Lee, R. M. (2003). The transracial adoption paradox: History, research, and counseling implications of cultural socialization. *The Counseling Psychologist, 31,* 711–744. http://dx.doi.org/10.1177/0011000003258087

Lee, R. M., Grotevant, H. D., Hellerstedt, W. L., Gunnar, M. R., & the Minnesota International Adaption Project Team. (2006). Cultural socialization in families with internationally adopted children. *Journal of Family Psychology, 20,* 571–580. http://dx.doi.org/10.1037/0893-3200.20.4.571

Leinaweaver, J. (2017, July 20). The international adoption rate has plummeted in the US. *TRT World.* Retrieved from https://www.adoptioninstitute.org/news/the-international-adoption-rate-has-plummeted-in-the-us/

Lindblad, F., Hjern, A., & Vinnerljung, B. (2003). Intercountry adopted children as young adults—A Swedish cohort study. *American Journal of Orthopsychiatry, 73,* 190–202. http://dx.doi.org/10.1037/0002-9432.73.2.190

Marcellus, L. (2010). Supporting resilience in foster families: A model for program design that supports recruitment, retention, and satisfaction of foster families who care for infants with prenatal substance exposure. *Child Welfare, 89,* 7–29.

Masten, A. S. (2001). Ordinary magic: Resilience processes in development. *American Psychologist, 56,* 227–238. http://dx.doi.org/10.1037/0003-066X.56.3.227

McMillen, J. C., Zima, B. T., Scott, L. D., Jr., Auslander, W. F., Munson, M. R., Ollie, M. T., & Spitznagel, E. L. (2005). Prevalence of psychiatric disorders among older youths in the foster care system. *Journal of the American Academy of Child & Adolescent Psychiatry, 44,* 88–95. http://dx.doi.org/10.1097/01.chi.0000145806.24274.d2

Miller, B. C., Fan, X., Christensen, M., Grotevant, H. D., & van Dulmen, M. (2000). Comparisons of adopted and nonadopted adolescents in a large, nationally representative sample. *Child Development, 71,* 1458–1473. http://dx.doi.org/10.1111/1467-8624.00239

Nadeem, E., Waterman, J., Foster, J., Paczkowski, E., Belin, T. R., & Miranda, J. (2017). Long-term effects of pre-placement risk factors on children's psychological symptoms and parenting stress among families adopting children from foster care. *Journal of Emotional and Behavioral Disorders, 25*(2), 67–81. http://dx.doi.org/10.1177/1063426615621050

Ollendick, T. H., & Cerny, J. A. (1981). *Clinical behavior therapy with children.* New York, NY: Plenum Press.

Pedro-Carroll, J. (2010). *Putting children first: Proven parenting strategies for helping children thrive through divorce.* New York, NY: Penguin/Avery.

Pilowsky, D. J., & Wu, L.-T. (2006). Psychiatric symptoms and substance use disorders in a nationally representative sample of American adolescents involved with foster care. *Journal of Adolescent Health, 38,* 351–358. http://dx.doi.org/10.1016/j.jadohealth.2005.06.014

Price, J. M., Chamberlain, P., Landsverk, J., Reid, J. B., Leve, L. D., & Laurent, H. (2008). Effects of a foster parent training intervention on placement changes of children in foster care. *Child Maltreatment, 13,* 64–75. http://dx.doi.org/10.1177/1077559507310612

Riley, D. (with Meeks, J.). (2005). *Beneath the mask: Understanding adopted teens.* Silver Spring, MD: C.A.S.E. Publications.

Rosenthal, J. A., & Groze, V. K. (1994). A longitudinal study of special-needs adoptive families. *Child Welfare, 73,* 689–706.

Rubin, D. M., Alessandrini, E. A., Feudtner, C., Mandell, D. S., Localio, A. R., & Hadley, T. (2004). Placement stability and mental health costs for children in foster care. *Pediatrics, 113,* 1336–1341. http://dx.doi.org/10.1542/peds.113.5.1336

Rushton, A., Monck, E., Upright, H., & Davidson, M. (2006). Enhancing adoptive parenting: Devising promising interventions. *Child and Adolescent Mental Health, 11,* 25–31.

Sanders, M. R., Markie-Dadds, C., Tully, L. A., & Bor, W. (2000). The triple P-positive parenting program: A comparison of enhanced, standard, and self-directed behavioral family intervention for parents of children with early onset conduct problems. *Journal of Consulting and Clinical Psychology, 68,* 624–640.

Sandler, I. N., Ayers, T. S., Wolchik, S. A., Tein, J.-Y., Kwok, O.-M., Haine, R. A., . . . Griffin, W. A. (2003). The family bereavement program: Efficacy evaluation of a theory-based prevention program for parentally bereaved children and adolescents. *Journal of Consulting and Clinical Psychology, 71,* 587–600. http://dx.doi.org/10.1037/0022-006X.71.3.587

Scott, S., Spender, Q., Doolan, M., Jacobs, B., & Aspland, H. (2001). Multicentre controlled trial of parenting groups for childhood antisocial behaviour in clinical practice. *BMJ: British Medical Journal, 323*(7306), 194–198. http://dx.doi.org/10.1136/bmj.323.7306.194

Sharma, A., McGue, M., & Benson, P. (1996a). The emotional and behavioral adjustment of United States adopted adolescents: Part I. An overview. *Children and Youth Services Review, 18,* 83–100. http://dx.doi.org/10.1016/0190-7409(95)00055-0

Sharma, A., McGue, M., & Benson, P. (1996b). The emotional and behavioral adjustment of United States adopted adolescents: Part II. Age at adoption. *Children and Youth Services Review, 18,* 101–114. http://dx.doi.org/10.1016/0190-7409(95)00056-9

Simmel, C. (2007). Risk and protective factors contributing to the longitudinal psychosocial well-being of adopted foster children. *Journal of Emotional and Behavioral Disorders, 15,* 237–249. http://dx.doi.org/10.1177/10634266070150040501

Simmel, C., Barth, R. P., & Brooks, D. (2007). Adoptive foster youths' psychosocial functioning: A longitudinal perspective. *Child & Family Social Work, 12,* 336–348. http://dx.doi.org/10.1111/j.1365-2206.2006.00481.x

Simmel, C., Brooks, D., Barth, R. P., & Hinshaw, S. P. (2001). Externalizing symptomatology among adoptive youth: Prevalence and preadoption risk factors. *Journal of Abnormal Child Psychology, 29,* 57–69. http://dx.doi.org/10.1023/A:1005251513130

Smith, S. L., Howard, J. A., Garnier, P. C., & Ryan, S. D. (2006). Where are we now? A post-ASFA examination of adoption disruption. *Adoption Quarterly, 9*(4), 19–44. http://dx.doi.org/10.1300/J145v09n04_02

Sturgess, W., & Selwyn, J. (2007). Supporting the placements of children adopted out of care. *Clinical Child Psychology and Psychiatry, 12,* 13–28. http://dx.doi.org/10.1177/1359104507071051

Testa, M. F., & Smith, B. (2009). Prevention and drug treatment. *The Future of Children, 19*, 147–168. http://dx.doi.org/10.1353/foc.0.0033

Tieman, W., van der Ende, J., & Verhulst, F. C. (2005). Psychiatric disorders in young adult intercountry adoptees: An epidemiological study. *The American Journal of Psychiatry, 162*, 592–598. http://dx.doi.org/10.1176/appi.ajp.162.3.592

Triseliotis, J. (2002). Long-term foster care or adoption? The evidence examined. *Child & Family Social Work, 7*, 23–33. http://dx.doi.org/10.1046/j.1365-2206.2002.00224.x

Trozzi, M. (1999). *Talking with children about loss*. New York, NY: Berkley Publishing Group of Penguin Putnam.

U.S. Department of Health and Human Services. (2010). *The Adoption and Foster Care Analysis and Reporting System* (AFCARS). Washington, DC: Author. Available at https://www.acf.hhs.gov/cb/research-data-technology/statistics-research/afcars

U.S. Department of Health and Human Services. (2016). *The AFCARS report*. Washington, DC: Author. Retrieved from https://www.acf.hhs.gov/sites/default/files/cb/afcarsreport23.pdf

U.S. Department of State. (2017). *Annual report on intercountry adoptions narrative*. Washington, DC: Author. Retrieved from https://travel.state.gov/content/dam/NEWadoptionassets/pdfs/AnnualReportonIntercountryAdoptions6.8.17.pdf

van IJzendoorn, M. H., & Juffer, F. (2005). Adoption is a successful natural intervention enhancing adopted children's IQ and school performance. *Current Directions in Psychological Science, 14*, 326–330. http://dx.doi.org/10.1111/j.0963-7214.2005.00391.x

van IJzendoorn, M. H., Juffer, F., & Poelhuis, C. W. (2005). Adoption and cognitive development: A meta-analytic comparison of adopted and nonadopted children's IQ and school performance. *Psychological Bulletin, 131*, 301–316. http://dx.doi.org/10.1037/0033-2909.131.2.301

Vega, W. A., Kolody, B., Hwang, J., & Noble, A. (1993). Prevalence and magnitude of perinatal substance exposures in California. *The New England Journal of Medicine, 329*, 850–854. http://dx.doi.org/10.1056/NEJM199309163291207

Verhulst, F. C., Althaus, M., & Versluis-den Bieman, H. J. (1990a). Problem behavior in international adoptees: I. An epidemiological study. *Journal of the American Academy of Child & Adolescent Psychiatry, 29*, 94–103. http://dx.doi.org/10.1097/00004583-199001000-00015

Verhulst, F. C., Althaus, M., & Versluis-den Bieman, H. J. (1990b). Problem behavior in international adoptees: II. Age at placement. *Journal of the American Academy of Child & Adolescent Psychiatry, 29*, 104–111. http://dx.doi.org/10.1097/00004583-199001000-00016

Verhulst, F. C., Althaus, M., & Versluis-den Bieman, H. J. (1992). Damaging backgrounds: Later adjustment of international adoptees. *Journal of the American Academy of Child & Adolescent Psychiatry, 31*, 518–524. http://dx.doi.org/10.1097/00004583-199205000-00020

Versluis-den Bieman, H. J., & Verhulst, F. C. (1995). Self-reported and parent reported problems in adolescent international adoptees. *Journal of Child Psychology and Psychiatry, 36*, 1411–1428. http://dx.doi.org/10.1111/j.1469-7610.1995.tb01672.x

Vinnerljung, B., & Hjern, A. (2011). Cognitive, educational and self-support outcomes of long term foster care versus adoption. A Swedish national cohort study.

Children and Youth Services Review, 33, 1902–1910. http://dx.doi.org/10.1016/j.childyouth.2011.05.016

Waterman, J., & Walker, E. (2009). *Helping at-risk students: A group counseling approach for grades 6–9*. New York, NY: Guilford Press.

Waterman, J. M., Nadeem, E., Paczkowski, E., Foster, J. C., Lavner, J. A., Belin, T., & Miranda, J. (2013). Pre-placement risk and longitudinal cognitive development for children adopted from foster care. *Child Welfare, 92*(4), 9–30.

Webster-Stratton, C. (1984). Randomized trial of two parent-training programs for families with conduct-disordered children. *Journal of Consulting and Clinical Psychology, 52,* 666–678. http://dx.doi.org/10.1037/0022-006X.52.4.666

Webster-Stratton, C. (2011). *The Incredible Years: Parents, teachers, and children's training series: Program content, methods, research and dissemination, 1980–2011*. Seattle, WA: The Incredible Years.

Welsh, J. A., Viana, A. G., Petrill, S. A., & Mathias, M. D. (2007). Interventions for internationally adopted children and families: A review of the literature. *Child & Adolescent Social Work Journal, 24,* 285–311. http://dx.doi.org/10.1007/s10560-007-0085-x

Wierzbicki, M. (1993). Psychological adjustment of adoptees: A meta-analysis. *Journal of Clinical Child Psychology, 22,* 447–454. http://dx.doi.org/10.1207/s15374424jccp2204_5

Wrobel, G. M., Grotevant, H. D., & McRoy, R. G. (2004). Adolescent search for birthparents: Who moves forward? *Journal of Adolescent Research, 19,* 132–151. http://dx.doi.org/10.1177/0743558403258125

Young, N. K., Gardner, S., Otero, C., Dennis, K., Chang, R., Earle, K., & Amatetti, S. (2009). *Substance-exposed infants: State responses to the problem* (HHS Pub. No. [SMA] 09-4369). Rockville, MD: Substance Abuse and Mental Health Services Administration. Available at https://www.ncsacw.samhsa.gov/files/Substance-Exposed-Infants.pdf

Index

T

About the Authors

Jill Waterman, PhD, is adjunct professor emerita in the University of California Los Angeles (UCLA) psychology department and for many years was coordinator of the UCLA Psychology Clinic, the training clinic for UCLA's top-ranked clinical psychology doctoral program. She was one of the initial developers of UCLA Training, Intervention, Education, and Services (TIES) for Adoption (now called UCLA TIES for Families), an interdisciplinary program to support successful adoption from foster care of children with prenatal substance exposure and other at-risk conditions, and she has been with TIES since its inception in 1995. Much of the content of the adoption-specific therapy (ADAPT) model was developed through her years of clinical work and supervision at TIES. Currently, Dr. Waterman is the director of Infant Mental Health at UCLA TIES for Families, where she oversees the clinical and research components of the program. Dr. Waterman's research involves various aspects of adoption and child trauma. She and her students have followed one cohort of children adopted from foster care for 15–20 years and are now following a cohort of infants with prenatal substance exposure who are in foster care with prospective adoptive parents. In addition, she has provided training and consultation both locally and nationally on issues related to parenting and treatment of children in or adopted from foster care. Dr. Waterman has cochaired 21 doctoral dissertations and is the author of two books on child sexual abuse as well as an evidence-based group treatment manual for at-risk middle school students.

Audra K. Langley, PhD, is a clinical child psychologist and associate professor at the UCLA Semel Institute for Neuroscience and Human Behavior and the UCLA David Geffen School of Medicine Department of Pediatrics. She is the director of UCLA TIES for Families, an innovative multidisciplinary program for children in or adopted from foster care and their families in Los Angeles County. Dr. Langley specializes in evidence-based treatments for children and adolescents with posttraumatic stress, anxiety, and related issues. Her body of work has sought to increase access to quality mental health interventions for underserved populations of children, including those in schools and involved with the child welfare system. Dr. Langley has been the director of training for the Substance Abuse and Mental Health Services Administration–funded Trauma Services Center for Resiliency, Hope, and Wellness in Schools since 2003 and served for 7 years as chair of the Schools Committee for the National Child Traumatic Stress Network. Nationally and locally, she provides training and consultation related to trauma-informed, child-welfare competent care to professionals in multiple fields and to parents and caregivers. Dr. Langley recently developed and evaluated Bounce Back, an intervention for ethnically and socioeconomically diverse elementary-aged children exposed to traumatic events, which has since been disseminated nationally. She is the author of four treatment manuals and a proud parent of biological and adopted children.

Jeanne Miranda, PhD, is a professor in the department of psychiatry and biobehavioral sciences at UCLA. Her major research contributions have been in evaluating mental health care for poor and minority women. She is evaluating an intervention her team developed for families adopting older children from foster care, adapting depression interventions for young women in Uganda, as well as evaluating governmental social programs there. She has developed and is evaluating a resilience intervention for low-income and minority lesbian, gay, bisexual, and transgender populations. She was the senior scientific editor of *Mental Health: Culture, Race and Ethnicity: A Report of the Surgeon General*. She became a member of the Institute of Medicine, now the National Academy of Medicine, in 2005. Dr. Miranda is the 2008 recipient of the Emily Mumford Award for Contributions to Social Medicine from Columbia University.

Debbie B. Riley, LCMFT, is a licensed clinical marriage and family therapist and CEO and cofounder of the Center for Adoption Support and Education (C.A.S.E.), an independent, nonprofit adoptive family support center in the Baltimore–Washington area. A nationally recognized adoption expert and dynamic public speaker, Ms. Riley has 35 years of professional experience, including extensive health care management, administrative expertise, designing and developing nationally acclaimed adoption-competent programs, and direct delivery of specialized counseling services, which affords her the broad knowledge and nationally respected expertise needed to promote mental health training, child advocacy, and public policy development. Ms. Riley created a continuum of innovative, culturally responsive, evidenced-informed programs to improve the behavioral outcomes of foster and adopted youth and their families, which has become a nationally recognized model. Ms. Riley consults with national child welfare agencies on complex child welfare issues and systems of care enhancement. For over a decade, she has built and implemented a framework for training an adoption-competent mental health workforce nationally and is the founder of the Training for Adoption Competency curriculum currently taught in 17 states. Through a recent federal 5-year grant awarded to C.A.S.E. from the U.S. Department of Health and Human Services, Administration for Children and Families, Ms. Riley serves as the principal investigator to establish a National Adoption Competency Mental Health Training Initiative (NTI). The initiative will build the adoption competency capacity of child welfare professionals and mental health practitioners who serve youth moving toward permanency as well as youth living in permanent adoptive or guardianship homes. The NTI will develop state-of-the-art, evidence-informed adoption competency web-based curricula for each group, with quality improvement components for use on a national basis. Ms. Riley is coauthor of *Beneath the Mask: Understanding Adopted Teens,* contributing author of the article "Adoption Competent Clinical Practice: Defining Its Meaning and Development" (*Adoption Quarterly, 16,* 2013), and contributing author of *Transracial and Intercountry Adoptions: Cultural Guidance for Professionals* (edited by Rowena Fong and Ruth McRoy, 2016).